Minding Movies

Minding Movies

OBSERVATIONS ON THE ART,

CRAFT, AND BUSINESS

OF FILMMAKING

David Bordwell and *Kristin Thompson*

THE UNIVERSITY OF CHICAGO PRESS ⁄ CHICAGO AND LONDON

DAVID BORDWELL is the Jacques Ledoux Professor Emeritus of Film Studies at the University of Wisconsin–Madison. With Kristin Thompson he has coauthored *Film Art: An Introduction* (9th ed., McGraw-Hill, 2010) and *Film History: An Introduction* (3rd ed., McGraw-Hill, 2009). His most recent book is *Poetics of Cinema* (Routledge, 2008).

KRISTIN THOMPSON holds an honorary fellowship in the Department of Communication Arts at the University of Wisconsin–Madison. In addition to the books she has coauthored with David Bordwell, she has written several other books, most recently *The Frodo Franchise: "The Lord of the Rings" and Modern Hollywood* (University of California Press, 2007).

The University of Chicago Press, Chicago 60637
The University of Chicago Press, Ltd., London
© 2011 by The University of Chicago
All rights reserved. Published 2011.
Printed in the United States of America
20 19 18 17 16 15 14 13 12 11   1 2 3 4 5

ISBN-13: 978-0-226-06698-1 (cloth)
ISBN-13: 978-0-226-06699-8 (paper)
ISBN-10: 0-226-06698-3 (cloth)
ISBN-10: 0-226-06699-1 (paper)

Library of Congress Cataloging-in-Publication Data

    Minding movies : observations on the art, craft, and business of filmmaking / David Bordwell and Kristin Thompson.
        p. cm.
    Includes index.
    ISBN-13: 978-0-226-06698-1 (hardcover : alk. paper)
    ISBN-10: 0-226-06698-3 (hardcover : alk. paper)
    ISBN-13: 978-0-226-06699-8 (pbk. : alk. paper)
    ISBN-10: 0-226-06699-1 (pbk. : alk. paper) 1. Motion pictures. I. Bordwell, David II. Thompson, Kristin, 1950–
    PN1994.M529 2011
    791.43—dc22

2010028025

♾ The paper used in this publication meets the minimum requirements of the American National Standard for Information Sciences—Permanence of Paper for Printed Library Materials, ANSI Z39.48-1992.

For Roger and Chaz Ebert

Contents

Preface

Our blog *Observations on Film Art* started small. We were in the process of revising our textbook *Film Art: An Introduction*, and our publisher sent us a big stack of comments from users. Buried in them was a suggestion that we start a blog.

We were intrigued. The idea was to supplement *Film Art* with discussions of current films and trends. Designed primarily as a resource for teachers, the entries might, we hoped, appeal to general readers too.

The blog launched in late September 2006 with David reporting from the Vancouver International Film Festival. Soon we recognized that there was no way to stick closely to the strictures of a textbook. Keeping up a blog means seizing inspiration where you find it: in a new film that sparks ideas, in a rash prediction made by an industry insider, in a DVD release of a restored film that deserves film lovers' attention. Blogging would be fun only if we could follow our enthusiasms.

The format allowed us to do some things we couldn't undertake elsewhere. No print publication, academic or mainstream, could afford us so much space. None would have entertained our open-ended reflections on film criticism, on the pleasures of silent cinema, on what counts as good acting, on freeze-framing Warner Bros. cartoons, or on how flashbacks work. Reviewers must say something about many current releases, and this dull compulsion can be a death march of the intellect. But the blog made us aristocrats; we could talk about anything we wanted and swiftly offer our thoughts to readers. In effect, the site became our self-published magazine. Soon after starting, we began writing informal essays that ran to an unblogly length and included a staggering number of illustrations.

We slipped into a thinly populated niche on the web. Some excellent blogger-critics like Roger Ebert, Jim Emerson, Matt Zoller Seitz, and Mike Barrier were already flourishing, but even they did not push into the regions that lured us. We are academics, with several scholarly books to our credit, so we hoped that the blog would allow us to reach not only students but also filmgoers interested in ideas. These are the people who go to local film festivals, search out obscure titles on Netflix, and scan the Internet Movie Database for information on classics. Outside the multiplex, they read quality nonfiction about politics, history, and the arts. They naturally want to consider films within an intellectual frame of reference.

One such frame considers film as an art. It's not the only way to think about movies, but it's the one we find most illuminating. We don't have all the answers about this still-new art form, but we have a lot of questions. How is the medium of cinema used in different times and places? How do narrative and other formal principles get deployed in particular films? What are the norms of what we think of as conventional cinema, and how have some filmmakers or groups of filmmakers recast them? How do style and form shape the experience of the movie viewer? And how can we research such matters historically—understanding them in the light of economic, technical, and social circumstances?

Readers interested in these questions aren't well served by the bulk of current film writing. On one side are academics housed in departments of film studies, whose audiences are principally other faculty and students. Surprisingly, a great many of these academics are not interested in film as an art form but instead treat it as a vehicle of social attitudes. At the other pole are journalist-critics, some of them grinding out daily copy, others writing belletristic essays. These writers usually think of film as an art, but they seldom probe it in the depth that we find in other areas of arts journalism. Even the most highbrow film writing usually looks superficial when put alongside the best mainstream criticism of painting (think of Robert Hughes), music (Gary Giddins, Alex Ross), and dance (Arlene Croce).

For example, Charles Rosen can authoritatively dissect the intricacies of musical composition in the *New York Review of Books*, but in the same pages Louis Menand can claim that Hollywood action movies rely on

… a concept which translates into lots of buildings exploding, vehicles flying through the air, thirty-foot fireballs, and so forth. A car chase, as they say, is the same in every language. So, for that matter, is a fart. The standard rhythm of an action movie today is ten minutes of "action," followed by two minutes of dialogue, followed by ten more minutes of "action"—exactly the rhythm of a television program, which pauses for commercials, or a video game, which pauses when you run out of chances. (Louis Menand, "Hollywood's Trap," *New York Review of Books*, September 19, 1996, 4)

How Menand discovered that rhythmic formula he doesn't bother to say, although the *NYRB* allows footnotes. More important, had Menand actually examined films in the action genre, or video games, or even the movie he's writing about (*The Rock*), he'd find his claims inaccurate—as well as inadequate to understanding how action pictures work. We're forced to conclude that literary intellectuals and workaday reviewers do not have the inclination or expertise to think about cinema as deeply as their counterparts routinely reflect on other arts.

This is the sort of thinking we aimed for. Our blog gained readers and links more quickly than we had dared to hope: over a million total visitors after three years. By now, each year brings us about 80,000 returning visitors. Perhaps our audience has, like us, been frustrated by the scarcity of substantive but accessible writing about film. Thanks to the interest of Rodney Powell and John Tryneski of the University of Chicago Press, some of our entries have now made their way into book form, revised and given fresh life through updates.

From over three hundred entries, we have picked ones that reflect the blog's range and some recurring concerns. For example, we think it's important to analyze the storytelling conventions of popular cinema, and essays like "Anatomy of the Action Picture" and "Times Go by Turns" do that. Perhaps surprisingly, we find that many of these conventions have been around a long time, as we suggest in "Slumdogged by the Past." Our turn to history shows up in other ways. Sometimes articles predicting the end of cinema or the universal availability of films online require a dose of counterevidence, as in "Movies Still Matter" and "The Celestial Multiplex." At other times a particular film teases us into wide-ranging speculation, as when *The Bourne Ultimatum* allows us to analyze the run-and-gun shooting technique that captivates some critics and nauseates others ("Unsteadicam Chronicles"). Speaking of critics, we air some of our reservations about current film writing in "In Critical Condition" and "Love Isn't All You Need."

One of our strategies is debunking, zeroing in on conventional wisdom that journalists, facing blank pages and looming deadlines, persistently fall back on.

Film as art inevitably clashes with film as a business. Not necessarily. For centuries art has served patrons and the market, and the fact that it takes money to make a film is only one enabling circumstance, not the mark of Cain. The real issue, as Rembrandt and Haydn and Dickens understood, is what the artist does with the constraints and opportunities afforded by making art for a market or a patron.

We can best understand cinema by seeing it as a reflection of society. Most journalists and academics think so. We think that the variants of this idea—zeitgeist thinking, national character, collective psyche, or identity politics—usually lead to vague and vacuous explanations, and they seldom illuminate the artistic power of cinema.

New moving-image technology—videotape, DVD, video games, 3-D—is killing the movies. Nope. As new media have grown, so has film consumption. Movies are viewed on several platforms, and many video games are based on films. Most new media don't replace older ones; innovations force old media to adjust by cannibalizing, piggybacking, or finding new things to do.

Still, this collection doesn't represent everything the blog does. Several online entries use dozens of frame enlargements to analyze sequences closely, but book publication makes this infeasible. Likewise, we have posted appreciations of Jean-Luc Godard, Jacques Tati, Shimizu Hiroshi, Tsui Hark, Johnnie To, Lewis Klahr, Béla Tarr, *The Prestige*, Kurosawa's early films, classic Disney animation, key films of the year 1960, and the avant-garde tradition. These appreciations run too long for inclusion here, but we have provided some briefer observations on David Cronenberg, Abbas Kiarostami, Pixar, Quentin Tarantino, and Bob Clampett. Nor have we reprinted reports on our visits to archives, our periodic explorations of cognitive film theory, our excursions into the neglected art of cinematic staging, and our coverage of mind-expanding lectures by scholars and film artists. For all these matters and more, you can visit http://www.david bordwell.net/blog/.

In both our blog and this sampling, we freeze-frame a mercurial art form long enough to offer fresh information and explore ideas at leisure. If the prospect of thinking seriously but not solemnly about movies intrigues you, read on. In any case, we promise never to send you a tweet.

Madison, Wisconsin
February 2010

Acknowledgments

McGraw-Hill publishers funded the creation of our blog and the redesign of http://www.davidbordwell.net/, and so we thank our friends there: Chris Freitag, Betty Chen, Pamela Cooper, and their colleagues. We're also grateful to our many collaborators and correspondents. Some are noted in the pages to come, but a full list of those who enhanced the essays here would include Mary Susan Britt, Colin Burnett, Noël Carroll, James Cortada, Corey Creekmur, John Damer, Bill Desowitz, Shan Ding, Paul Duncan, James Fiumara, Manuel Garin, Patrick Colm Hogan, Fred Holliday, Michael Kerpan, Nate Kohn, Justin Mory, Lalita Pandit, and Cathy Root.

We are especially grateful to our colleagues in the blogosphere who have welcomed us into the conversation through replies and, not incidentally, links. The list of such netizens includes David Cairns (*Shadowplay*), David Chute (*Hungry Ghost*), Roger Ebert, Jim Emerson (*Scanners*), David Hudson (*GreenCine Daily, The Auteurs*), Henry Jenkins (*Confessions of an Aca-Fan*), Luke McKernan (*The Bioscope*), Jason Mittell (*Just TV*), Michael Newman (*Zigzigger*), David Poland (*Movie City News*), Catherine Russell (*Film Studies for Free*), the Self-Styled Siren, Matt Zoller Seitz (*Moving Image Source, IFC.com*), Yvonne Teh (*Webs of Significance*), Anne Thompson (*Thompson on Hollywood*), and Harry Tuttle (*Screenville*).

Central to the whole enterprise has been our web tsarina, Meg Hamel, a voice of calm during Internet upheavals (*The bottom of the post got chopped off! I can't get rid of boldface!*). She steers this cruise boat; we just provide the buffet.

The Business

World Rejects Hollywood Blockbusters!?

FEBRUARY 28, 2007

(T)Raumschiff Surprise–Periode I

Kristin here:
I've just returned from two weeks in Egypt, and on the ten-hour flight from Cairo to New York, I had plenty of time to absorb the contents of the February 24–25 edition of the *International Herald Tribune*. One of its articles, "Hollywood Rides Off into the Setting Sun," proclaimed the imminent decline of Hollywood.

The coauthors of this article are Nathan Gardels, editor of *New Perspectives Quarterly* (*NPQ*) and *Global Viewpoint*, and Michael Medavoy, CEO of Phoenix Pictures and producer of, among many others, *Miss Potter*. These two men are, according to the biographical blurb accompanying the article, writing "a book about the role of Hollywood in the rise and fall of America's image in the world."

The *Tribune* piece is a slightly abridged version of an essay that appeared on the *Huffington Post* on February 21, 2007, under the title "Hearts and Minds vs. Shock and Awe at the Oscars" (http://www.huff ingtonpost.com/nathan-gardels-and-mike-medavoy/hearts-and-minds -vs-shock_b_41748.html). The subject is not really the Oscars, though, but the supposed decline in interest in American blockbusters, both in the United States and abroad. The authors make a series of claims to suggest that Hollywood is about to lose its "century-long" status as the center of world filmmaking. (Actually, American films didn't gain dominance in world markets until early 1916, but that's a quibble in the face of the other shaky claims made here.)

1. *Foreign films are getting all the awards and prestige this year.* "Films by foreigners such as 'Babel,' 'The Queen' and 'Volver' that make little at the box office are winning the top awards while the big Hollywood blockbusters, which make all the money, much of it abroad, are being virtually ignored." Gardels and Medavoy point out that even veteran director Clint Eastwood figured prominently in the nominations by making a Japanese-language film.

Several objections can be made to this. Technically *The Queen* is foreign, but it's not foreign-language. British films have figured in the Oscars since Charles Laughton won as Best Actor by playing a king in *The Private Life of Henry VIII* back in 1933. Let's factor out British films, shall we?

Of course Gardels and Medavoy couldn't know this when they wrote the piece, but none of those "foreign" films won. *The Departed*, an American genre film, did, and its much-respected Hollywood director finally got an Oscar as best director. He remade a Hong Kong film, secure in the knowledge that most Americans won't watch a foreign-language import like *Infernal Affairs*.

Plenty of nonforeign films get awards and prestige. There have been years—like 2005—when most of the Best Picture nominees were English-language art-house films like *Crash* and *Brokeback Mountain*. If *The Departed* hadn't been crowned Best Picture this year, one other good contender would have been *Little Miss Sunshine*. Think back over how many indies have won Best Picture in the last decade or so. *The English Patient* and *Chicago* (both Miramax) come to mind. (Gardels and Medavoy never make mention of independent American films, since their argument presumes that nonformulaic films come only from abroad.)

2. *Foreign films show "the world in transition as we are living it."* That is, they reflect the real world and hence are more admired and more admirable. In contrast, "American filmmakers too often grind out formulaic, shock and awe blockbusters."

Again, there are plenty of American films that don't fall into the "blockbuster" category. Directors like Quentin Tarantino, David Lynch, Tim Burton, the Coen Brothers, and Christopher Nolan are admired internationally for their unconventional films. Conversely, most films made in foreign countries are no less formulaic than ours. Other countries' popular comedies, crime films, and horror pics are almost never imported into the United States. Nowadays they're remade in English with Hollywood stars.

3. *Hollywood's blockbusters "may be winning the battle of Monday morning grosses, but are losing the war for hearts and minds."* Whose hearts and minds are the authors talking about? Doesn't a film win hearts and minds by drawing people into theaters? So if blockbusters are popular, aren't they, at least in some sense, winning hearts and minds? Obtaining Oscar nominations means these films have won the Academy members' hearts and minds, or in the case of the many critics' awards, the hearts and minds of journalists.

4. *"Audience trends for American blockbusters are beginning to show a decline as well, both at home and abroad."* According to Gardels and Medavoy, the fact that films now gross more abroad than at home suggests that the American public is tired of these big pictures.

This claim is self-contradictory. If blockbusters make more in foreign countries than in the United States, then there would not appear to be evidence for a decline of audiences for such films abroad—unless, of course, there has been an overall decline in box-office income worldwide. That's not true. In the past four years, two films, *The Lord of the Rings: The Return of the King* and *Pirates of the Caribbean: Dead Man's Chest*, have made over a billion dollars each internationally. They now stand at, respectively, second and third on the all-time box-office chart (in unadjusted dollars).

Even if we assume that just Americans are getting tired of their own formulaic films, the authors' argument doesn't work. Gardels and Medavoy lump *Titanic*, *Jurassic Park*, and *Star Wars: Episode I–The Phantom Menace* together with *Mission: Impossible III* and *Poseidon* as having earned large percentages of their worldwide box-office income outside the United States. Clearly, though, the cases are not comparable. The first three were enormously successful in the United States as well as abroad. Similarly, the *Lord of the Rings* and *Harry Potter* series have brought in around two-thirds of their income from outside the United States, but one would hardly claim that Americans didn't like them. *The Da Vinci Code* earned over 71 percent of its total gross abroad, but in 2006 it was also the fifth-highest-grossing film in the American market.

The authors have chosen two films, *Mission: Impossible III* and *Poseidon*, to support their case. Yet in general big action films that perform poorly or even flop in the American market tend to do better in foreign countries, especially if they have auteur directors and big stars. Other examples of recent years have been Oliver Stone's *Alexander* and Ridley Scott's *Kingdom of Heaven*. Indeed, the importance of stars in selling Hollywood films can hardly be overemphasized. For instance, Tom Cruise is enormously popular in Japan, where *Mission: Impossible III* grossed $44 million of its $398 million worldwide income. There are few comparable international stars working in foreign-language films.

The rising proportion of receipts abroad results largely from reasons other than any putative decline in the popularity of American cinema. For one thing, rising prosperity in developing countries has made movie-going more affordable, and hence there are more moviegoers. The fall of Communism in the Eastern bloc and the new profit orientation in China have opened large new markets for American films. Most crucially, a huge boom in the construction of multiplexes in South America, Europe, and much of Asia during the 1990s and early 2000s raised the number and cost of tickets sold outside the United States. It isn't the American market that has shrunk. It's the foreign market that has expanded.

Moreover, comparisons between the total box-office incomes of films within the American market and in foreign ones are often misleading due to currency fluctuations. The recent weakness of the American dollar against many other currencies has made it considerably easier for those in other countries to see Hollywood's products. Theatrical income does not necessarily reflect the number of tickets sold or the price of those tickets in local currencies. Hence raw statistics may not accurately indicate the actual popularity of any given title. Unfortunately, figures on numbers of tickets sold are not available for many countries.

5. *Countries increasingly are favoring their domestically produced films.* "Even long-time American cultural colonies like Japan and Germany are beginning to turn to the home screen."

This isn't a new and consistent trend. Some countries have been doing quite well in their own markets for years, partly due to government subsidies for the film industry. France is one such market. Germany had a good year in 2006, but 2005 was a bad one. Many such successes are cyclical. Recently, films made in Denmark and South Korea have gained remarkable portions of their domestic film markets, and if they decline, other countries will take their places for a period of relative prosperity.

We should also keep in mind that some countries have exhibition quotas for domestic films. South Korea, which provides government subsidies for filmmaking, in recent years has also required that 40 percent of exhibition days be given over to domestic films. That quota was halved to 20 percent last July 1, with filmmakers fearing a surge in competition from Hollywood. In fact, September saw the Korean share of the domestic market rise to 83 percent, but this was largely due to two big hits: *The Host* and *Tazza: The High Rollers*. Such success can be ephemeral, however, and the government has recently imposed a tax on movie tickets designed to generate a fund for supporting local filmmaking. *Variety* has recently predicted a slump in South Korea for 2007 ("Biz Adapts to Uncertain 2007," http://www.variety.com/article/VR1117959030.html).

Moreover, German or Danish films doing well in their own markets doesn't mean that they're beating Hollywood at its own game. American films are truly international products, and blockbusters play in most foreign markets. A non-English-language market like Denmark may produce films that gain considerable screen time at home, but they do not circulate outside the country on nearly the scale of the American product.

Take, for example, the most successful German filmmaker of recent years, actor-director Michael "Bully" Herbig (on the left in the frame above). Within Germany his wildly popular comedy *Der Schuh des Manitu* (2001) sold almost as many tickets as *Harry Potter and the Sorcerer's Stone*, and his over-the-top gay *Star Trek/Star Wars* parody *(T)Raumschiff Surprise–Periode 1* (2004) grossed more than twice as much as *Spider-Man 2*. Most people outside of Germany have never heard of him or his films. There are comic stars like him in many countries. In general, popular local comedies—many of them as formulaic as any Hollywood product—don't travel well.

More evidence for my claims that successful foreign-language films often don't circulate widely outside their countries of origin comes in the February 23 issue of *Screen International*. In an essay entitled "Calling on the Neighbours," Michael Gubbins discusses new funding that the European Union is putting into cinema specifically to promote the wider distribution of films. "The performance of European films outside their home markets remains one of the thorniest issues for the EU's policy-makers," Gubbins writes. "Last year's box-office recovery in many European territories was largely built on the success of local films in local markets and a number of Hollywood blockbusters."

In 1995, production within Europe totaled 600 films, and it rose to 800 films in 2005. Yet "that rise in production has not been matched by admissions, which have fluctuated strongly over the last five years. There has been little to suggest that increased production has helped European films travel beyond their borders."

6. *The competition from increasingly successful national cinemas "suggests that we may be seeing the beginning of the end of the century-long honeymoon of Hollywood, at least in its American incarnation, with the world."*

I don't know what the authors mean by "Hollywood, at least in its American incarnation." Has Hollywood existed elsewhere?

Hollywood may well be geographically in decline, at least as a center for planning, shooting, and post-producing a movie. That isn't happening, however, for the reasons that Gardels and Medavoy offer in their article.

One factor is the globalization of film financing. Many films these days are coproductions between companies in different countries. It's sometimes hard to determine the nationality of a film, given its several participants. The English language, however, remains central to most internationally successful films, and that is unlikely to change anytime soon. The most popular stars still tend to come from English-speaking countries or to be able to speak English well, as actors like Juliette Binoche and Penélope Cruz can.

Another factor in globalization is the increasing tendency to make American-based productions partly or entirely abroad. Offshore production has actually been fairly common since World War II. In the postwar austerity, many countries restricted how much currency could be taken out, and Hollywood firms spent their income by covering the production costs of films made abroad.

Even with the easing of such restrictions, the trend continued. These days, the most common reason is simply cost-cutting through inexpensive labor and other expenses—advantages that have long been found in Eastern European countries. More recently, countries have seen the economic advantages of filmmaking as an environmentally friendly enterprise. More and more of them have put tax and other financial benefits into place in an effort to be competitive in the search for offshore productions. For example, the February 2–8, 2007, issue of *Screen International* contains an ad placed by the Puerto Rico Film Commission (p. 40) declaring that "Puerto Rico is Ready for Action" and offering a remarkable 40 percent rebate on local expenditures. It also touts the country's "experienced bilingual local crews" and its "infrastructure."

One important cause for the offshore trend that I deal with in the closing section of *The Frodo Franchise* is the fact that technological change now offers the possibility of making films entirely abroad, from planning to post-production. Ten years ago it would have been almost unthinkable to have sophisticated special effects created by anyone other than the big American specialty firms like Rhythm & Hues or Industrial Light & Magic. Now world-class digital effects houses are springing up around the globe, and one of the top firms, Weta Digital, is located in a small suburb of Wellington, New Zealand. When a huge, complex production like *The Lord of the Rings* can be almost entirely made in a country with a minuscule production history, there is far less reason for American producers to confine any phase of their projects to the traditional capital of filmmaking.

There may indeed be an ongoing decline in Hollywood's importance in world cinema, but it isn't happening quickly. For one thing, there is no reason to think that U.S. firms will soon cease to be the main sources of financing and organization of filmmaking. Even if Hollywood stopped making films and just distributed the most popular American indies and overseas imports, it would remain the most important locale for the film industry. As anyone who studies or works in that industry knows, distribution is the financial core of the whole process.

Finally, we shouldn't forget that since early in the history of the cinema, the United States has been far and away the largest exhibition market for films. No other single country can match it, and Europe's attempts to create a united multinational market to rival it have so far made slow progress. With such a firm basis, the Hollywood industry can simply afford to spend more on its films than can firms in most countries. Expensive production values help create movies that have international appeal, in part precisely because they are blockbusters of a type that are rarely made anywhere else.

In the international cinema, "shock and awe" and "hearts and minds" aren't always as far apart as one might think.

Gardels and Medavoy's analysis of Hollywood versus foreign films falls into a common pattern within journalistic writing on entertainment. As soon as some trend or apparent trend is spotted, the commentator turns to the content of the films to explain the change. If foreign or indie films dominate the awards season, it must be because blockbusters have finally outworn their welcome. If foreign or indie films decline, it must be because audiences want to retreat from reality into fantasy. It's an easy way to generate copy that sounds like it's saying something and will be easily comprehensible to the general reader.

Such explanations depend on considerable generalizations that are usually made without taking into account the context of industry circumstances. Fluctuations involving currency rates, tax loopholes, genre cycles, quotas, labor-union agreements, and similar factors interact in complex ways. All these are really difficult to keep track of and analyze, and most writers don't bother, even though that would seem to be part of their job.

Almost inevitably commentators also fail to note that films typically take a very long time to get from conception to screen. Most releases of today actually reflect industry trends that were happening a few years ago. The world film industry is just too cumbersome to turn on a dime, or even on a few billion dollars.

• •

The book that Gardels and Medavoy were working on was *American Idol after Iraq: Competing for Hearts and Minds in the Global Media Age* (Wiley-Blackwell, 2009). Their thesis is that American films and other media products need, on moral and practical political grounds, to project a better, more realistic image of our culture abroad. Moreover, on financial grounds, Hollywood risks losing its dominance abroad by not doing so—which really is the authors' main concern.

The first point is debatable. I am all for avoiding stereotyped Islamic villains in films or portrayals of American society as invariably sex-obsessed and riddled with gruesome violence. I'm skeptical, though, that most blockbusters contain such elements or that blockbusters as they exist now risk losing their appeal abroad. I'm quite comfortable with having *Up* represent us abroad, and the *Ice Age* and *Harry Potter* and *Pirates of the Caribbean* series seem unlikely to turn populations against us.

After three years, the claims the authors made in their article seem even less well-grounded. For example, Gardels and Medavoy imply that all Islamic countries are up in arms against American films. Yet many Iranians, for example, stealthily watch American blockbusters on video because they can't see them in theaters, thus risking arrest to see our latest hits. Admittedly most of those videos are bootleg, so the studios aren't benefiting financially. But many hearts and minds in the Middle East admire America specifically because of its popular culture. (For a vivid account of how devoted to American movies some Iranians are and how much they cling to them in the face of considerable danger, see Brian T. Edwards, "Watching *Shrek* in Iran," *The Believer* [March/April 2010]: http://www.believermag.com /issues/201003/?read=article_edwards.)

Studios certainly have not made any of the changes the pair advocate. There-fore, if the authors' arguments had captured an ongoing trend, by now American blockbusters would be even less popular abroad and foreign films more successful than they were in 2007. Yet the most globally successful foreign-language films are usually in the same genres as mainstream American films—action, mystery, historical epic, and so on. Few take long, hard looks at the social realities of their respective countries. Hayao Miyazaki's animated films are among the most successful non-English-language films, but they have little to do with social reality (apart from the recent ones' environmental theme). China is currently turning out historical epics like John Woo's *Red Cliff*—a trend launched by an American coproduction, *Crouching Tiger, Hidden Dragon*. In contrast, films that examine contemporary Chinese society too closely end up being banned.

As of late February 2010, four American films released in 2009 have made over $600 million outside their domestic market. Seven additional titles have grossed over $200 million. The most successful foreign-language film, Miyazaki's *Ponyo on a Cliff by the Sea* (technically a 2008 release but brought out in the United States in 2009), made $199 million internationally. *Red Cliff*, a 2009 release, made $102 million.

As to local hits, in 2008 Michael "Bully" Herbig's *Der Schuh des Manitu*, still the top-grossing locally-made film in Germany, became a hit stage musical in Berlin—imitating a recent trend in American pop culture. (A scene is available at http://www .youtube.com/watch?v=l8hY_sdyLX8.)

For those who don't remember who the "much-respected" director was, Martin Scorsese finally won an Oscar for *The Departed* after several nominations.

Live with It! There'll Always Be Movie Sequels. Good Thing, Too.

MAY 20, 2007

David here:

You've heard it before. Facing a summer packed with sequels, a journalist gets fed up. This time it's Patrick Goldstein in the *Los Angeles Times*, and his lament (in his blog The Big Picture, http://articles.latimes.com/2007 /may/08/entertainment/et-goldstein8) strikes familiar chords. Sequels prove that Hollywood lacks imagination and is interested only in profits. Sequel films are boring and repetitive. They rarely match the original in quality. And when good directors sign on to do sequels, they get a big payday but they compromise their talents.

Me, I want more original and plausible ideas. So, I expect, do you. Time to call in the Badger squad, an ensemble drawn from various generations of UW–Madison grad students and faculty. I asked them if we can't understand sequels in a more thoughtful and sophisticated way—historically, artistically, in relation to other media. The result is another virtual roundtable, like the one on B-films held on our blog a few months ago (http:// www.davidbordwell.net/blog/?p=438).

There were enough ideas for several blog entries, and I've regretfully had to drop a whole thread devoted to comics and video games. Maybe I'll compile those remarks into a sequel. For now, the participants are Stew Fyfe, Doug Gomery, Jason Mittell (of *Just TV*, http://justtv.wordpress .com/), Michael Newman (of *Zigzigger*, http://zigzigger.blogspot.com), Paul Ramaeker, and Jim Udden. I throw in some ideas as well.

Are all sequels in the arts automatically second rate?

DB: The *Odyssey* is a sequel to the *Iliad*, and the second, better part of *Don Quixote* is a sequel to the first. Tolkien's *The Lord of the Rings* trilogy is explicitly a follow-up to *The Hobbit*. After killing off Sherlock Holmes in "The Adventure of the Final Problem," Conan Doyle resurrected him for more exploits. *The Merry Wives of Windsor* brings back Sir John Falstaff after his death in *Henry IV, Part 2*, because, supposedly, Queen Elizabeth wanted to see him again, this time in a romance plot.

MICHAEL NEWMAN: Sequels exist in all narrative forms—novels, plays, movies, television, video games, comics, operas. What is the Bible but a series of sequels? Didn't Shakespeare follow up *Henry IV* with a *Part 2*? What of Wagner's Ring Cycle and Updike's Rabbit novels? Many novelists of high reputation have written sequels, including Thackeray, Trollope, Faulkner, and Roth. There is nothing intrinsically unimaginative about continuing a story from one text to another. Because narratives draw their basic materials from life, they can always go on, just as the world goes on. Endings are always, to an extent, arbitrary. Sequels exploit the affordance of narrative to continue.

What about film sequels? What's their track record?

DB: Goldstein grants the excellence of *The Godfather II*, but what about *Aliens*, *The Empire Strikes Back*, *Toy Story 2*, and *Indiana Jones and the Last Crusade* (arguably the best entry in the franchise)? We have art-house examples too, provided by Satyajit Ray (*Aparajito* and *The World of Apu*), Bergman (*Saraband* as a sequel to *Scenes from a Marriage*), and Truffaut (the Antoine Doinel films). If we allow avant-garde sequels, we have James Benning's *One-Way Boogie Woogie / 27 Years Later*. As for documentaries, what about Michael Moore's *Pets or Meat?*, the pendant to *Roger and Me*?

The world of film would be a poorer place if critics had by fiat banned all the fine Hong Kong sequels, notably those spawned by *Police Story*, *A Better Tomorrow*, *Drunken Master*, *Once Upon a Time in China*, *Swordsman*, and so on, up to Johnnie To's *Election 2* and Andrew Lau's *Infernal Affairs 2*. And art-house fave Wong Kar-wai hasn't been shy about making sequels.

STEW FYFE: Other sequels of quality: *The Bride of Frankenstein*, *Mad Max 2 (The Road Warrior)*, *Spider-Man 2*, *X-Men 2*, *Dawn of the Dead*, *Sanjuro*, *Quatermass and the Pit*. Personally, I'd also add *Blade 2*, *Babe 2*, and *The Devil's Rejects*, but I'm sure those are arguable. Would *The Limey* be a sequel to *Poor Cow*? Del Toro speaks of *Pan's Labyrinth* as a companion piece or "sister-film" to *The Devil's Backbone*. If you want to include docs, there's always the *Up* series.

Why are there film sequels in the first place?

DB: Most film industries need to both standardize and differentiate their products. Audiences expect a new take on some familiar forms and materials. Sequels offer the possibility of recognizable repetition with controlled, sometimes intriguing, variation. This logic can be found in sequels in other media, which often respond to popular demand for the same again, but different. Remember Conan Doyle reluctantly bringing back Holmes, and Queen Elizabeth asking to see Sir John Falstaff in love.

DOUGLAS GOMERY: Sequels happen because the studio owners have never figured out any business model to predict success. If number 1 is popular, perhaps number 2 will be almost as popular. Until recently, producers seldom expected the follow-up's revenues to equal the first. The basics were to keep costs low, keep risks low, and make a profit. Maybe not as large as the breakthrough initial film—but at least a profit.

But they're not a contemporary development. As part of the Hollywood studio system, they have existed in all eras—the Coming of Sound, the Classical Era, and the Lew Wasserman era. They surely seem to be surviving Wasserman as well. Indeed, as much as I admire Wasserman, who can defend *Jaws 2* and its successors?

In the classic era, it may seem that there were fewer sequels as such, but there was a variant called rewrites in another genre. Years ago as I did my first book, a study of *High Sierra*, I watched *Colorado Territory* with something close to awe. It's a gangster film turned western almost line by line. After all, Warner owned the literary rights: why not recycle it?

Given the mercenary impulse behind sequels, does a director's willingness to make one mean that he or she has sold out?

Look at the great talent who's on the sequel beat: Steven Soderbergh has done two *Ocean's* sequels. Bryan Singer, the wunderkind behind *The Usual Suspects*, has done *X-Men 2* and is at work on a sequel to *Superman Returns*. Christopher Nolan has left behind the raw originality of *Memento* to do *Batman* movies. Robert Rodriguez, who burst on the scene with *El Mariachi*, has done two sequels for *Spy Kids*, with a *Sin City* sequel on its way. After making *Darkman* and *A Simple Plan*, Sam Raimi seemed poised to be our generation's dark prince of meaty thrillers but has turned himself into an impersonal *Spider-Man* ringmaster instead. (Patrick Goldstein, "Part 2, Waste of Directing Talent," *The Big Picture*, May 8, 2007)

PAUL RAMAEKER: To assume that the *Spider-Man* films must necessarily be less personal than *Darkman* or *A Simple Plan* (both of which are heavily indebted to the strictures of their genres) is to perpetuate a culturally snobbish perspective on comic books. I've not seen *S-M3*, but Raimi is a genuine fan of the character, a character with a long and complex narrative history, and given the way *S-M2* continues and develops threads from the first film, I see no reason to assume he didn't have some artistic investment in presenting his interpretation of the character over three films (or however many) to present a larger "story" about the character. Why should this not be seen as "personal" filmmaking to the same extent as any other kind of adaptation?

Moreover, speaking as a Soderbergh fan: I may not like *Ocean's 12* as much as *Ocean's 11*, but it seems like an experiment made in good faith to me. It is a stranger movie than you would think from the way it gets picked up in articles like Goldstein's. In fact, the way it plays with audience expectations is both dependent upon familiarity with the first film, and radically divergent from it—in many ways, it does the exact opposite of what sequels are supposed to do, which is to provide a "cozy" (Goldstein's word) repetition of familiar pleasures. Perhaps it failed (again, I remain sort of fond of the film, which I think was best described as being like an issue of *Us Weekly* as put together by the editors of *Cahiers du cinéma*), but even so I think you'd have to call it a failed experiment rather than a rehashing.

STEW FYFE: At a guess, I'd say that audiences or critics might evaluate the worthiness/mercenary nature of sequels by asking three questions:

1. Has the sequel been made because there's more story to tell?
2. Has the sequel been made because the characters are great and people want to see them again?
3. Has the sequel been made because there's more money to be made?

Obviously, any combination of all three can be answered in the affirmative for any sequel, and presumably the sequel wouldn't get made if the answer to (3) was no. But with something like *The Two Towers*, (1) gets priority, while with *Pirates* 2 and 3, (3) nudges out (2). Even with (3), money, as the primary motivation, one could still make a good film. The suspicion of milking the franchise just makes the movie an easier target for critics.

Do sequels automatically equal predictability?

JASON MITTELL: The line that most interests me in Goldstein's piece is the last: "When it comes to entertainment, I'll take excitement and unpredictability over familiarity every time." This sets up a false dichotomy between the known and the unknown. As David and I both blogged about a few months ago (http://www.davidbordwell.net/blog/?p=300, justtv .wordpress.com/2007/03/09/spoiling-suspense), knowing a story doesn't preclude suspense and excitement. (For some viewers, it might actually enhance it.) And arguably, knowing a storyworld actually allows for greater opportunities for excitement and unpredictability—a film/ episode/entry in any series that doesn't need to spend much time introducing already-established settings, characters, conflicts, etc., can literally cut to the chase. Think of the second *Bourne* film as a good example, or *Spider-Man 2*, as a chance to deepen character once basic exposition is accounted for.

PAUL RAMAEKER: I have a theory. In the contemporary comic-book blockbuster, the sequels will always be better than the first entries. *Spider-Man 2* is better than *Spider-Man*, *X-Men 2* is better than *X-Men*, and I will bet that *The Dark Knight* will be better than *Batman Begins*, just as *Batman Returns* was better than *Batman*. The pattern seems to me to be that the first film in the series is relatively impersonal—the franchise must be established as a franchise, meaning that few boats will be rocked, and the director must prove that he or she can handle a film on that scale and can be trusted with the property with all the investment it represents.

But once the director has done so, in the above cases where the first films enjoyed significant economic (and critical) success, he or she is given a bit more leeway, is allowed to drive the family car a little further and a little faster. In each case, the second film in the series by the same director has been significantly more idiosyncratic. *Batman Returns* has much more of Burton's sense of humor and interest in the grotesque; *X-Men 2* is a much more serious and ambitious film narratively and thematically, more obviously the product of a prestige filmmaker. (Singer's never been an auteur by any stretch, so that will have to do.) *Spider-Man* seemed fairly anonymous in terms of style, but *Spider-Man 2* had a much more extensive and playful use of classic Raimi techniques: short, fast zooms; canted angles; rapid camera movements; whimsical motivations for techniques, like the mechanical-tentacle POV shot (virtually a repeat of his flying-eyeball POV from *Evil Dead 2*).

Who knows what *The Dark Knight* will be like, but I'm prepared to put money on the claim that it will have something to do with how people construct elaborate narratives around themselves to explain, justify, or obscure their actions and motives.

Are sequels part of a larger trend toward serial narrative?

DB: We can continue a story in another text within the same medium, but we can also spread the storyline across many platforms—novels, films, comic books, video games. Henry Jenkins has called this process "transmedia storytelling" (http://www.henryjenkins.org/2007/03/transmedia _storytelling_101.html).

MICHAEL NEWMAN: Compared with literary fiction, there seems to be a strong propensity toward the never-ending story in genres like sci-fi and fantasy and superhero comics and spy novels and soap operas. Much of the cinematic sequel-based storytelling today might be considered as this kind of serialized genre storytelling. Such serials tend to have a low aesthetic reputation in comparison to more respectable genres. (The cinematic comparison would be summer blockbusters versus fall Oscar bait.) Serial forms have historically been associated with children (e.g., comic books) and women (e.g., soaps). In other words, there is cultural distinction, a system of social hierarchy, at play.

STEW FYFE: In fact, the longer-standing comics universes have made regular use of serial continuity to forge after-the-fact connections. It's a form of what fans call *retcon*, or "retroactive continuity."

Moreover, in the current crop of movie sequels featuring superheroes, one thing that has been noticeable is the casting of minor characters who might serve as springboards for later storylines. We've seen Dylan Baker play Dr. Connors in two Spidey films, for example, so if they decide to go with the Lizard as a villain in one of the later films, they've already set him within the film series' continuity. Aaron Eckhart's casting as Harvey Dent in *The Dark Knight* could similarly be used to set up Two-Face as a villain for film 3.

This is similar to the idea of leaving a film "open for a sequel," but it seems more closely integrated into the planning and execution of the initial film. It also points to a middle ground between the "We're going into this making three unified films" model (*Lord of the Rings*) and the "We can make more money, so let's see what plot elements we can build off" (*Pirates of the Caribbean*). This is more of a "We're probably going to make more films, let's give ourselves something to work with" model.

It also raises the question, I guess, if you want to start speaking of dangling causes extending past the end of a film, or in the case of *Pirates*, the conversion of plot elements into something like dangling causes. In *Pirates 1*, we hear of Bootstrap Bill Turner getting chained to a cannonball and shot out into the ocean, but wasn't it after he was made immortal by the curse of the Aztec gold? I guess you could call this a retroactive cause. Or, noting the similarity to "retcon," a "retcause." Never mind, that sounds lame.

MICHAEL NEWMAN: In the contemporary era of media convergence, serialized storytelling is becoming a mainstay across media and genres. Serial narratives supposedly facilitate spreading franchises out across multiple platforms. The media franchise demands long-format storytelling that can be spun off in multiple iterations. The rise of sequels is a much larger issue than a bunch of directors trying to make lots of money or audiences having unadventurous tastes. Sequel/serial franchises are a central business model in the media industry today, supported and encouraged by the structure of conglomeration and horizontal integration.

The real point of the *LAT* article is that Hollywood is all commerce and no art, and sequels are a symptom. But this is such old news. And to connect it to a Squeeze summer tour is really stretching.

JASON MITTELL: I think Michael's cross-media point is crucial. Continuity of a narrative world is a core part of nearly every storytelling form, but the language of "sequel" is applied predominantly to film. "Series" seems a more respectable term, as it suggests an organic continuity rather than a reactive stance of "Hey, let's do that again!"

Are some serial/sequel forms better suited to different media?

JASON MITTELL: I think the *LAT* article is ultimately trying to valorize cinema's potential to introduce something new, in reaction to the presumed rise of legitimate and praised series narratives on television (*The Sopranos, Six Feet Under, Lost*, etc.). And perhaps Goldstein has a point. Maybe film should stick to presenting compelling stand-alone short stories, since television has emerged as the leader in narrating persistent worlds? Or maybe I'm just saying that to pick a fight . . .

JIM UDDEN: I disagree that films should stick with one-off feature-length productions and leave ongoing series work to TV. Television has long had its made-for-TV movies, so why shouldn't cinema think more in terms of series than it does? After all, if these are truly hard times for the film industry, as we're always told, doesn't it make more economic sense to adapt, just as TV has done in the last couple of decades?

True, there are things that cannot be matched on either side. I cannot imagine any film ever matching the daunting complexity of *Deadwood* or *The Wire*. Then again, some things work best as a stand-alone concern. Try to imagine a sequel to *Pan's Labyrinth* or *Children of Men*, or try to imagine either film being made only for TV, for that matter. Moreover, some sequels should never be made. (Remember *2010*?) On the other hand, some films would have been better off had they been pitched as an HBO series. (*Syriana* comes to mind.)

Yet film has proven its ability to take on a series format even when it is not called that. In a sense the oeuvres of most of the great art cinema auteurs are series of sorts. Aren't Tati's films a series with the ongoing presence of Hulot (or Hulots, if we include the false ones in *Play Time*)? And does anybody castigate Wong Kar-wai for following up *Chungking Express* with *Fallen Angels*, or *In the Mood for Love* with *2046*, which are not series, but mere (gasp!) sequels? Clearly these examples were based not only on aesthetic visions, but on banking on previous success. Why do we give them a pass, but not more mainstream fare?

I think the more closely we look, the more we might find there are series and sequels even if they are not tagged by those names. It does happen in documentary, and not just in the *7 Up!* series. For example, *American Dream* does seem to me to a continuation of *Harlan County USA*, if not an outright sequel. *Bowling for Columbine* and *Fahrenheit 9/11* combined make for a more complex argument about the relation of the defense industry to class issues than each one does on its own.

In other words, none of these formats has any value on its own. Everything depends on the types of stories to be told and the talent and economic wherewithal to find the best format for that story (or argument). The most appropriate format could be just a two-hour film, or it could be a television series going on for years. Or it could be something in between, such as the first two *Infernal Affairs* films, which got clumsily condensed into one film in *The Departed*. Both television and film can equally participate in such in-between formats.

DB: I don't agree with all of these arguments and opinions, and I don't expect you to either. The point is that compared to journalists' rote dismissal of sequels, these writers offer more stimulating and more probing arguments. These guys are researchers and teachers, and they offer detailed evidence for their claims. They also write clearly, a point to remember when people say that film academics always talk in jargon and propound gaseous theories.

To end on an upbeat note, I find that some journalists avoid the conventional wisdom. Consider Manohla Dargis's recent and welcome defense of the blockbuster (http://query.nytimes.com/gst/fullpage.html?res=980 DE6DE103EF935A35756C0A9619C8B63). Her case doesn't seem to me spanking new: the artistic possibilities of the format have been defended for several years by film historians, as well as in Tom Shone's lively book

Blockbuster (Scribner, 2005). Still, in the pages of the good, gray *Times*, Dargis's piece remains something of a breakthrough. Maybe someday the paper will host a defense of sequels as well. If so, consider this communal blog a prequel.

• •

On average, for the period 2000–2010, sequels amounted to four of each year's top ten North American releases. In two years, six of the top ten films were sequels. And for six successive years, the top-grossing film was a sequel, from *The Lord of the Rings: The Return of the King* (2003) to *The Dark Knight* (2008). Clearly the public's bias against sequels is over; people look forward to further adventures of characters they have come to know.

Formerly we could distinguish between a *series*, like the James Bond movies, which included recurring characters but which could be viewed in any order because the plots didn't carry over, and a string of *sequels*, such as the successors to the initial *Back to the Future* and *Lethal Weapon* movies. But then came integral, through-composed series like the Harry Potter adaptations. Today, the very idea of a franchise seems to depend not only on continuing characters but also on sustaining plotlines across installments. Even the rebooting of the James Bond brand in *Casino Royale* (2006) let a major line of action carry over to the follow-up, *Quantum of Solace* (2008).

Paul Ramaeker's prediction that *The Dark Knight* would center on self-justifying narratives was borne out, especially in the Joker's inconsistent references to his past. For more on whether a story's "predictable" shape diminishes suspense, see "This Is Your Brain on Movies, Maybe" (pp. 96–102). Jason Mittell followed up the question of sequels and financial success on his blog (http://justtv.wordpress.com/2007/05/28/box-office-misreadings).

• •

Superheroes for Sale

AUGUST 16, 2008

David here:

After a day at the movies, maybe I am living in a parallel universe. I go to see two films praised by people whose tastes I respect. I find myself bored and depressed. I'm also asking questions.

Over the twenty years since *Batman* (1989), and especially in the last decade or so, some tentpole pictures, and many movies at lower budget levels, have featured superheroes from the golden and silver ages of comic books. By my count, since 2002, there have been between three and seven comic-book superhero movies released every year. (I'm not counting other movies derived from comic books or characters, like *Richie Rich* or *Ghost World*.)

Until quite recently, superheroes haven't been the biggest money-spinners. Only eleven of the top 100 films on Box Office Mojo's current worldwide-grosser list are derived from comics, and none ranks in the top ten titles (http://boxofficemojo.com/alltime/world/). But things are changing. For nearly every year since 2000, at least one title has made it into the list of top twenty worldwide grossers. For most years two titles have cracked this list, and in 2007 there were three. This year three films have already arrived in the global top twenty: *The Dark Knight*, *Iron Man*, and *The Incredible Hulk* (four, if you count *Wanted* as a superhero movie).

These 2008 successes have vindicated Marvel's long-term strategy to invest directly in movies and have spurred Warner to slate more comic-book titles. David S. Cohen analyzes this new market in a *Variety* article (http://weblogs.variety.com/thompsononhollywood/2008/08/marvel

-vs-dc.html). So we are clearly in the midst of a Trend.[1] My trip to the multiplex got me asking, what has enabled superhero comic-book movies to blast into a central spot in today's blockbuster economy?

Enter the Comic-book Guys

It's evidently not due to a boom in reading. Comic books have not commanded a huge audience for a long time. Statistics on comic-book readership are closely guarded, but the expert commentator John Jackson Miller (http://blog.comichron.com/2008_08_01_archive.html) reports that back in 1959, at least 26 million comic books were sold every month. In the highest month of 2006, comic shops ordered, by Miller's estimate, about 8 million books (and this total includes not only periodical comics but graphic novels, independent comics, and non-superhero titles). There have been upticks and downturns over the decades, but the overall pattern is a steep slump.

Try to buy an old-fashioned comic book, with staples and floppy covers, and you'll have to look hard. You can get albums and graphic novels at the chain stores like Borders, but very few of the monthly periodicals. For those you have to go to a comic shop, and Hank Luttrell, one of my local purveyors of comics, estimates there aren't more than 1,000 of them in the United States.

Moreover, there's still a stigma attached to reading superhero comics. Even beach novels have a slightly higher cultural standing than comic books. Admitting you had read *The Devil Wears Prada* would be less embarrassing than admitting you read *Daredevil*.

For such reasons and others, the audience for superhero comics is far smaller than the audience for superhero movies. The movies seem to float pretty free of their origins; you can imagine a young *Spider-Man* fan who loved the series but never knew the books.

What's going on?

Men in Tights and Iron Pants

The films that disappointed me on that moviegoing day were *Iron Man* and *The Dark Knight*. The first seemed to me an ordinary comic-book movie endowed with verve by Robert Downey Jr.'s performance. While he's thought of as a versatile actor, Downey also has a star persona—he's the guy who's wound a few turns too tight, putting up a good front with rapid-fire patter (see *Home for the Holidays, Wonder Boys, Kiss Kiss Bang Bang, Zodiac*). Downey's cynical chatterbox makes *Iron Man* watchable. When he's not onscreen we get excelsior.

Christopher Nolan showed himself a clever director in *Memento* and a promising one in *The Prestige*. So how did he manage to make *The Dark Knight* such a portentously hollow movie? Apart from enjoying seeing Hong Kong in IMAX, I was struck by the repetition of gimmicky situations—disguises, hostage-taking, ticking bombs, characters dangling over a skyscraper abyss, who's dead really once and for all? The fights and chases were as spatially unintelligible as most such sequences are nowadays, and the usual roaming-camera formulas were applied without much variety. Shoot lots of singles, track slowly in on everybody who's speaking, spin a circle around characters now and then, and transition to a new scene with a quick airborne shot of a cityscape. Like Jim Emerson (http://blogs.suntimes.com/scanners/2008/08/the_shorter_the_longer.html), I thought that everything hurtled along at the same aggressive pace. If I want an arch-criminal caper aiming for shock, emotional distress, and political comment, I'll take Benny Chan's *New Police Story*.

Then there are the mouths. This is a movie about mouths. I couldn't stop staring at them. Given Batman's cowl and his husky whisper, you practically have to lip-read his lines. Harvey Dent's vagrant facial parts are especially engaging around the jaws, and of course the Joker's double rictus dominates his face. Gradually I found Maggie Gyllenhaal's spoonbill lips starting to look peculiar.

The expository scenes were played with a somber knowingness I found stifling. Quoting lame dialogue is one of the handiest weapons in a critic's arsenal and I usually don't resort to it; many very good movies are weak on this front. Still, I can't resist feeling that some weighty lines were doing duty for extended dramatic development, trying to convince me that enormous issues were churning underneath all the heists, fights, and chases. "Know your limits, Master Wayne." Or: "Some men just want to watch the world burn." Or: "In their last moments people show you who they really are." Or: "The night is darkest before the dawn."

I want to ask: "Why so serious?"

Odds are you think better of *Iron Man* and *The Dark Knight* than I do. That debate will go on for years. My purpose here is to explore a historical question: why comic-book superhero movies now?

Z as in Zeitgeist

More superhero movies after 2002, you say? Obviously 9/11 so traumatized us that we feel a yearning for superheroes to protect us. Our old friend the zeitgeist furnishes an explanation. Every popular movie can be read as taking the pulse of the public mood or the national unconscious.

I've argued against zeitgeist readings elsewhere, so I'll just mention some problems with them:

1. A zeitgeist is hard to pin down. There's no reason to think that the millions of people who go to the movies share the same values, attitudes, moods, or opinions. In fact, all the measures we have of these things show that people differ greatly along all these dimensions. I suspect that the main reason we think there's a zeitgeist is that we can find it in popular culture. But we would need to find it independently, in our everyday lives, to show that popular culture reflects it.

2. So many different movies are popular at any moment that we'd have to posit a pretty fragmented national psyche. Right now, it seems, we affirm heroic achievement (*Indiana Jones and the Kingdom of the Crystal Skull*, *Kung Fu Panda*, *Prince Caspian*) except when we don't (*Get Smart*, *The Dark Knight*). So maybe the zeitgeist is somehow split? That leads to vacuity, since that answer can accommodate an indefinitely large number of movies. (We'd have to add the fractions of our psyche that are solicited by *Sex and the City* and *Horton Hears a Who!*)

3. The movie audience isn't a good cross-section of the general public. The demographic profile tilts very young and moderately affluent. Movies are largely a middle-class teenage and twentysomething form. When a producer says her movie is trying to catch the zeitgeist, she's not tracking retired guys in Arizona wearing white belts; she's thinking mostly of the tastes of kids in baseball caps and draggy jeans.

4. Just because a movie is popular doesn't mean that people have found the same meanings in it that critics do. Interpretation is a matter of constructing meaning out of what a movie puts before us, not finding the buried treasure, and there's no guarantee that the critic's construal conforms to any audience member's.

5. Critics tend to think that if a movie is popular, it reflects the populace. But a ticket is not a vote for the movie's values. I may like or dislike it, and I may do either for reasons that have nothing to do with its projection of my hidden anxieties.

6. Many Hollywood films are popular abroad, in nations presumably possessing a different zeitgeist or national unconscious. How can that work? Or do audiences on different continents share the same zeitgeist?

Wait, somebody will reply, *The Dark Knight* is a special case! Nolan and his collaborators have strewn the film with references to post-9/11 policies about torture and surveillance. What, though, is the film saying about those policies? The blogosphere is already ablaze with discussions of whether the film supports or criticizes Bush's White House. And the editorial board of the *Times* has noticed: "It does not take a lot of imagination to see the new Batman movie that is setting box office records,

The Dark Knight, as something of a commentary on the war on terror" (http://theboard.blogs.nytimes.com/2008/07/21/batman-and-the-war -on-terror/). You said it! Takes no imagination at all. But what is the commentary? The board decides that the water is murky, that some elements of the movie line up on one side, some on the other. The result: "Societies get the heroes they deserve," which is virtually a line from the movie.

I remember walking out of *Patton* (1970) with a hippie friend who loved it. He claimed that it showed how vicious the military was, by portraying a hero as an egotistical nutcase. That wasn't the reading offered by a veteran I once talked to, who considered the film a tribute to a great warrior.

It was then that I began to suspect that Hollywood movies are usually strategically ambiguous about politics. You can read them in a lot of different ways, and that ambivalence is more or less deliberate.

A Hollywood film tends to pose sharp moral polarities and then fuzz or fudge or rush past settling them. For instance, take *The Bourne Ultimatum*, which says, yes, the espionage system is corrupt, but there is one honorable agent who will leak the information, and the press will expose it all, and the malefactors will be jailed.

The constitutive ambiguity of Hollywood movies helpfully disarms criticisms from interest groups ("Look at the positive points we put in"). It also gives the film an air of moral seriousness ("See, things aren't simple; there are gray areas"). That's the bait the *Times* writers took.

I'm not saying that films can't carry an intentional message. Bryan Singer and Ian McKellen (http://www.montereycountyweekly.com/archives /2003/2003-May-08/9055/1/@@index) claim the *X-Men* series criticizes prejudice against gays and minorities. Nor am I saying that an ambivalent film results from its makers delicately implanting counterbalancing clues. Sometimes they probably do. More often, I think, filmmakers opportunistically pluck out bits of cultural flotsam, stir it all together, and offer it up to see if we like the taste. It's in filmmakers' interests to push a lot of our buttons without worrying whether what comes out is a coherent intellectual position. *Patton* grabbed people and got them talking, and that was enough to create a cultural event. Ditto *The Dark Knight*.

Back to Basics

If the zeitgeist doesn't explain the flourishing of the superhero movie in the last few years, what does? I offer some suggestions. They're based on my hunch that the genre has brought together several trends in contemporary Hollywood film. These trends, which can commingle, were around before 2000, but they seem to be developing in a way that has created a niche for the superhero movie.

The changing hierarchy of genres. Not all genres are created equal, and they rise or fall in status. As the Western and the musical fell in the 1970s, the urban crime film, horror film, and science-fiction film rose. For a long time, it was unthinkable for an A-list director to do a horror or science-fiction movie, but that changed after Polanski, Kubrick, Ridley Scott, et al., gave those genres a fresh luster just by their participation. More recently, I argue in *The Way Hollywood Tells It* (University of California Press, 2006), the fantasy film arrived as a respectable genre, as measured by box-office receipts and critical respect. It seems that the sword-and-sorcery movie reached its full rehabilitation when *The Lord of the Rings: The Return of the King* scored its eleven Academy Awards.

The comic-book movie has had a longer slog from the B and sub-B regions. Superman, Flash Gordon, and Dick Tracy were all fodder for serials and low-budget fare. *Prince Valiant* (1954) was the only comics-derived movie of any standing in the 1950s, as I recall, and you can argue that it fitted into a cycle of widescreen costume pictures. (Though it looks like a pretty camp undertaking today.) Much later came revivals of the two most popular superheroes, *Superman* (1978) and *Batman* (1989).

The success of the Batman film, which was carefully orchestrated by Warner and its DC comics subsidiary, can be seen as preparing the grounds for today's superhero franchises. The idea was to avoid simply reiterating a series, as the Superman movie did, or mocking it, as the Batman TV show did. The purpose was to "reimagine" the series, to "reboot" it, as we now say, the way Frank Miller's *The Dark Knight Returns* re-launched the Batman comic. Rebooting modernizes the mythos by reinterpreting it in a thematically serious and graphically daring way.

During the 1990s, less famous superheroes filled in as the Batman franchise tailed off. Examples were *The Rocketeer* (1991), *Timecop* (1994), *The Crow* (1994) and *The Crow: City of Angels* (1996), *Judge Dredd* (1995), *Men in Black* (1997), *Spawn* (1997), *Blade* (1998), and *Mystery Men* (1999). Most of these managed to fuse their appeals with those of another parvenu genre, the kinetic action-adventure movie.

Significantly, these were typically medium-budget films from semi-independent companies. Although some failed, one or two were big hits, and many earned well, especially once home video was reckoned in. Moreover, the growing number of titles, sometimes featuring name actors, fueled a sense that this genre was becoming important. As often happens, marginal companies developed the market more nimbly than the big ones, who tend to move in once the market has matured.

I'd also suggest that *The Matrix* (1999) helped legitimize the cycle. (Neo isn't a superhero? In the final scene he can fly.) The pseudo-philosophical aura this movie radiated, as well as its easy familiarity with comics, video games, and the web, made it irrevocably cool. Now ambitious young directors like Nolan, Singer, and Brett Ratner could sign such projects with no sense that they were going downmarket.

The importance of special effects. Arguably there were no fundamental breakthroughs in special-effects technology from the 1940s to the 1960s. But with motion-control cinematography, showcased in the first *Star Wars* installment (1977), filmmakers could create a new level of realism in the use of miniatures. Later developments in matte work, blue- and green-screen techniques, and digital imagery were suited to, and driven by, the other genres that were on the rise—horror, science fiction, and fantasy—but comic-book movies benefited as well. The tagline for *Superman* was, "You'll believe a man can fly."

Special effects thereby became one of a film's attractions. Instead of hiding the technique, films flaunted it as a mark of big budgets and technological sophistication. The fantastic powers of superheroes cried out for CGI (computer-generated imagery), and it may be that convincing movies in the genre weren't really ready until the software matured.

The rise of franchises. Studios have always sought predictability, and the classic studio system relied on stars and genres to encourage the audience to return for more of what it liked. But as film attendance waned, producers looked for other models. One that was successful was the branded series, epitomized in the James Bond films. With the rise of the summer blockbuster, producers searched for properties that could be exploited in a string of movies. A memorable character could tie the installments together, and so filmmakers turned to pop literature (e.g., the Harry Potter series) and comic books. Today, Marvel Enterprises is less concerned with publishing comics than with creating film vehicles for its characters. Indeed, to get bank financing it put up ten of its characters as collateral (http://www.variety.com/article/VR1117921854.html).

Yet a single character might not sustain a robust franchise. Henry Jenkins has suggested that popular culture is gravitating to multi-character "worlds" that allow different media texts to be carved out of them.[2] Now that periodical sales of comics have flagged, the tail is wagging the dog. The 5,000 characters in the Marvel Universe furnish endless franchise opportunities. If you stayed for the credit cookie at the end of *Iron Man*, you saw the setup for a sequel that will pair the hero with at least one more Marvel protagonist.

Merchandising and corporate synergy. It's too obvious to dwell on, but superhero movies fit neatly into the demand that franchises should spawn books, TV shows, soundtracks, toys, apparel, and so on. Time Warner's acquisition of DC Comics was crucial to the cross-platform marketing of the first *Batman*.[3] Moreover, most comics readers are relatively affluent (a big change from my boyhood), so they have the income to buy action figures and other pricey collectibles, like a Batbed.

The shift from an auteur cinema to a genre cinema. The classic studio system maintained a fruitful, sometimes tense, balance between directorial expression and genre demands. Somewhere in recent decades that balance has split into polarities. We now have big-budget genre films that are made by directors of no discernible individuality, and small "personal" films that showcase the director's sensibility. There have always been impersonal craftsmen in Hollywood, but the most distinctive directors could often bring their own sensibilities to projects big or small.

David Lynch could make *Dune* part of his own oeuvre, but since then we have many big-budget genre pictures that bear no signs of directorial individuality. In particular, science-fiction, fantasy, and superhero movies demand so much high-tech input, so much preparation, so much logistical oversight in shooting, and such intensive post-production, that economy of effort favors a standardized look and feel. Hence perhaps the recourse to well-established techniques of shooting and cutting; what I've called "intensified continuity" provides a line of least resistance. A comic-book movie can succeed if it doesn't stray from the fanbase's expectations and swiftly initiates the newbies. Not much directorial finesse is needed, as *300* shows.

The development of the megapicture may have led the more talented directors to the "one for them, one for me" motto. Think of the difference between Burton's *Planet of the Apes* or even *Sweeney Todd* and, say, *Ed Wood* or *Big Fish*. Or think of the moments of elegance in *Memento* and *The Prestige*, as opposed to the blunt handling of *Batman Begins* and *The Dark Knight*.

Shock and awe in presentation. The rise of the multiplex meant not only an upgrade in comfort (my back appreciates the tilting seats) but also a demand for big pictures and big sound. Smaller, more intimate movies look woeful on your megascreen, and what's the point of Dolby surround channels if you're watching a Woody Allen picture? Like science fiction and fantasy, the adventures of a superhero in yawning landscapes fill the demand for immersion in a punchy, visceral entertainment. Scaling the film for IMAX, as *Superman Returns* and *The Dark Knight* have, is the next step in this escalation.

Too much is never enough. Since the 1980s, mass-audience pictures have gravitated toward ever more exaggerated presentation of momentary effects. In a comedy, if a car is about to crash, everyone inside must stare at the camera and shriek in concert. Extreme wide-angle shooting makes faces funny in themselves. Action movies shift from slo-mo to fast-mo to reverse-mo, all stitched together by ramping, because somebody thinks these devices make for eye candy. Steep high and low angles, familiar in 1940s noir films, were picked up in comics, which in turn reinfluenced movies.

Movies now love to make everything airborne. Things fly out at us, and thanks to surround channels we can hear them after they pass. It's not enough simply to fire an arrow or bullet; the camera has to ride the projectile to its destination—or, in *Wanted*, from its target back to its source. In *21* of earlier this year, blackjack is given a monumentality more appropriate to buildings slated for demolition: giant playing cards whoosh like Stealth fighters or topple like brick walls.

I'm not against such one-off bursts of imagery. There's an undoubted wow factor in seeing spent bullet casings shower into our face in *The Matrix*. I just ask: What do such images remind us of? My answer: comic book panels, those graphically dynamic compositions that keep us turning the pages. In fact, we call such effects "cartoonish." On the following page is an example from the graphic novel *Watchmen*, where the slow-motion effect of the Smiley pin floating down toward us is sustained by a series of lines of dialogue from the funeral service.

With comic-book imagery showing up in non-comic-book movies, one source may be greater reliance on storyboards and animatics. Special effects demand intensive planning, so detailed storyboarding is a necessity. Once you're planning shot by shot, why not create very fancy compositions in previsualization? Spielberg seems to me the live-action master of "storyboard cinema." And of course storyboards look like comic-book pages.

The hambone factor. In the studio era, star acting ruled. A star carried her or his persona (literally, mask) from project to project. Parker Tyler once compared Hollywood star acting to a charade; we always recognized the person underneath the mime. This is not to say that the stars were mannequins or dead meat. Rather, like a sculptor who reshapes a piece of wood, a star remolded the persona to the project. Cary Grant was always Cary Grant, with that implausible accent, but the Cary Grant of *Only Angels Have Wings* is not that of *His Girl Friday* or *Suspicion* or *Notorious* or *Arsenic and Old Lace*. Or compare Barbara Stanwyck in *The Lady Eve*, *Double Indemnity*, and *Meet John Doe*. *Young Mr. Lincoln* is not the same character as *Mr. Roberts*, but both are recognizably Henry Fonda.

Dress them up as you like, but their bearing and especially their voices would always betray them. As Mr. Kralik in *The Shop Around the Corner*, James Stewart talks like Mr. Smith on his way to Washington. In *The Little Foxes*, Herbert Marshall and Bette Davis sound only a little like southern gentry.

Star acting persisted into the 1960s, with Fonda, Stewart, Wayne, Crawford, and other granitic survivors of the studio era finishing out their careers. Star acting continues in what scholar Steve Seidman has called "comedian comedy," from Jerry Lewis to Adam Sandler and Jack Black.[4] Their characters are usually the same guy, again. Arguably some women, like Sandra Bullock and Meg Ryan, continued the tradition.

On the whole, though, the most highly regarded acting has moved closer to impersonation. Today your serious actors shape-shift for every project—acquiring accents, burying their faces in makeup, gaining or losing weight. We might be inclined to blame the Method, but classical actors went through the same discipline. Olivier, with his false noses and endless vocal range, might be the impersonators' patron saint. His followers include Streep, Our Lady of Accents; and the self-flagellating young De Niro. Ironically, although today's performance-as-impersonation aims at greater naturalness, it projects a flamboyance that advertises its mechanics. It can even look hammy. Thus, as so often, does realism breed artifice.

Horror and comic-book movies offer ripe opportunities for this sort of masquerade. In a straight drama, confined by realism, you usually can't go over the top, but if you're playing Hannibal Lecter, there is no top. The awesome villain is a playground for the virtuoso, or the virtuoso in training. You can overplay, underplay, or over-underplay. You can also shift registers with no warning, as when hambone supreme Orson Welles would switch from a whisper to a bellow. More often now we get the flip from menace to gargoylish humor. Jack Nicholson's "Heeere's Johnny" in *The Shining* is iconic in this respect. In classic Hollywood, humor was used to strengthen sentiment, but now it's used to dilute violence.

Such is the range we find in *The Dark Knight*. True, some players turn in fairly low-key work. Morgan Freeman plays Morgan Freeman, Michael Caine does his usual punctilious job,[5] and Gary Oldman seems to have stumbled in from an ordinary crime film. Maggie Gyllenhaal and Aaron Eckhart provide a degree of normality by only slightly overplaying; even after Harvey Dent's fiery makeover, Eckhart treats the role as no occasion for theatrics.

All else is Guignol. The Joker's darting eyes, waggling brows, chortles, and restless licking of his lips send every bit of dialogue special delivery. Ledger's performance has been much praised, but what would count as a bad line reading here? The part seems designed for scenery chewing. By contrast, poor Bale has little to work with. As Bruce Wayne, he must be stiff as a plank, kissing Rachel while keeping one hand suavely tucked in his pocket, *GQ* style. In his Bat-cowl, he's missing as much acreage of his face as Dent is, so all Bale has is the voice, over-underplayed as a hoarse bark.

In sum, our principals are sweating through their scenes. You get no strokes for making it look easy, but if you work really hard you might get an Oscar.

A taste for the grotesque. Horror films have always played on bodily distortions and decay, but *The Exorcist* (1973) raised the bar for what sorts of enticing deformities could be shown to mainstream audiences. Thanks to new special effects, movies like *Total Recall* (1990) were giving us cartoonish exaggerations of heads and appendages.

But of course the caricaturists got here first, from Hogarth and Daumier onward. Most memorably, Chester Gould's *Dick Tracy* strip offered a parade of mutilated villains like Flattop, the Brow, the Mole, and the Blank, a gentleman who was literally defaced. The Batman comics followed Gould in giving the protagonist an array of adversaries who would raise an eyebrow even in a Manhattan subway car.

Eisenstein once argued that horrific grotesquerie was unstable and hard to sustain. He thought that it teetered between the comic-grotesque and the pathetic-grotesque. That's the difference, I suppose, between Beetlejuice and Edward Scissorhands, or between the Joker and Harvey Dent. In any case, in all its guises the grotesque is available to our comic-book pictures, and it plays nicely into the oversize acting style that's coming into favor.

You're thinking that I've gone on way too long, and you're right. Yet I can't avoid mentioning two more factors contributing to the superhero trend.

The global recognition of anime and Hong Kong swordplay films. During the climactic battle between Iron Man 2.0 and 3.0, so reminiscent of *Transformers*, I thought, "The mecha look has won."

Learning to love the dark. That is, filmmakers' current belief that "dark" themes, rendered by monochrome cinematography, somehow carry more prestige than light ones in a wide palette. This parallels comics' urge for legitimacy by treating serious subjects in somber hues, especially in graphic novels.

Time to stop! This is, after all, just a list of preconditions that occurred to me after my day in the multiplex. I'm sure we can find others. Still, converging factors like these seem to me more precise and proximate causes for the surge in comic-book films than a vague sense that we need these heroes now. These heroes have been around for fifty years, so in some sense they've always been needed, and somebody may still need them. The major media companies, for sure. Gazillions of fans, apparently. Me, not so much. But after *Hellboy II: The Golden Army*, I live in hope.

Notes

1. For a thoughtful essay written just as the trend was starting, see Ken Tucker's 2000 *Entertainment Weekly* piece "Caped Fears," http://www.ew.com/ew/article/0,,276435,00.html.

2. Henry Jenkins, *Convergence Culture: Where Old and New Media Collide* (New York: New York University Press, 2007), 113–122.

3. The process is discussed in detail in Eileen R. Meehan, "'Holy Commodity Fetish, Batman!': The Political Economy of a Commercial Intertext," in *The Many Lives of the Batman*, ed. Roberta E. Pearson and William Uricchio (New York: Routledge, 1991), 47–65. Other essays in this collection offer information on the strategies of franchise-building.

4. Steve Seidman, *Comedian Comedy: A Tradition in Hollywood Film* (Ann Arbor: UMI Research Press, 1981).

5. Just as *Star Wars* helped legitimate itself by including Alec Guinness in its cast (surely he wouldn't be in a potboiler), several superhero movies have a proclivity for including a touch of British class: McKellen and Stewart in *X-Men*, Caine in the Batman series. These old reliables like to keep busy and earn a spot of cash.

• •

This post attracted some intriguing responses. At *Scanners*, Jim Emerson elaborated on the zeitgeist motif (http://blogs.suntimes.com/scanners/2008/08/batman_vs_the_zeitgeist.html). At *Crooked Timber*, John Holbo examined how much the film's dark look owes to the 1990s (http://crookedtimber.org/2008/08/21/dark-knight/).

Since this blog entry was published, one comic-book adaptation entered the all-time top-ten theatrical releases: *The Dark Knight*. Another sign of the ongoing viability of comic-book movies came in September 2009, when the Disney Company purchased Marvel, presumably spurred by the success of Marvel's first film, *Iron Man*. The success of films like *The Dark Knight* and *Iron Man* and *X-Men Origins: Wolverine* (2009), however, seems to have had little economic impact on comic-book publishing. John Jackson Miller reports that sales of the top 300 titles distributed by Diamond (the massively dominant market leader) fell from 85 million copies in 2007 to 81 million in 2008 and then to about 75 million in 2009—the lowest circulation since 2004. (See http://www.comichron.com/yearlycomicssales.html). It seems that superheroes still sell better in movies than in print.

• •

What Won the Weekend? Or, How to Understand Box-Office Figures

OCTOBER 12, 2006

Kristin here:

For nearly a decade now, morning talk shows and round-the-clock cable news channels have routinely announced the weekend box-office rankings. Why? Partly because they can. In 1997 and 1998, the websites that now provide overnight BO figures went online, and typically they post estimates for the weekend on Sunday afternoons. That's great for those of us who write about films for a living. During the years when *The Lord of the Rings* was coming out, I looked in on Box Office Mojo (http://box officemojo.com) almost daily as part of my research for *The Frodo Franchise*. But why would a college student or a lawyer or a dentist care about what film "won" the weekend?

I suppose it's partly the notion that box-office takes are like scores in a contest. The number-one film is the winner, and people tend to like to hear about winners. The news covers big lottery results, even though virtually none of us is affected by them. I suppose, too, that there's a vague assumption that if a film is packing them in, people must like it and therefore it's worth seeing. Thus reports of big-ticket sales in many cases may prolong a film's success.

The trouble with this is: Although gross BO returns are all that gets reported on TV news, they are far from the only gauge of a film's success. There's a lot more to be learned by browsing through a site like Box Office Mojo.

First, consider the total number of screens a film is playing on. These days big films routinely start out in around 3,000 theaters, and a few that are virtually guaranteed to be hits start out in even more (3,858 theaters for *Harry Potter and the Goblet of Fire*, 4,223 for *Shrek 2*). In multiplexes, big films play on two or even three screens. Unless a blockbuster is released on the same weekend as another blockbuster (and the studios juggle their schedules to avoid such confrontations), it's almost bound to win the weekend.

But how many people are in each of those theaters? If you were the owner of a small local chain of movie-houses, you'd care more about that than the total gross. Anything over $5,000 per theater is considered reasonably successful, but usually the top films do better than that. This past weekend, for example, the chart's topper, *The Departed*, averaged $8,911, and runner-up *Texas Chainsaw Massacre: The Beginning* pulled in $6,563. Not great, but decent.

Judged by per-screen averages, quite a few independent and foreign films playing in art houses do very well indeed. The current indie hit *Little Miss Sunshine* opened in only seven theaters its first weekend (July 28–30), but it brought in $52,999 in each. (It had opened July 26, so that was actually a five-day count.) It was only number twenty in the weekend BO race, but on the basis of its early success, it eventually topped out at 1,602 theaters and is still playing in 824.

Even now, though, after eleven weeks in release, *Little Miss Sunshine* has "only" grossed $55,010,203. Does that mean it's actually not a hit? The same news sources that announce the top films of the weekend often mention when a film crosses the $100 million mark. That's a sort of benchmark for a blockbuster to be labeled a success—or it used to be, before production budgets ballooned into the multi-hundred-million-dollar range.

That's the other big figure, of course: the budget. *Miami Vice* makes for an interesting comparison with *Little Miss Sunshine*. *Miami Vice* just went out of distribution a week ago, on October 5. It had been in theaters for ten weeks, and its domestic total gross was $63,450,470. *Little Miss Sunshine* has now been in theaters for eleven weeks and is number eleven on the BO chart. Its total may creep up to a point somewhere close to *Miami Vice*'s by the time it leaves theaters. The difference is, *Miami Vice* cost about $135 million, and *Little Miss Sunshine* was bought by its distributor, Fox Searchlight, for a reported $8 million at the Sundance Film Festival. So although *Miami Vice* topped the chart on its opening weekend and *Little Miss Sunshine* never climbed higher than the number-three slot (on its fifth weekend), it's pretty clear which one was a hit.

That strategy of opening a film in only a small number of theaters is called "platforming." It's done with small films that the distributors think will get good reviews and word-of-mouth. If it fails, at least the company will have saved on prints and advertising (P&A).

P&A create costs for the distributor that often go well beyond the announced production budget. A major Hollywood company can spend tens of millions of dollars on them. In extreme cases P&A add 50 percent to the total cost of making, marketing, and distributing a film. The public seldom hears figures for P&A, so people may get the impression that a film is more profitable for its maker than it really is.

Of course not all the money in those high-gross figures announced on Monday mornings goes back to the studio. Across a film's run, on average about half of its ticket income stays with the theater owner (and slightly more than that overseas). So a Hollywood film has to gross roughly twice its production and P&A costs just to break even on the theatrical run. That actually doesn't happen all that often, so the studio makes its real profits on ancillary income, principally the DVD (which costs little to make and brings in about $11 in profit per disc to its maker).

The horse-race figures announced by news sources are just for domestic grosses (that is, the United States and Canada). These days, big blockbusters tend to make more abroad than domestically. *The Lord of the Rings*, for example, took in about two-thirds of its gross BO outside North America. *Little Miss Sunshine*, however, probably won't do so well abroad. Comedies tend not to, given that different cultures have different senses of humor, and comedies also depend on dialogue that may not be conveyed well by subtitles.

All these factors (except P&A costs) can be traced on Box Office Mojo. Follow links on the menu at the left to find BO summaries for any weekend since the site began. These include numbers of theaters, the percentage of change in each film's earnings, the film's production budget (where known), per-theater averages, and total earnings to date. (Weekly charts are also available.) The site also covers "international" BO (i.e., outside North America) and "worldwide" (i.e., really worldwide).

That "percentage of change in each film's earnings" is another key to why winning the first weekend isn't the most important factor. If a film has legs, as *Little Miss Sunshine* has, its percentage change from one weekend to the next will be low. A drop of over 50 percent is generally bad news. *Miami Vice* dropped 60.2 percent its second weekend, from first to fourth place on the chart, while the surprise hit *The Devil Wears Prada* went down only 38.6 percent. After *Brokeback Mountain* earned a record-breaking

$109,485 per screen on its opening weekend, it expanded from five to sixty-nine screens, and its second weekend percentage rose 358.2 percent.

On a grander scale are Box Office Mojo charts of all-time BO winners. These can be accessed for domestic, international, or worldwide, and even broken down by genre and other categories. Newscasters like these charts, too, and occasionally when a new film breaks into the top ten, as *Pirates of the Caribbean: Dead Man's Chest* recently did, they announce the fact.

Dead Man's Chest is currently number three in the elite group of films that have grossed over a billion dollars worldwide, with *Titanic* at number one and *The Lord of the Rings: The Return of the King* at number two. Usually that's taken to mean that these three have earned more than any other film ever made. Uh, not exactly . . .

That's only in unadjusted dollars. Inflation has driven ticket prices gradually up, and naturally films released at a time when one commonly pays around $8 to get into a movie will make more on average than those released thirty years ago. Unfortunately it's impossible to adjust all the miscellaneous currencies for all the countries where movies are shown, so Box Office Mojo can only offer a chart of domestic BO grosses adjusted for inflation. Ticket prices sometimes rise for reasons other than inflation, as when theaters charge extra for 3D screenings, fancy seating, and other factors not reflected in the gross numbers.

On the unadjusted domestic chart (http://boxofficemojo.com/alltime /domestic.htm), *Titanic* is number one, *Dead Man's Chest* number six, and *Return of the King* number nine. Adjusted for inflation, though, they are at numbers six, forty-four, and forty-nine, respectively. The real top three moneymakers in theatrical release are *Gone with the Wind*, *Star Wars*, and *The Sound of Music*.

Box Office Mojo is a fun site to click around, either to trace the fortunes of your favorite titles or to get a general sense of how the film industry works. You can search any title and get a set of basic figures on it. And you can talk back to your TV on Monday mornings and say, "Ha! But what about the per-screen averages?"

• •

In general what I said in this entry remains true. Some updates and caveats are in order, though.

For big-budget blockbusters, studios now spend in the neighborhood of $100 million on publicity.

Edward Jay Epstein's *The Hollywood Economist: The Hidden Financial Reality*

Behind the Movies (2010) assembles a lot of information known within the industry but less so by the public.

By now studios probably make less than $11 profit per DVD, due to falling retail prices; still, the takings are high proportionate to costs. Downloaded and streamed movies, clearly the wave of the immediate future, will bring in less, but studios have little choice but to cooperate with online suppliers like Netflix. This partly explains why we're seeing a rash of DVDs released with elaborate extras, like Blu-ray, DVD, and downloadable versions in the same box.

American comedies may be raising their international profile. In 2009, *The Hangover* brought in nearly 41 percent of its gross income overseas, despite its R rating. *Little Miss Sunshine* earned almost exactly the same percentage abroad, perhaps boosted by the Oscar attention.

Studios have become increasingly reluctant to release their official budget figures for films, so often Box Office Mojo and other websites don't list them. At any rate, budgets divulged by the studios should be viewed with skepticism. The real budgets are usually larger.

Getting worldwide (as opposed to domestic and international) figures on Box Office Mojo is now difficult and often doesn't allow for useful comparisons among, say, American versus foreign films. One often now has to search the individual film title to find its worldwide gross, broken down by domestic and foreign.

A caution about "adjusted dollars" comparisons. Obtaining accurate box-office figures on older successful films like *Gone with the Wind* (1939) or *The Big Parade* (whose first Broadway run in 1926 lasted over a year) is impossible. Many of these films were re-released, and figures on their issues on various video formats are not made public, even in industry trade publications. Finding even a rough estimate of what such films have really earned would require considerable research on each title. One such search, conducted by someone going by the nom de net DC2010, uncovered preliminary figures for *Gone with the Wind*. It was posted in Box Office Mojo's own discussion forums (http://boxofficemojo.com/forums/viewtopic.htm?t= 82668&sid=632d11ce1cc179b02320a9131bb2091f).

In short, an actual ranking of the most popular films across history is probably impossible to concoct. Box Office Mojo's "adjusted dollars" charts are merely rough estimates that serve mainly as reminders that the most successful contemporary films haven't left all the classic hits in the dust. With the current hype about *Avatar* becoming the most successful film of all time, it is salutary to realize that that's only by current measures.

In general, Box Office Mojo's figures are not precise enough to be used unquestioningly in a careful historical study. As a way of gauging the most successful films of the weekend, though, they're sufficient.

Snakes, No; Borat, Yes: Not All Internet Publicity Is the Same

JANUARY 7, 2007

Kristin here:

This past summer I had my first experience of being quoted as a pundit. The *Los Angeles Times* was planning a story on the Internet buzz around *Snakes on a Plane* and more specifically around the fact that some of that buzz had actually influenced New Line to change the film.

In late July I had completed the final revision and updating of *The Frodo Franchise*. Two chapters cover the official and unofficial Internet publicity for *The Lord of the Rings*. The last thing I had added to those chapters was a reference to the *Snakes* Internet phenomenon—which was still ongoing, since the film was not released until August 18. The connection is closer than it may appear, since New Line distributed both films.

Dawn Chmielewski of the *LA Times* got wind of my work on fans and the Internet. She called me, and we had a pleasant 40-minute conversation. The result was one pretty uncontroversial statement from me near the end of the story (http://articles.latimes.com/2006/jun/29/business /fi-snakes29) describing how studios have a mixed attitude toward fan sites on the Internet: "It is a phenomenon where the studios are having to keep a delicate balance between, on the one hand, wanting to use this enormous potential for publicity, and on the other hand having control over copyrighted materials and over spoilers."

This story was part of the huge amount of attention paid to the *Snakes* phenomenon, with Brian Finkelstein, webmaster of the main fan site, *Snakes on a Blog* (http://www.snakesonablog.com), widely quoted about how New Line had cooperated with him and even invited him to LA for the premiere. One of the main points of interest to the media was that New Line had added a line of dialogue for Samuel L. Jackson's character that had originated on a fan site. The studio also added some sex and gore, moving the film's rating from PG-13 to R.

Fans' influencing films was not entirely new at this point. After *The Fellowship of the Ring* came out in 2001, two fans elevated a nonspeaking elf extra from the Council of Elrond to fame by dubbing him "Figwit" and starting a website devoted to him (*Figwit Lives*, http://www.figwitlives.net/). As a salute to the fans, the filmmakers brought the extra back and gave him one line to say in *The Return of the King*, where he is credited as an "Elf escort." That phenomenon, however, didn't get much notice beyond fan circles. The *Snakes* revisions got far more attention.

Much was made of the fact that industry officials were eager to see whether wide Internet buzz—especially when covered by mainstream news media—would translate into boffo box-office figures. As we all now know, *Snakes* was deemed a failure. New Line said that its opening gross was typical for a low-budget genre film. *Snakes* cost a reported $33 million. So far it has grossed just under $60 million worldwide. I suspect that New Line spent a great deal more on advertising that it ordinarily would have, hoping in vain to expand the enthusiasm. The film's box-office takings would certainly not bring in a profit, but doubtless New Line hopes for better things on DVD. That DVD was released on January 2, so no sales figures are available yet, but the widescreen edition is doing reasonably well at number 19 in DVD sales on Amazon.com.

The film's disappointing ticket sales led to questions. Why would fans spend so much time on the Internet generating such hype and then not go to the film? After all, fans created parody posters, music videos, comic strips, and photos on their sites, as well as designing T-shirts and other mock-licensed products. The DVD supplement *Snakes on a Blog* presents a generous sampling of such homages; see also *Snakes on Stuff* (http://www.snakesonstuff.com). And if that much free hype—even aided and abetted by the studio—didn't translate into ticket sales, was the Internet all that useful for publicizing films?

Of course fan sites had already proven their worth for New Line's own *Austin Powers: Man of Mystery* and *The Lord of the Rings*. Other films had benefited from free fan labor and enthusiasm. Famously, *The Blair Witch Project* became a massive hit primarily because of the Internet. But anytime a hitherto dependable formula results in even a single failure, the studio publicity departments go into a tizzy of doubt. It's true of genres, stars, and just about any other factor you can name. *Snakes* fails, so maybe the Internet isn't that powerful a publicity force.

Borat: Cultural Learnings of America for Make Benefit Glorious Nation of Kazakhstan came along to confuse things even further. It, too, had a huge fan presence on the Internet. In this case, the main activity was posting clips on YouTube. Well before the film was released on November 3, hundreds of clips—deleted-scenes footage and extracts from the film—were showing up. There were about 2,000 items by then, and as of yesterday a search for "Borat" on YouTube yielded 6,293 clips.

It came to be a joke on the Internet: "What is the difference between Google and Borat? The latter knows how to make money from YouTube." ("Borat" was recently reported by the website CNET News to be one of the top search terms on Google in 2006 [article no longer available online].) Webmasters and chat-room denizens who were already fans of Sacha Baron Cohen from *Da Ali G Show*, where the Borat character originated, promoted the film. The Internet buzz probably led to more coverage of the film in mainstream infotainment outlets than would have otherwise occurred.

Borat's reported budget was $18 million. To date, it has grossed $126 million domestically and a total of $241 million worldwide.

The timing of these two releases triggered much press coverage and show-business hand-wringing. What did it all mean? Is the fan-based sector of the Internet good for films or not?

This isn't some idle question as far as the industry is concerned. Twentieth Century Fox wisely encouraged all the *Borat* uploaders at YouTube. Far from threatening to sue over copyright, the company leaked footage. Then, however, shortly before the film's release, audience research (that dubious tool in which studios put such faith) revealed that many members of the public had never heard of Borat. What to do? At the last minute Fox cut back the number of theaters in which the film would be shown. Did anyone else in the world think that was a good idea?

Back on November 11, with *Borat* freshly successful and speculation about Internet coverage rife, I promised to explore how the two films differed when it came to Internet hype and success (see "Borat Make Benefit Glorious Multinational of Murdoch," http://www.davidbordwell.net /blog/?p=64). That exploration would be possible without seeing either film. I saw both, though. Like many others, I watched *Borat* in a theater and *Snakes* on DVD.

Others have offered reasons for the difference. On NPR, Kim Masters (http://www.npr.org/templates/story/story.php?storyId=6413410) made some plausible observations. *Snakes*, she points out, "was a film with a very broad concept—Samuel L. Jackson battles snakes on a plane. The buzz took off on thousands of websites as the film became the butt of many jokes. The problem is that the movie wasn't really meant to be that funny. *Borat*, on the other hand, is meant to be funny." True enough. In fact, *Snakes* has a weird mixture of tones, starting off with a highly non-humorous scene of a gangster killing a man with a baseball bat. It goes on to interject funny moments in the midst of grim ones in a seemingly random way.

Moreover, Masters claims, the buzz for *Snakes* "took off too fast" and in the wrong places. The sites making all the jokes and parodies weren't the same ones that horror fans frequent, and the humor may in fact have created a negative reaction among what would ordinarily have been the film's target audience. *Borat* had no such problem. Fans of comedy and especially of Cohen spread the word to likeminded fans through what is termed viral marketing in the publicity business.

All true, and yet, having studied *Lord of the Rings* fan sites for a long time, I think there was another crucial factor that never occurred to the anxious studios. That factor was what the fans were doing with the films on their websites, in chat rooms, and on YouTube.

Many popular films, especially in genres like fantasy, science fiction, action, and horror, generate fanfiction, fanart, spoofs, and other creative responses. *Snakes on a Plane* offered the inspiration for all sorts of clever writing and drawing and video making through its title alone. As was pointed out over and over, from that title and the casting of Jackson, everyone knew what the film would be like. It could be parodied without even being seen. Indeed, I suspect that after months of posting and mutually enjoying hundreds of amusing riffs on "Snakes on a Plane," many fans realized that they could never have as much fun watching the film as they had playing around with its title and concept. It had never been the movie itself they were really interested in.

Borat's full, unwieldy title was also an attention-getter, but no one could possibly predict much about the film from it, let alone parody it. Here the focus was primarily on how funny Cohen was as Borat and how funny the film was going to be. What circulated were samples that seemed to prove exactly that. People would go to this film and have more fun than they could possibly make for themselves by messing around on the Internet with its title. The words "snakes on a plane" could inspire just about anybody with a creative bone in their body, but only Cohen could do Borat.

Print and broadcast media spread the same message. For *Snakes*, they had zeroed in on the Internet coverage and stuck with that. End message: there is a lot of fan attention being paid to a rather silly-sounding film. For *Borat*, the media presented Cohen as an interviewee.

Cohen brilliantly manipulated the infotainment outlets, especially the chat shows, by appearing in character as Borat. As the film's release approached, Cohen was a hot property, a ratings booster. Talk-show hosts and soft-news reporters presumably couldn't alienate him by insisting that he speak as himself. Maybe they didn't want to. As a result, three things happened. First, the endlessly talkative Borat dominated each interview. On *The Daily Show*, the ordinarily in-charge Jon Stewart was totally unable to control the situation and frequently cracked up, once badly enough that he had to turn his back on the audience momentarily (this video clip is available at http://www.milkandcookies.com/link/53378 /detail/).

The second result was that each appearance by "Borat," supposedly there to talk about the film, ended up being a hilarious performance by Cohen, ad-libbing on everything around him—the chairs, the coffee mugs, the cameras, the audience. Spectators came away with one impression about the film: it was about this incredibly funny guy doing incredibly funny things.

Third, there could be no discussion of the less savory aspects of *Borat*, the ones that surfaced mostly after the film was already a hit. These included allegations that people had been manipulated by false claims into signing consent forms and "performing" in the film. One has to suspect that when Cohen was explaining his project to them, he may have appeared as his own rational self and not in the wild-and-crazy persona of Borat. The stylistics of the film itself betray many points at which encounters with real people could have been manipulated. Who knows what the crowds at the rodeo where Borat butchers the national anthem were actually reacting to? None of their responses is ever visible in the shots of Borat. How many non-bigoted interviews were thrown out for every bigoted one that could be used?

The point is that the interviews were like the Internet clips, furnishing more evidence of how entertaining the film would be. *Borat* could provide a sort of creativity that was all his own, and fans could never imagine it ahead of seeing the film or create a more fun version of it themselves. Many, many of the people who posted or read stuff about *Borat* on the Internet went to the film.

Ultimately the studios have yet to emerge from their early love-hate relationship with fan-generated publicity on the Internet. Naturally they dread the early posting of bad reviews and crave good ones. But they still seem to believe that most online publicity means the same thing: eyeballs on monitors should equal bottoms in theater seats. Publicists have not yet grasped that fans don't go to the web just to talk about films and learn about films. They do things with films, and different films inspire different sorts of activities. Those different activities may or may not mean that the fan ultimately wants to see the film itself.

In most cases they probably do end up seeing the film. *Snakes on a Plane* is most likely an aberration, as *Blair Witch* was. But *Snakes* does prove one other thing. Fawning attention paid to the webmasters and bloggers who launch these unofficial campaigns is no guarantee of success. The *Snakes on a Blog* DVD supplement displays some interesting aspects of New Line's wooing of the main fans involved in the online hype. The documentary seems to have been made at just about the time *Snakes* was released. It ends with the bloggers, by invitation, on the red carpet at the Chinese Theater for the film's premiere and later at the bloggers' party put on by New Line at a bar. The whole tone is very enthusiastic about the Internet's impact on the film's success; there is no sense that the film will disappoint and raise doubts about the value of fan publicity. There is also the implicit suggestion that fans starting future film-related blogs might get similar encouragement and hospitality from studios.

Clearly no amount of studio cooperation and attention to fans' interests will make a film succeed if the right blend of ingredients isn't there. Nevertheless, fans' enthusiasm and willingness to spend great amounts of time, effort, and even their own money to create what amounts to free online publicity for films is of incalculable value to the studios. Yet for the most part those studios are still making only grudging, limited use of this amazing resource. The resentment they garner from fans as a result may be squandering part of that resource's potential.

Gradually, though, the studios are giving up their policy of stifling the fans by making vague threats about copyright and trademark violations. If studios go further and actually learn how fans use all the vast access the Internet has given them, maybe movie executives can relax and recognize the obvious answer to the current debate: yes, fans on the Internet are good for the movie business.

· ·

When I wrote this entry, *Snakes on a Plane* had already left theaters, but *Borat* was still in release. Now I can compare their financial results. The final worldwide grosses are reported as, *Snakes*, $62,022,014; and *Borat*, $261,572,744. The announced budget for *Snakes* was $33 million, for *Borat* $18 million. Given that theaters keep part of the take and the budget doesn't cover publicity and other distribution costs, *Snakes* probably fell short of breaking even until the DVD release. *Borat* probably went into the black after a few weeks in theaters.

The relative performance of the two films is evident in other ways. *Snakes* opened in 3,555 theaters, with an opening weekend per-screen average of $3,883; the opening weekend gross was 40.6 percent of its final total. It never expanded into more theaters and was in distribution for 84 days. *Borat* opened in 857 theaters to a per-screen average of $31,607. It expanded to 2,611 theaters at its widest release and stayed in distribution for 147 days. Its opening weekend take was 20.6 percent of the final tally. A long distribution period and a small percentage on the opening weekend indicate that a film has legs, with good word-of-mouth and prob-ably some repeat visits. While *Borat* had legs, *Snakes*, as it were, didn't.

Years later, studios don't seem to be any closer to cooperating with the fan sites that provide them with so much publicity. One interesting exception may prove the rule. Melissa Anelli, one of the main contributors to the leading Harry Potter fan site (http://www.the-leaky-cauldron.org/), wanted to write a book on the history of HP fandom. She wanted to deal with both the books and the films. Despite the fact that Anelli was a trained journalist and a key figure responsible for the most accurate, respected, and popular Potter fan site, Warner Bros. refused to cooperate with her. Only the insistence of J. K. Rowling, who *was* cooperating with Anelli, led them to allow her access to the production, the actors, and the publicity events. (Indeed, she gained such access without having to sign a confidentiality agreement or allow Warner to vet the manuscript.) The result, *Harry: A History* (Simon & Schuster, 2008), sold very well and cannot have been anything but positive for a series that admittedly doesn't need much boosting. It says something about the studios' ap-parent paranoia if an established, reputable enthusiast like Anelli needs a backer as powerful as Rowling to be allowed to create valuable free publicity.

Chapters 5 and 6 of my *The Frodo Franchise* deal with official and fan sites devoted to *The Lord of the Rings*, including the uneasy and unpredictable relation-ship of New Line Cinema with representatives of *TheOneRing.net* and *Ain't It Cool News*, as well as less prominent sites. The situation I describe there, current as of 2005, has changed little.

Don't Knock the Blockbusters

OCTOBER 22, 2009

Kristin here:

When was the last time you heard someone complaining about the high cost of the latest Toyota prototype? Probably not recently, since car manufacturers don't tend to boast about how much it costs them to design a new model. In fact, I couldn't find any information on how much the development of automobile prototypes costs. Some new models catch on, some don't. Presumably some don't make a profit for their makers. The same tends to be true for other big-ticket items.

In a way, a film's negative is like a prototype. It costs a lot for a mainstream commercial film to be made, tens or hundreds of millions of dollars in many cases, before the first distribution print is struck and the first ticket sold. Yet once that prototype exists, any number of distribution prints can be struck, and a film may make back many times its negative cost.

For some reason, the cost of making that negative is often public knowledge—to some extent, at least, since we all know that the budget as acknowledged by a studio may be considerably less than the actual costs. The notion that a movie set its company back by $200 million can be a selling point. I'm sure that back in 1922, Universal wasn't happy that Erich von Stroheim's *Foolish Wives* ended up costing more than a million dollars. Still, the studio turned it to an advantage by advertising it as the first million-dollar movie, and studios have been using the same tactic ever since.

The producers and makers of other kinds of artworks don't tend to make such information public. What kind of money goes into the creation of a large stone sculpture? How much does it cost to put on a symphonic concert or publish a book? We may hear about big advances paid to an author, but an advance is basically a lump sum against future royalties, and the author doesn't get any more until the advance is paid off—if ever. But how much do editorial supervision, printing, and binding set a publisher back?

Journalists looking for a hook for an article about movies find a sturdy one in the idea that today's film budgets are bloated. They point to classic movies of decades past that cost only a few million to make and then compare these to the loud, overblown summer tentpoles of today, with their multi-hundred-million-dollar costs. Journalists who use this gambit almost invariably overlook the inflation of the dollar over the years. In the 1950s the average family income was about $5,000 and an average house cost under $20,000. A penny bought a gumball and could be used in parking meters. Just about everything costs a lot more now.

To be sure, other factors have raised the budgets of films well beyond what they would be through inflation alone. The key factors have been star salaries and computer-generated special effects. The latter can account for half the cost of an effects-heavy film. Beyond the negative cost, typical budgets for prints and advertising have skyrocketed.

Some people seem to see an innate immorality in today's biggest budgets, as well as an almost inevitable lack of quality in the films that result. Here's one of the first results of a search on "big budget movies," from Dmitry Sheynin on the website *suite101.com*. He even makes the car comparison:

The film industry has had a good summer this year—action sequences were bigger than ever, and expensive displays of pyrotechnics and CGI showcased new and exciting ways to destroy cinematic credibility.

With the economic crisis forcing many companies to scale down or even discontinue some of their more opulent product lines (think GM), it's comforting to know Hollywood studios are still spending inordinate sums of money producing bad movies. (http://filmtvindustry.suite101 .com/article.cfm/the_five_worst_bigbudget_movies_of_summer_2009#ixzz0Uoe5qzQm)

I think that's fairly typical of the grousing you find on the Internet and in print. No doubt Hollywood produces many bad movies. But actually, it *is* comforting to know that Hollywood still spends great sums of money, ordinate or in-, if you think of the welfare of the country as a whole.

Every now and then I've pondered the possibility that American movies must be one of the products, if not *the* product, that has the most favorable balance of trade. While the United States doesn't have quite the stranglehold on world film markets that it used to, most significant Hollywood films get exported to numerous countries. Conversely, very few films are imported from abroad, and those that come in, especially the foreign-language ones, play in far fewer theaters and sell far fewer tickets than do domestic films. In 2006, according to U.S. census figures, foreign films took in $216 million in the United States, while domestic films sold $7.1 billion worth of tickets. So that's 3 percent of the U.S. market for imported films, which is the figure I've heard pretty consistently for decades.

(In passing, I note from the same report that theaters made 66 percent of their income on tickets, meaning that we moviegoers spend a lot of cash on all that stuff in the lobby.)

It turns out my ponderings have been correct. On the Motion Picture Association of America's "Research and Statistics" web page, there appears the claim, "We are the only American industry to run a positive balance of trade in every country in which we do business" (quote no longer available online). (The "industry" includes both film and television.) In April the MPAA put out its latest annual report on "The Economic Impact of the Motion Picture & Television Industry on the United States" (http://www .mnddc.org/asd-employment/pdf/09-TEI-MPAA.pdf). The trade surplus in the moving-picture industry for 2007 was $13.6 billion, or 10 percent of the U.S. trade surplus in private-sector services. According to the report, "the motion picture and television surplus was larger than the combined surplus of the telecommunications, management and consulting, legal, and medical services sectors, and larger than sectors like computer and information services and insurance services."

Lest anyone think these figures are mere industry propaganda, the MPAA's information, though made public, is gathered for the benefit of the film studios, which collectively own the association. *Screen Digest*, a highly respected trade publication, summarized some of the report's material in its September issue ("Film and TV Are Key to US Economy," p. 265).

For better or worse, most films that are really successful abroad are big-budget items, with lots of expensive special effects and (usually) pricey stars. Back in 1997 people were aghast at the first $200 million movie, *Titanic*—until it brought in nearly $2 billion around the world. Here, in unadjusted dollars, are the top foreign earners for the past nine years (not including domestic box-office):

2008	*Indiana Jones and the Kingdom of the Crystal Skull*	$469,534,914
2007	*Pirates of the Caribbean: At World's End*	$651,576,067
2006	*Pirates of the Caribbean: Dead Man's Chest*	$642,863,913
2005	*Harry Potter and the Goblet of Fire*	$605,908,000
2004	*Harry Potter and the Prisoner of Azkaban*	$546,093,000
2003	*The Lord of the Rings: The Return of the King*	$742,083,616
2002	*Harry Potter and the Chamber of Secrets*	$616,655,000
2001	*Harry Potter and the Sorcerer's Stone*	$657,158,000
2000	*Mission: Impossible II*	$330,978,216

Add in the DVDs and ancillary products, and the balance of trade gets even more favorable.

Yes, it may sound absurd that it requires $200 million to make a movie, especially one that gets mediocre reviews from critics and fans. Still, from a business point of view, it makes sense and it's good for the country. It's especially important in a period of financial crisis, when the movie industry's income seems considerably less affected than many others. Our overall trade deficit is falling, since Americans are saving more and buying less from abroad. This year the film and television industry's proportion of the surplus will presumably grow.

Apart from the balance of trade, according to the MPAA report, in 2007 the moving-image industry also employed 2.5 million people, paid $41.1 billion in wages, spent $38.2 billion at vendors and suppliers, and handed over $13 billion in federal and local taxes.

If you think the trade deficit doesn't affect you, think again the next time you travel abroad and curse the exchange rate with the Euro or the yen.

No doubt there's a great deal of waste and slippery dealing involved in those huge budgets, but there are definite advantages that don't get considered often enough.

I do see a lot of foreign cars on the roads.

• •

A few days after this entry went online, a friend of mine privy to information about car manufacturing informed me that an ordinary prototype runs $50 million to $250 million. A radically new product like an electric car could run over a billion. And car companies do keep those figures secret, so it's no wonder I couldn't find them.

Coincidentally, $50 million to $250 million is pretty much the range of budgets for mainstream commercial Hollywood features these days.

My friend told me other things about car manufacturing that make it sound as though the comparison between the two industries is a reasonable one. For example, auto companies can save money by releasing new, slightly modified versions of a popular model, such as the Honda Civic, rather than designing a new model from the ground up. It's rather like sequels in the film industry.

More recently, something appeared that will probably help our overall balance of trade as much as just about any single manufactured item produced recently. One word: *Avatar*. And as with *Titanic*, Cameron got grief for his huge budget—part of which involved experimental technology that can now be applied to other blockbusters. In an interview in the March 2010 issue of *Empire*, Cameron said, "There was always this notion that it made sense from a business standpoint that if we invested all this money in the first film, that our margin would be less than it would be on the second film, where all the assets existed" ("I've Got a Road Map for Avatar 2," p. 17). *Avatar* would be the film above *Indiana Jones and the Kingdom of the Crystal Skull* in my list of top-grossers, having already passed the $2 billion mark worldwide as of mid-February 2010, but final figures are not yet available.

One last point. In the "Golden Age" of the Hollywood studio system, each big filmmaking company had its own facilities and held workers under contract. These were fixed costs, and a lot of things like special effects and costume construction that are outsourced today would have been done cheaper in-house. Now those studio facilities are a shadow of their former selves, workers are mostly freelance, and many tasks are contracted out. This change, alongside expensive CGI and ballooning star salaries, helps explain why film budgets are so much higher now.

Writing about Movies

In Critical Condition

MAY 14, 2008

David here:

A web-prowling cinephile couldn't escape all the talk about the decline of film criticism. First, several daily and weekly reviewers left their print publications, as Anne Thompson points out (http://www.variety.com/article/VR1117983482.html?categoryid=2508&cs=1). Then one of our brightest critics, Matt Zoller Seitz, suspended writing in order to return to film production. This and the departure of another web critic, Raymond Young of *Flickhead*, has prompted Tim Lucas to ponder, at length and in depth, why one would maintain a film blog (http://talkingmoviezzz.blogspot.com/2008/05/decline-of-film-blogging.html).

I've been teaching film history and aesthetics since the early 1970s, but before that I wrote criticism for my college newspaper, the *Albany Student Press*, and then for *Film Comment*. When I set out for graduate school, film criticism was virtually the only sort of film writing I thought existed. Auteurism was my faith, and Andrew Sarris its true apostle. In grad school, I learned that there were other ways of thinking about cinema. Since then, I've tried to steer a course among film criticism, film history, and film theory—sometimes doing one, sometimes mixing them. But criticism has remained central to my interest in cinema.

What, though, does the concept mean? I think that some of the current discussions about the souring state of movie criticism would benefit from some thoughts about what criticism is and does.

Watch Your Language

Consider criticism as a language-based activity. What do critics do with their words and sentences? Long ago, the philosopher Monroe Beardsley laid out four activities that constitute criticism in any art form, and his distinctions still seem accurate to me.[1]

1. Critics *describe* artworks. Film critics summarize plots, describe scenes, characterize performances or music or visual style. These descriptions are seldom simply neutral summaries. They're usually perspective-driven, aiding a larger point that the critic wants to make. A description can be coldly objective or warmly partisan.

2. Critics *analyze* artworks. For Beardsley, this means showing how parts go together to make up wholes. If you simply listed all the shots of a scene in order, that would be a description. But if you go on to show the functions that each shot performs, in relation to the others or some broader effect, you're doing analysis. Analysis need not concentrate only on visual style. You can analyze plot construction. You can analyze an actor's performance; how does she express an arc of emotion across a scene? You can analyze the film's score; how do motifs recur when certain characters appear? Because films have so many different kinds of "parts," you can analyze patterns at many levels.

3. Critics *interpret* artworks. This activity involves making claims about the abstract or general meanings of a film. The word "interpret" is used in many ways, but in the sense I mean here, figuring out the chronological order of scenes in *Pulp Fiction* wouldn't count. If, though, you claim that *Pulp Fiction* is about redemption, both failed (Vincent) and successful (Jules's decision to quit the hitman trade), you're launching an interpretation. If I say that *Cloverfield* is a symbolic replay of 9/11, that counts as an interpretation too.

4. Critics *evaluate* artworks. This seems pretty straightforward. If you declare that *There Will Be Blood* is a good film, you're evaluating it. For many critics, evaluation is the core critical activity; after all, the word *critic* in its Greek origins means *judge*. Like all the other activities, however, evaluation turns out to be more complicated than it looks.

Why break the process of criticism into these activities? I think they help us clarify what we're doing at any moment. They also offer a rough way to understand the critical formats that we usually encounter.

In paper media, on TV, or on the Internet, we can distinguish three main platforms for critical discussion. A *review* is a brief characterization of the film, aimed at a broad audience who hasn't seen the film. Reviews come out at fixed intervals—daily, weekly, monthly, quarterly. They track current releases, and so have a sort of news value. For this reason, they're a type of journalism.

An *academic article or book of criticism* offers in-depth research into one or more films, and it presupposes that the reader has seen the film (or doesn't mind spoilers). It isn't tied to any fixed rhythm of publication.

A *critical essay* falls in between these types. It's longer than a review, but it's usually more opinionated and personal than an academic article. It's often a "think piece," drawing back from the daily rhythm of reviewing to suggest more general conclusions about a career or trend. Some examples are Pauline Kael's "On the Future of Movies" and Philip Lopate's "The Last Taboo: The Dumbing Down of American Movies."[2] Critical essays can be found in highbrow magazines like *The New Yorker* and *Artforum*, in literary quarterlies, and in film journals like *Film Comment*, *Cinema Scope*, and *Cahiers du Cinéma*.

Any critic can write on all three platforms. Roger Ebert is known chiefly for his reviews, but his *Great Movies* books consist of essays.[3] J. Hoberman usually writes reviews, but he has also published essays and academic books. And the lines between these formats aren't absolutely rigid, as I'll try to show later.

Reviewing Reviewers

How do these forums relate to the different critical activities? It seems clear that academic criticism, the sort published in research articles or books, emphasizes description, analysis, and interpretation. Evaluation isn't absent, but it takes a backseat. Usually the academic critic is concerned to answer a question about the films. How, for instance, is the theme of gender identity represented in *Rebecca*, and what ambiguities and contradictions arise from that process? In order to pursue this question, the critic needn't declare *Rebecca* a great film or a failure.

Of course, the academic piece could also make a value judgment, either at the outset (I think *Rebecca* is excellent and want to scrutinize it) or at the end (I'm forced to conclude that *Rebecca* is a narrow, oppressive film). But the academic critic need not pass judgment. I have written about plenty of ordinary films in my life. They became interesting because of the questions I brought to them, not because they had a lot going for them intrinsically.

The academic article has considerable space to examine its question— several thousand words, usually—and of course a book offers still more real estate. By contrast, a review is pinched by its format. It must be brief, often a couple of hundred words. Unlike the academic critique, the review's purpose is usually to act as a recommendation or warning. Most readers seek out reviews to get a sense of whether a movie is worth seeing or whether they would like it.

Because evaluation is central to reviewers' roles, they tend to focus their descriptions on certain aspects of the film. A reviewer is expected to describe the plot situation, but without revealing major twists in the action and of course the ending. The writer also typically describes the performances, perhaps also the look and feel of the film, and its tone or tenor. Descriptions of shots, cutting patterns, music, and the like are neglected. And what is described will often be colored by the critic's evaluation. You can, for instance, retell the plot in a way that makes your opinion of the film's value pretty clear.

Reviews seldom indulge in analysis, which typically consumes space and inevitably gives away too much. Nor do reviewers usually float interpretations, but when they do, the most common tactic is reflectionism. A current film is read in relation to the mood of the moment, a current political controversy, or a broader zeitgeist. A cynic might say that this is a handy way to make a film seem important and relevant, while offering a ready-made way to fill a column. Reviewers don't have a monopoly on reflectionism, though. It's present in the essayistic think-piece and in academic criticism too.[4]

The centrality of evaluation, then, dictates certain conventions of film reviewing. Those conventions obviously work well enough. But we can learn things about cinema through wide-ranging descriptions and detailed analyses and interpretations, as well. We just ought to recognize that we're unlikely to get them in the review format.

The Good, the Bad, and the Tasty

Let's look at evaluation a little more closely. If I say that I think that *Les Demoiselles de Rochefort* is a good film, I might just be saying that I like it. But not necessarily. I can like films I don't think are particularly good. I enjoy mid-level Hong Kong movies because I can see their ties to local history and film history, because I take delight in certain actors, because I try to spot familiar locations. But I wouldn't argue that because I like them, they're good. We all have guilty pleasures—a label that was coined exactly to designate films which give us enjoyment even if by any wide criteria they aren't especially good.

They needn't be disastrously bad, of course. I do like *Les Demoiselles de Rochefort*, inordinately. It's my favorite Demy film and a film I will watch anytime, anywhere. It always lifts my spirits. I would take it to a desert island. But I'm also aware that it has its problems. It is very simple and schematic, and it probably tries too hard to be both naive and knowing. Artistically, it's not as perfect as *Play Time* or as daring as *Citizen Kane* or as . . . well, you go on. It's just that somehow, this movie speaks to me.

The point is that evaluation encompasses both judgment and taste. Taste is what gives you a buzz. There's no accounting for it, we're told, and a person's tastes can be wholly unsystematic and logically inconsistent. Among my favorite movies are *The Hunt for Red October, How Green Was My Valley, Choose Me, Back to the Future, Song of the South, Passing Fancy, Advise and Consent, Zorns Lemma,* and *Sanshiro Sugata.* I'll also watch June Allyson, Sandra Bullock, Henry Fonda, and Chishu Ryu in almost anything. I'm hard-pressed to find a logical principle here.

Taste is distinctive, part of what makes you you, but you also share some tastes with others. We teachers often say we're trying to educate students' tastes. True, but we should admit that we're trying to broaden tastes, not necessarily replace them with better ones. The more different kinds of things we can like, the better life becomes.

The difference between taste and judgment emerges in this way: You can recognize that some films are good even if you don't like them. You can declare *The Birth of a Nation* or *Citizen Kane* or *Persona* an excellent film without finding it to your liking.

Why? Most people recognize some general criteria of artistic excellence. These would include originality, thematic significance, subtlety, technical skill, formal complexity, and intensity of emotional effect. There are also moral and social criteria, as when we object to films full of stereotypes. All of these criteria and others can help us pick out films worthy of admiration. These aren't fully "objective" standards, but they are intersubjective—many people with widely varying tastes accept them.

So critics not only have tastes; they judge. The term *judgment* aims to capture the comparatively impersonal quality of this sort of evaluation. A judge's verdict is supposed to answer to principles going beyond his or her own preferences. Judges at a gymnastic contest provide scores on the basis of their expertise and in recognition of technical criteria, and we expect them to back their judgment with detailed reasons.

One more twist and I'm done with distinctions. At a higher level, your tastes may make you weigh certain criteria more heavily than others. If you most enjoy movies that wrestle with philosophical problems, you may favor the thematic-significance criterion. So you'll love Bergman *and* think he's a great director. In other words, you can have tastes in films that you also consider excellent. Presumably this is what we teachers are trying to cultivate as well: to teach people, as Plato urged, to love the good.

Of course we can disagree about relevant criteria, particularly about what criteria to apply to a particular movie. I'd argue that profundity of theme isn't a very plausible criterion for judging *Cloverfield*; but formal originality, technical skill, and intensity of emotional appeal are plausible criteria to apply. Many of the best Hong Kong films don't rank high on subtlety of theme or character psychology, but they do well on technical originality and intensity of visceral and emotional response. You may disagree, but now we're arguing not about tastes but about what criteria are appropriate to a given film. To get anywhere, our conversation will appeal to both intersubjective standards and discernible things going on in the movie—not to the fact that you got a buzz from it and I didn't.

There's a Reason They Call that DVD Series "Criterion"

Now back to film reviewing. Judgment certainly comes into play in a film review, because the critic may invoke criteria in evaluating a movie. Such criteria are widely accepted as picking out "good-making" features. For instance:

> *The plot makes no sense.* Criterion: Narrative coherence helps make a film, or at least a film of this sort, good.
>
> *The acting is over the top.* Criterion: Measured performance helps make a film, or at least a film of this sort, good.
>
> *The action scenes are cut so fast that you can't tell what's going on.* Criterion: Intelligibility of presentation helps make a film, or at least a film of this sort, good.

Most reviewers, though, can't resist exposing their tastes as well as their judgments. This is a convention of reviewing, at least in the most high-profile venues. Readers return to reviewers with strongly expressed tastes.

Some readers want to have their own tastes reinforced. If you think Hollywood pumps out shoddy product, Joe Queenan will articulate that view with a gonzo relish that gives you pleasure. Other readers want to have their tastes educated, so they seek out a strong personality with clear-cut tastes to guide them. Still other readers want to have their tastes challenged, so they read critics whose tastes vary widely from theirs.

Celebrity critics—the reviewers who attract attention and controversy—are usually vigorous writers who have pushed their tastes to the forefront. Andrew Sarris and Pauline Kael are famous partly because they flaunted their tastes and championed films that they liked. (Of course they also thought that the films were good, according to widely held criteria.) It isn't only a matter of praise, either. Every so often critics launch all-out attacks on films, directors, or other critics, and some are permanently cranky. Hatchet jobs assure a critic notoriety, but they also prove Valéry's maxim that "taste is made of a thousand distastes."

At a certain point, celebrity critics may even give up justifying their evaluations altogether, simply asserting their preferences. They trust that their track record, their brand name, and their forceful rhetoric will continue to engage their readers. It seems to me that after decades of stressing the individuality of their tastes, many of the most influential reviewers are emitting two main messages: *You see it or you don't*, and *Differ if you dare*. I'd like to see more argument and less strutting. But then, that's my taste.

Stuck in the Middle, with Us

There's much more to say about the distinctions I've floated. They are rough and need refining. But they'll do for my purpose today, which is to indicate that everything I've said can apply to web writing.

For instance, it seems likely that one cause of current critical burnout is the fact that reviews dominate the net. They're typically highly evaluative, mixing taste and judgment. Many people will find a bombardment of such items eventually too much to take. I could imagine somebody abandoning Internet criticism simply because of the cacophony of shrieking one-liners. We're all interested in somebody else's opinions, but we can't be interested in everybody else's opinions.

In addition, the distinguishing feature among these thousands of reviews won't necessarily be wit or profundity or expertise, but style. I think that, years ago, the urge toward self-conscious critical style arose from the drudgery of daily reviewing. Faced with a dreadful new movie, you could make your task interesting only by finding a fresh way to slam it. In addition, magazines that wanted to appear smart encouraged writers to elevate attitude above ideas. In the overabundance of critical talk on the net, saying "It's great" or "It stinks" in a clever way will draw more attention than plainer speaking.

Fortunately, there are other formats available to cybercriticism. At first glance, the web seems to favor the snack size, the 150-word sally that's all about taste and attitude. In fact, the net is just as hospitable to the long piece. There are no space limitations, so one can launch arguments at length. (It's too long to read scrolling down? Print it out. Maybe you have to do that with *this* piece.) Thanks to the indefinitely large acreage available, one of the heartening developments of web criticism is the growth of the mid-range format I've mentioned: the critical essay.

Historically, that form has always been closer to the review than to the academic piece. It relies more on evaluation. That's centrally true of the Kael and Lopate essays I mentioned above, both of which warn about disastrous changes in Hollywood moviemaking. But the tone can be positive too, most often seen in the *appreciative essay*, which celebrates the accomplishment of a film or filmmaker. Dwight Macdonald's admiring piece on 8½ and Susan Sontag's 1968 essay on Godard, despite their differences, seem to me milestones in this genre.[5]

The critical essay is, I think, the real showcase for a critic's abilities. We say that good critics have to be good writers, usually meaning that their style must be engaging, but it doesn't have to explode at the end of every paragraph. More generally, in a long essay, you are forced to use language differently than in a snippet. You need to build and delay expectations, and find new ways to restate and modify your case.

Just as important, the long piece separates the sheep from the goats because it shows a critic's ability to sustain a case. The short form lets you pirouette, but the extended essay—unless it's simply a rant—obliges you to show all your stuff. In the long form, your ideas need to have heft. Stepping outside film for a moment, consider Gary Giddins on Jack Benny, or Geoffrey O'Brien on Burt Bacharach, or Robert Hughes on Goya, and in each you will see a sprightly, probing, deeply informed mind develop an argument in surprising ways.[6] Strikingly, all these writers venture into analysis, putting them close to the academic model.

Above all, the critical essay can develop new depth on the web. Given more space, the web can ask critics to lay out their assumptions and evidence more fully. After years of "writing short," of firing off invectives, put-downs, and passing paeans to great filmmakers unknown to most readers, critics now have an opportunity—not to rant at greater length but to go deeper. If you think a movie is interesting or important, please show us. Don't simply assert your opinion with lots of hand-waving, but back it up with some homework. The web allows analysis and interpretation, which take a lot of effort, to come into their own.

Need an example? Jim Emerson, time and again at *Scanners* (http://blogs.suntimes.com/scanners/). There are plenty of other instances hosted by journals like *Rouge* (http://www.rouge.com.au/index.html) and the extraordinary *Senses of Cinema* (http://www.sensesofcinema.com), and many solo efforts.

Some will object that this is a pretty unprofitable undertaking. Who'll pay people to write in-depth critical studies on the movies they find compelling? Well, who's paying for all those 100-word zingers? And who has paid those programmers who continue to help Linus Torvalds develop Linux? People do all kinds of things for love of the doing and for the benefit of strangers. Besides, no one should expect that writing web criticism will pay the bills. If Disney can't collect from people who have downloaded *Pirates of the Caribbean 3* for free, why should you or I expect to be paid for talking about it? Maybe only idlers, hobbyists, obsessives, and retirees (count me among all four) have the leisure to write long for the web.

I envision another way to be in the middle. If most critical essays have been akin to reviews, what about essays that lie closer to the other extreme, the academic one? I'd like to see more of what might be called "research essays." If the critical essay of haut journalism tips toward reviewing while being more argument-driven, the research essay leans toward academic writing but doesn't shrink from judgment, and even parades tastes. I've tried my hand at several research essays, in books as well as in pieces you'll find on this site; and occasionally one of our blog entries moves in this direction.

This isn't to discourage people from jotting down opinions about movies and triggering a conversation with readers. The review, professional or amateur, shouldn't go extinct. But we also benefit from ambitious critical essays, pieces that illuminate movies through detailed analysis and interpretation. Web critics could write less often, but longer. In an era of slow food, let's try slow blogging. It might encourage slow reading.

Notes

1. Monroe K. Beardsley, *Aesthetics: Problems in the Philosophy of Art Criticism* (New York: Harcourt, Brace and World, 1958), 75–78.

2. Pauline Kael, "On the Future of Movies," in *Reeling* (New York: Warner Books, 1977), 415–444; Philip Lopate, "The Last Taboo: The Dumbing Down of American Movies," in *Totally Tenderly Tragically: Essays and Criticism from a Lifelong Love Affair with the Movies* (New York: Anchor, 1998), 259–279.

3. In addition, Ebert often manages to build his daily pieces around a general idea, not necessarily involving cinema, so he can be read with enjoyment by people not particularly interested in film. I talk about this a little in my introduction to his collection *Awake in the Dark*.

4. Reflectionist interpretation usually seems to me unpersuasive, for reasons I've discussed in *Poetics of Cinema* (New York: Routledge, 2008), 30–32. I realize that I'm tilting at windmills. Reflectionism will be with us forever.

5. Dwight Macdonald, "*8 1/2*: Fellini's Obvious Masterpiece," in *On Movies* (Englewood Cliffs, NJ: Prentice-Hall, 1969), 15–31; Susan Sontag, "Godard," in *Styles of Radical Will* (New York: Delta, 1969), 147–189.

6. Gary Giddins, "'This Guy Wouldn't Give You the Parsley off His Fish,'" in *Faces in the Crowd: Musicians, Writers, Actors, and Filmmakers* (New York: Da Capo Press, 1996), 3–13; Geoffrey O'Brien, "The Return of Burt Bacharach," in *Sonata for Jukebox: Pop Music, Memory, and the Imagined Life* (New York: Counterpoint, 2004), 5–28; and Robert Hughes, "Goya," in *Nothing If Not Critical: Selected Essays on Art and Artists* (New York: Penguin, 1992), 50–64.

Elsewhere on our site I speculated that our most abiding tastes are formed in adolescence (http://www.davidbordwell.net/blog/?p=1484). "Weather Bird Flies Again" (http://www.davidbordwell.net/blog/?p=358) is my homage to Gary Giddins, one of our finest critical essayists.

This piece stands as a sort of declaration of principles about what I find valuable in film criticism, on and off the net. The distinctions aren't deep, but I think they're necessary points of departure if we're to understand what sort of critical writing achieves lasting value. The idea that anything published on the net will last long will strike some as naïvely idealistic, but I continue to hope that not everything on display there is immediately swept under the next wave.

Love Isn't All You Need

APRIL 3, 2009

David here:
Last week the Hong Kong International Film Festival hosted Gerry Peary's *For the Love of Movies: The Story of American Film Criticism*. It's a lively and thoughtful survey, interspersing interviews with contemporary critics with a chronological account that runs from Frank E. Woods to Harry Knowles. It goes into particular depth on the controversies around Pauline Kael and Andrew Sarris, but it even spares some kind words for Bosley Crowther.

Some valuable points are made concisely. Peary indicates that the alternative weeklies of the 1970s and 1980s were seedbeds for critics who moved into more mainstream venues like *Entertainment Weekly*. I also liked the emphasis on fanzines, which too often get forgotten as precedents for Internet writing. In all, *For the Love of Movies* offers a concise, entertaining account of mass-market movie criticism. I think a lot of universities would want to use it in film and journalism courses.

Gerry's documentary comes along at a parlous time, of course. Most of the footage was taken before the wave of downsizings that lopped reviewers off newspaper staffs, but already tremors were registered in some interviewees' remarks. Apart from this topical interest, the film set me thinking: Is love of movies enough to make someone a good critic? It's a necessary condition, surely, but is it sufficient?

Gerry's film includes the inevitable query, what movie imbued each critic with a passion for cinema? I have to say that I have never found this an interesting question, or at least any more interesting when asked of a professional critic than of an ordinary cinephile. Watching Gerry's documentary made me think that everybody has such formative experiences, and nearly everybody loves movies. But what sets a critic apart?

A piece of critical writing ideally should offer ideas, information, and opinion—served up in decent, preferably absorbing prose. This is a counsel of perfection, but I think the formula *ideas + information + opinion + good or great writing* isn't a bad one.

You really can't write about the arts without having some opinion at the center of your work. Too often, though, a critic's opinions come down simply to evaluations. Evaluation is important, but it has several facets, as I've tried to suggest in another entry (pp. 53–62). And your opinions need not be about the film's value. You can have an opinion about its place in history, or its contribution to a trend, or its most original moments. Opinions like these allow you to build an argument, drawing on evidence in or around the movie in question. Several of our blog entries are opinion-driven pieces, but not necessarily evaluations of the movies.

Most people think that film criticism is largely a matter of stating evaluations of a film, based either on criteria or personal taste, and putting those evaluations into user-friendly prose. If that's all a critic does, why not find bloggers who can do the same, and maybe better and surely cheaper than print-based critics? We all judge the movies we see, and the world teems with arresting writers, so with the Internet why do we need professional critics? We all love movies, and many of us want to show our love by writing about them.

In other words, the problem may be that film criticism, in both print and the net, is currently short on information and ideas. Not many writers bother to put films into historical context, to analyze particular sequences, to supply production information that would be relevant to appreciating the movies. Above all, not many have genuine ideas—not statements of judgments, but notions about how movies work, how they achieve artistic value, how they speak to larger concerns. The One Big Idea that most critics have is that movies reflect their times. This, I've suggested earlier (pp. 23–25), is a weak idea at best.

Once, critics were driven by ideas. The earliest critics, like Frank Woods and Rudolf Arnheim, were struggling to define the particular strengths of this new art form. Later writers like André Bazin and the *Cahiers* crew tried to answer tough idea-based questions. What is distinctive about sound cinema? How can films creatively adapt novels and plays? What are the dominant "rules" of filmmaking? (And how might they be broken?) What constitutes a cinematic modernism worthy of that in other arts?

You could argue that without Bazin and his younger protégés, we literally couldn't see the artistry in the elegant staging of a film like George Cukor's *Pat and Mike*. Manny Farber, celebrated for his bebop writing style, also floated wider ideas about how the Hollywood industry's demand for a flow of product could yield unpredictable, febrile results.

One of the reasons that Sarris and Kael mattered, as Gerry's documentary points out, was that they represented alternative ideas of cinema. Sarris wanted to show, in the vein of *Cahiers*, that film was an expressive medium comparable in richness and scope to the other arts. One way to do that (not the only way) was to show that artists had mastered said medium. Kael, perhaps anticipating trends in cultural studies, argued that cinema's importance lay in being opposed to high art and part of a raucous, occasionally vulgar popular culture. The Sarris-Kael dispute isn't only a matter of taste or jockeying for power: it is genuinely about something bigger than the individual movie.

In the same period, critics' ideas had an impact on filmmaking. Sarris's promotion of the director as prime creator, with a bardic voice and a personal vision, was quickly taken up by Hollywood. Now every film is "a film by . . ." or "a . . . film": auteur theory shows up in the credits. Similarly, the concept of film noir was constructed by French critics and imported to the United States by Paul Schrader. Suddenly, unheralded films like *The Big Combo* popped up on the radar. Today viewers routinely talk about film noir, and filmmakers produce "neo-noirs." It seems to me as well that Hollywood became somewhat more sensitive to representation of women after Molly Haskell had brought feminist ideas to bear on the American studio tradition, avoiding simple celebration or denunciation. Film criticism had a robust impact on the industry when it trafficked in ideas.

You can argue that these are old examples. What new ideas are forthcoming from mainstream film criticism? In the Q&A after the screening, Gerry, like the rest of us, couldn't come up with many. On reflection, I wonder if the rise of academic film studies forced ideas to migrate to specialized journals and monographs. These ideas also had a different ambit—sometimes not particularly focused on cinema, or on aesthetics, or on creative problem solving.

Of course ideas don't move on their own. A more concrete way to put this is that bright, intellectually oriented young people who in an earlier era would have become journalistic critics became professors instead. The division of labor, it seems, was to aim film studies at an increasingly esoteric elite, and let film reviewers address the masses. It's an unhappy state of affairs that we still confront: recondite interpretations in the university, snap evaluations in the newspapers. You can also argue that print reviewers, by becoming less idea driven, paved the way for DIY criticism on the net.

What about information, the other ingredient I mentioned? If we think of mainstream film criticism as a part of arts journalism, we have to admit that most of it can't compare to the educational depth offered by the best criticism of music, dance, or the visual arts. You can learn more from Richard Taruskin on a Rimsky performance or Robert Hughes on a Goya show than you can learn about cinema from almost any reviewer I can think of. These writers bring a lifetime of study to their work, and they can invoke relevant comparisons, sharp examples, and quick analytical probes that illuminate the work at hand. Even academically trained film reviewers don't take the occasion to teach.

Most of the journalistic criticism I see today is uninformative about the range and depth of the art form, its traditions and capacities. Perhaps editors think that film isn't worthy of in-depth writing, or they fear that their readers would resist. As if to recall the battles that Woods, Arnheim, and others were fighting, cinema is still not taken seriously as an art form by the general public or even, I regret to say, by most academics.

Yet other aspects of information could be relevant. Close analysis offers us information about how the parts work together, how details cohere and motifs get transformed. For an example of how analysis can be brought into a newspaper's columns, see Manohla Dargis on one scene in *Zodiac* (http://www.nytimes.com/2008/01/06/movies/awardsseason/06darg.html?_r=2).

I'd also be inclined to see description—close, detailed, loving, or devastating—as providing information. It's no small thing to capture the sensuous surface of an artwork, as Susan Sontag put it. Good critics seek to evoke the tone or tempo of a film, its atmosphere and center of gravity. We tend to think that this is a matter of literary style, but it's quite possible that sheer style is overrated. (Yes, I'm thinking of Agee.) Thanks to our old friends adjective and metaphor, even a less-than-great writer can inform us of what a film looks and sounds like.

In any event, I'm coming to the view that the greatest criticism combines all the elements I've mentioned. As so often in life, love isn't always enough.

• •

Soon after this piece was posted, I moderated a panel on which several journalistic critics, from the press, television, and the net, chatted about their craft. During the question period, a student declared that he wanted to be a film critic. How could he achieve his dream?

The panelists' responses were pro forma. *See lots of movies. Argue with your friends. Above all, keep writing! The more you write, the better writer you will become.* (Oddly, that didn't help the Unabomber.) I wish I had had time to tell him something else. *Forget becoming a film critic. Try to become an intellectual. Read history, politics, and the sciences. Study art history, music history, theater, and literature. With a sense of the heritage of world culture, you might develop ideas and opinions that would shed light on film.*

I suppose that the pieces in this collection aim at something like this—blending pursuit of specialized knowledge with a broader sense of why movies matter to the history of the arts and to contemporary life. A dry run of this argument appeared in "Against Insight," a piece I wrote for the journal *Cinema Scope* (http://cinema-scope .com/wordpress/?page_id=717).

Do Filmmakers Deserve the Last Word?

OCTOBER 10, 2007

David here:

On December 3, 1913, this advertisement appeared in the *New York Dramatic Mirror*. D. W. Griffith had left the American Biograph company and set out on an independent path. Because Biograph never credited directors, casts, or crews, he wanted to make sure that the professional community was aware of his contributions. Not only did he point out that he had made several of the most noteworthy Biograph films; he also took credit for new techniques. He introduced, he claims, the close-up, powerful suspense, restrained acting, "distant views" (presumably picturesque long shots of the action), and the "switchback," his term for crosscutting—that editing tactic that alternates shots of different actions occurring at the same time.

Griffith's bid for credit was a shrewd career move, and it had repercussions after the stunning success of *The Birth of a Nation* two years later. Journalists took up the cry. An advertisement in *Wid's Year Book 1918*, a trade annual, quotes *The New Republic*, claiming, "As inventor of the 'close-up' and 'cut-back' and half a dozen other technical devices, he might be content to occupy the position of a Masolina, discoverer of perspective and the art of painting" (n.p.). Soon historians were taking Griffith at his word and crediting him with the breakthroughs he listed. He became known as the father of "film grammar" or "film language."

The idea hung on for decades. Here's the normally perceptive Dwight Macdonald, criticizing Dreyer's *Gertrud* for being anachronistic: "He just sets up his camera and photographs people talking to each other, usually sitting down, just the way it used to be done before Griffith made a few technical innovations."[1]

Filmmakers believed the Griffith story too. Orson Welles said of the "founding father" in 1960: "Every filmmaker who has followed him has done just that: followed him. He made the first close-up and moved the first camera."[2]

In the late 1970s a new generation of early-cinema scholars gave us a more nuanced account of Griffith's place in history. They pointed out that most of the innovations he claimed either predated his work,[3] or appeared simultaneously and independently in Europe and in other American films. Some Griffith partisans had already conceded this, but they maintained that he was the great synthesizer of these devices, and that he used them with a vigor and vividness that surpassed the sources.

That judgment seems right in part. Still, Eileen Bowser, Tom Gunning, Barry Salt, Kristin Thompson, Joyce Jesionowski, and other early-cinema researchers have drawn a more complicated picture.[4] Griffith did speed up cutting and devote an unusual number of shots to characters entering and leaving locales. But these innovations weren't usually recognized as original by previous historians. More interestingly, much of what Griffith did was not taken up by his successors. His technique was idiosyncratic in many respects. By 1915 younger directors like Walsh, Dwan, and De Mille were forging a smoother style that would be more characteristic of mainstream storytelling cinema than Griffith's somewhat eccentric scene breakdowns. Instead of creating film language, he spoke a forceful but often unique dialect.

The New York Dramatic Mirror ad coaxes me to reflect on how filmmakers have shaped critics' and historians' responses to their work. Hawks and Hitchcock developed a repertory of ideas, opinions, and anecdotes to be trotted out on any occasion. Today, directors write books, give interviews, appear on infotainment shows, and provide DVD commentary. We know that many of the talking points are planned as part of the film's publicity campaign, and journalists dutifully follow the lead. (In chapter 4 of The Frodo Franchise, Kristin discusses how this happened with The Lord of the Rings.) For many decades, in short, filmmakers have been steering critics and viewers toward certain ways of understanding their films. How much should we be bound by the way the filmmaker positions the film?

Deep Focus and Deep Analysis

Determining intentions is tricky, of course. Still, in many cases we can reconstruct a plausible sense of an artist's purposes on the basis of the art-

work, the historical context, surviving evidence, and other information.[5] This may or may not correspond to what the artist says on a particular occasion. For now, I want simply to point to one instance in which film-makers have shaped critical uptake, with results that are both illuminat-ing and limiting.

In the late 1940s and early 1950s, André Bazin, one of the great theo-rists and critics of cinema, argued that Orson Welles and William Wyler created a revolution in filmmaking. They staged a shot's action in several planes, some quite close to the camera, and maintained more or less sharp focus in all of them. Bazin claimed that Welles's *Citizen Kane* and *The Mag-nificent Ambersons* and Wyler's *The Little Foxes* and *The Best Years of Our Lives* constituted "a dialectical step forward in film language."

Their "deep-focus" style, he claimed, produced a more profound real-ism than had been seen before because they respected the integrity of physical space and time. According to Bazin, traditional cutting breaks the world into bits, a series of close-ups and long shots. But Welles and Wyler give us the world as a seamless whole. A scene unfolds in all its actual duration and depth. Moreover, the new style captured the way we see the world; given deep compositions, we must choose what to look at, foreground or background, just as we must choose in reality. Bazin wrote of Wyler: "Thanks to depth of field, at times augmented by action taking place simultaneously on several planes, the viewer is at least given the opportunity in the end to edit the scene himself, to select the aspects of it to which he will attend."[6] While granting differences between the directors, Bazin said much the same about Welles, whose depth of field "forces the spectator to participate in the meaning of the film by distinguishing the implicit relations" and creates "a psychological realism which brings the spectator back to the real conditions of perception."[7]

In addition, Bazin pointed out, this sort of composition was artistically efficient. The deep shot could supply both a close-up and a long shot in the same framing—a synthesis of what traditional editing had given in separate shots. Bazin wove all these ideas into a larger theory that cinema was inherently a realistic medium, bound to photographic recording, and Welles and Wyler had discovered one path to artistic expression without violating the medium's biases.

There are many objections to Bazin's argument, some of which I've rehearsed in *On the History of Film Style*. My point here is that Bazin was elaborating on analytical points that stemmed from publicity put out by Welles, Wyler, and especially their talented cinematographer Gregg Toland.

In a 1941 article in *American Cinematographer*, Toland talked freely about how he sought "realism" in *Citizen Kane*. The audience must feel it is "looking at reality, rather than merely a movie." Key to this was avoiding cuts by means of long takes and great depth of field, combining "what would conventionally be made as two separate shots—a close-up and an insert—into a single, non-dollying shot."[8] Toland defended his sometimes extreme stylistic experimentation on grounds of realism and production efficiency, criteria that carried some weight in his professional community of cinematographers and technicians.[9]

Toland's campaign for his style addressed the general public too. For *Popular Photography* he wrote an article explaining again that his "pan-focus" technique captured the conditions of real-life vision, in which everything appears in sharp focus.[10] A still broader audience encountered a *Life* feature in the same year,[11] explaining Toland's approach with specially made illustrations. Two samples show selective focus: one focused on the background, the other on the foreground. An accompanying photo shows pan-focus at work, with Toland in frame center, an actor in the background, and Toland's camera assistant in the foreground.

In sum, Toland's publicity prepared viewers, both professional and nonprofessional, for an odd-looking movie.

Throughout the 1940s, Welles and Wyler wrote articles and gave more interviews, often insisting that their films invited greater participation on the part of spectators. In a crucial 1947 statement, Wyler noted:

Gregg Toland's remarkable facility for handling background and foreground action has enabled me over a period of six pictures he has photographed to develop a better technique for staging my scenes. For example, I can have action and reaction in the same shot, without having to cut back and forth from individual cuts of the characters. This makes for smooth continuity, an almost effortless flow of the

scene, for much more interesting composition in each shot, and lets the spectator look from one to the other character at his own will, do his own cutting.[12]

Some of this publicity material made its way into French translation after the liberation of Paris, just as *Kane*, *The Little Foxes*, and other films were arriving.[13] Bazin and his contemporaries picked up the claims that these films broke the rules. Deep-focus cinematography became, in the hands of critics, a revolutionary new technique. They presented it as their discovery, not something laid out in the films' publicity.

But the case involved, as Huck Finn might say, some stretchers. Watching the baroque and expressionist *Kane*, it's hard to square it with normal notions of realism,

and we may suspect Toland of special pleading. Some of Toland's purported innovations, such as low-angle shots showing ceilings, had been seen before. Even the signature Toland look, with cramped, deep compositions shot from below, can be found across the history of cinema before *Kane*. Here is a shot from the 1939 Russian film *The Great Citizen, Part 2*, by Friedrich Ermler.

More seriously, some of Toland's accounts of *Kane* swerve close to deception. For decades people presupposed that dazzling shots like those below were made with wide-angle lenses.

Yet the deep focus in the first image was accomplished by means of a back-projected film showing the boy Kane in the window, while the second image is a multiple exposure. The glass and medicine bottle were shot separately against a black background, then the film was wound back and the action in the middle ground and background were shot. (And even the

middle-ground material, Susan in bed, is notably out of focus.) I suspect that the flashy deep-focus illustration in *Life*, shot with a still camera, is a trick shot too. In any event, much of the depth of field on display in *Kane* couldn't have been achieved by straight photography.[14]

RKO's special-effects department had years of experience with back projection and optical printing, notably in the handling of the leopard in *Bringing Up Baby*, so many of *Kane*'s boldest depth shots were assigned to them. But here is all that Toland has to say on the subject: "RKO special-effects expert Vernon Walker, ASC, and his staff handled their part of the production—a by no means inconsiderable assignment—with ability and fine understanding."[15]

Kane's reliance on rephotography deals a blow to Bazin's belief in cinema as a medium committed to recording an event in front of the camera. Instead, the film becomes an ancestor of the sort of extreme artificiality we now associate with computer-generated imagery.

Despite these difficulties, Toland's ideas sensitized filmmakers and critics to deep space as an expressive cinematic device. Modified forms of the deep-focus style became a major creative tradition in black-and-white cinema, lasting well into the 1960s. Bazin's analysis certainly developed Toland's ideas in original directions, and he creatively assimilated what Toland and his directors said into an illuminating general account of the history of film style. None of these creators and critics were probably aware of the remarkable depth apparent in pre-1920 cinema, or in Japanese and Soviet film of the 1930s. Their claims taught us to notice depth, even though we could then go on to discover earlier examples that undercut Toland's claims to originality.

Some Little Things to Grasp At

I assume that Toland and his directors were sincerely trying to experiment, however much they may have packaged their efforts to appeal to viewers' and critics' tastes. But sometimes artists aren't so sincere. In the 1950s, there emerged directors who started out as film critics, and they realized that they could guide the agenda. Here is Claude Chabrol:

I need a degree of critical support for my films to succeed: without that they can fall flat on their faces. So, what do you have to do? You have to help the critics over their notices, right? So, I give them a hand. "Try with Eliot and see if you find me there." Or "How do you fancy Racine?" I give them some little things to grasp at. In *Le Boucher* I stuck Balzac there in the middle, and they threw themselves on it like poverty upon the world. It's not good to leave them staring at a blank sheet of paper, not knowing how to begin…. "This film is definitely Balzacian," and there you are; after that they can go on to say whatever they want.[16]

Chabrol is unusually cynical, but surely some filmmakers are strategic in this way. I'd guess that a good number of independent directors pick up on currents in the culture and more or less self-consciously link those to their film.

Today, in press junkets directors can feed the same talking points to reporters over and over again. An example I discuss in *Poetics of Cinema* is the way that chaos theory has been invoked to give weight to films centering on networks and fortuitous connections. As I read interview after interview, I thought I'd scream if I encountered one more reference to a butterfly flapping its wings.

It's always vital to listen to filmmakers, but we shouldn't limit our analysis to what they highlight. We can detect things that they didn't deliberately put into their films, and we can sometimes find traces of things they don't know they know. For example, virtually no director has explained in detail his or her preferred mechanics for staging a scene, indicating choices about blocking, entrances and exits, actors' business, and the like. Such craft skills are presumably so intuitive that they aren't easy to spell out. Often we must reconstruct the director's intuitive purposes from the regularities of what we find onscreen. And it doesn't hurt, especially in this age of hype, to be a little skeptical and pursue what we think is interesting, whether or not a director has flagged it as worth noticing.

Notes

1. Dwight Macdonald, "*Gertrud*," *Esquire*, December 1965, 86.

2. Quoted in Orson Welles and Peter Bogdanovich, *This is Orson Welles*, ed. Jonathan Rosenbaum (New York: HarperCollins, 1992), 21.

3. Such would seem to be the case of the close-up, which of course is found very early in film history. But Griffith's idea of a close-up may not correspond to ours. See my book *On the History of Film Style* (Cambridge, MA: Harvard University Press, 1997), 121–23.

4. I give an overview of this rich body of research in chapter 5 of *On the History of Film Style*. See also various entries in the *Encyclopedia of Early Cinema*, ed. Richard Abel (New York: Routledge, 2005).

5. The most detailed argument for this view I know is Paisley Livingston's *Art and Intention: A Philosophical Study* (New York: Oxford University Press, 2007).

6. "William Wyler, or the Jansenist of Directing," in *Bazin at Work: Major Essays and Reviews from the Forties and Fifties*, ed. Bert Cardullo (New York: Routledge, 1997), 8.

7. *Orson Welles: A Critical View*, trans. Jonathan Rosenbaum (New York: Harper and Row, 1978), 80.

8. Toland, "Realism for *Citizen Kane*," *American Cinematographer* 22, no. 2 (February 1941): 54, 80.

9. See the discussion in David Bordwell, Janet Staiger, and Kristin Thompson, *The Classical Hollywood Cinema: Film Style and Mode of Production to 1960* (New York: Columbia University Press, 1985), 345–49.

10. Toland, "How I Broke the Rules in *Citizen Kane*," *Popular Photography*, June 1941, 55, 90–91.

11. "Orson Welles: Once a Child Prodigy, He Has Never Quite Grown Up," *Life*, May 26, 1941, 110–11.

12. Wyler, "No Magic Wand," *The Screen Writer* 2, no. 9 (February 1947): 10.

13. *Citizen Kane* had been heralded by Sartre even before it appeared in Paris; see "Quand Hollywood veut faire penser: 'Citizen Kane' film d'Orson Welles," *L'Écran français*, no. 5 (August 1, 1945), 3–5, 15. After the release, *La Revue du cinéma* promoted the film, printing an article in which Toland explained pan-focus through stills from *Kane* and *The Little Foxes*. See "L'Opérateur de prise de vues," *La Revue du cinéma*, no. 4 (January 1947), 16–24. Bazin was affiliated with the *Revue* and would have known these ideas intimately before he published his crucial essay "La Technique du *Citizen Kane*," *Les Temps modernes* 2, no. 17 (1947): 943–49.

14. Peter Bogdanovich was to my knowledge the first person to publish some of this information; see "The Kane Mutiny," *Esquire*, October 1972, 99–105, 180–90.

15. Toland, "Realism," 80.

16. "Chabrol Talks to Rui Noguera and Nicoletta Zalaffi," *Sight and Sound* 40, no. 1 (Winter 1970–1971): 6.

"Bazin was never naïve," wrote a web commentator after this entry appeared. Of course I wasn't claiming he was. He simply followed up claims by Welles and Toland about their intentions. But he had no information about the mechanics behind many of the images he considered photographically pristine. For more on those mechanics, see Robert Carringer, *The Making of Citizen Kane*, revised edition (Berkeley: University of California Press, 1996).

Just as Griffith's claims to originality spurred critics and historians to take a closer look at the development of technique in his period, Toland's stretchers about *Kane* have led to a very productive research into cinematic depth. I examine this tradition in chapters 3, 5, and 6 of *On the History of Film Style*. Bazin is clearly the central figure in this line of inquiry. He wrote penetrating analyses of the films of Welles, Wyler, and Renoir, and out of these prototypes he built a productive and provocative theory of cinema. But he did still more. He went beyond the examples he had at hand to consider the historical implications of a trend that promoted camera movement and deep space as substitutes for traditional editing. He enriched our understanding of film by advancing powerful ideas and by analyzing form and style—activities that I think give his writing an enduring claim on our attention.

Crix Nix *Variety*'s Tics

OCTOBER 24, 2007

THE INTERNATIONAL ENTERTAINMENT WEEKLY ■ JANUARY 22-28, 2001

WHY DID THEY NUKE-A DE LUCA?

Exit signals 'tamer' New Line under AOL

By CHARLES LYONS

H e's been surely one of the most approachable of studio chiefs. Also the most empathetic and creative, which is why talent is drawn to him.

Yet at 35, the Brooklyn-born, street-smart De Luca is temporarily Hollywood's youngest has-been. Last week, his long-time mentor, the irascible Bob Shaye, fired De Luca as New Line president.

De Luca had been with New

story department, rising over the years to prexy.

In that post, which he held for nearly eight years, the exec came to symbolize the swaggering, high-risk New Line, a self-proclaimed anti-studio known for a shrewd eye for movies that

De Luca began building larger-budgeted films and some of them, alas, have failed.

Insiders have speculated over the past two months about De Luca's possible departure. Now the industry is wondering why chairman-CEO Shaye and prexy-chief operating officer Michael Lynne cut De Luca loose, how the studio will change without him and what the exec will do next.

Time Warner. And it's no secret

Kristin here:

Today Anne Thompson's blog contains a short entry (http://weblogs .variety.com/thompsononhollywood/2007/10/blogger-attacks.html) linking to an "acerbic Brit Blogger" who has objected to the language used in *Variety*. The writer in question is Ronald Bergan, whose title sums up his claim: "It's time Variety started speaking English" (http://www.guardian .co.uk/film/filmblog/2007/oct/23/variety).

Bergan acknowledges that *Variety* is the best source of news on film, film festivals, and reviews. (The journal also covers TV and theater, as well as occasionally music and video games.) But, he adds, "pity then that it is unreadable." Bergan attributes the cause to "Varietyese." "Sticks Nix Hick Pix," which he cites from the 1930s, is the sort of joke that has "now worn thin."

Bergan also quotes a passage rife with what *Variety* itself terms "slanguage": "The rookie self-distribbed indie pic, helmed and lensed by Alan Smithee, is geared for upscale fest auds and urban markets, particularly in Euro zones west and east. But the protags are too high-hat for wider BO appeal. Most perfs are boffo and tech contributions are on the money." His opinion is that "this sort of writing not only degrades film criticism and demeans reviewers but debases the English language."

Thompson, unfazed, responds, "I enjoy throwing around slanguage like prexy, helmer, boffo and pics with legs. They're ingrained in my brain. What's not to like?"

What, indeed? Anne, there's plenty of mitting for your position, despite a few sour comments agreeing with Bergan that have been posted in response to your entry. As you point out, the heavier use of terms that might be unfamiliar to many comes in the print versions of *Variety*. The website, available to a broader public, tones them down distinctly. Given how much it costs to subscribe to the print edition, presumably mostly industry insiders (and some film historians) are reading it. Speaking as one who looks forward to the arrival of *Variety* every week and reads the film parts immediately, I enjoy its distinctive prose.

I occasionally run across a slanguage term I don't recognize. Usually they're pretty easy to figure out. As a hypothetical headline, "Thesp Ankles Ten-Percenter" is odd, but couldn't a reader figure out that an actor has left his or her agent? OK, it's a little obscure, but I for one find it charming rather than annoying. And if I can't figure a term out, I can check *Variety*'s online "Slanguage Dictionary" (http://www.variety.com /index.asp?layout=slanguage).

Indeed, I'd like to suggest that slanguage is only one element in *Variety*'s style. It's partly the breezy tone, whether slanguage is employed or not. It's most evident in the headlines, which can draw upon a number of devices. I can think of at least three. These examples come from the October 22–28, 2007, print edition.

There's rhyming, as most famously represented by "Sticks Nix Hick Pix." Most aren't that spectacular, but there's the subtler "Studios try slower pace to kudos race." (That's for one of Thompson's own stories.)

There is insistent alliteration, which is a pretty common tactic. Three instances: "Super-size Skeins Shrink Skeds," "Brooks Book is Biz's Bible," and "Claques Click with Canucks."

Finally, there's the pun on a familiar title or phrase: "Puttin' on the Snits."

These are all fairly ordinary Varietyese. I wish I could remember some of the past titles that have made me laugh out loud. Glancing through my files, I could find only one of those, on a story concerning studio head Michael De Luca's abrupt departure from New Line Cinema in early 2001 (above).

Dignified? No, but *Variety* covers the entertainment industries, and why should it not take on a little of the spirit of its subject?

When I was writing *The Frodo Franchise*, I wanted to make its style appealing. I wanted it to be clear that it wasn't just an academic tome but one aimed at the general reader—especially fans of the *Lord of the Rings* trilogy. Of course there are the standard tricks, such as starting chapters with an intriguing anecdote or with a surprising fact. It occurred to me that maybe I could lighten the tone with some amusing titles for the chapters and their subsections. What better model to follow than *Variety*?

I began to appreciate the challenges a *Variety* title-writer must face. In some cases I came up with some decent ones, falling into the three types I listed above—not that I thought about the categories while waiting for inspiration to strike. I've read the trades long enough to know what an authentic Varietyese title sounds like.

Rhyme: "Last Ditch for PJ Pitch" for the section where I talk about Peter Jackson's presentation of his project to New Line head Bob Shaye.

Alliteration: The book title itself, and the chapter "Flying Billboards and FAQs."

Puns on familiar phrases: "In the Darkness Spellbind Them," on the release and success of the films, and my personal favorite, "Zaentz and Zaentz-ability," on Miramax's negotiations with producer Saul Zaentz for the *Rings* production rights. A zinger of a *Variety* headline should make you groan at the silliness and yet at the same time shake your head with admiration.

But I couldn't think of such headline titles for every chapter and subsection. Many of them ended up being just plain and descriptive. Still, I tried in every case. It was fun.

That brings us back to the Bergan blog entry. He seems to believe that *Variety*'s writers are forced to write such stuff by their employers and ends his entry by urging them to "go on strike for more textual flexibility. I can see the headline now: Hax Nix Variety Lingo."

The author presumably thinks that that headline typifies Varietyese, but it really doesn't. It has no rhyme, no alliteration, no pun, and no slanguage words. Bergan just made up "hax" to echo the "Sticks" title quoted above. (Pretty insulting to *Variety* scribes, too.) I'll never be good enough or quick enough at this to get a job at *Variety*. Still, I offer the title of this entry as more in the magazine's true spirit.

• •

Since I wrote this entry, *Variety* has undergone many changes, though it has not abandoned slanguage. Anne Thompson has moved to the *indieWIRE Blog Network* (http://blogs.indiewire.com/thompsononhollywood/).

• •

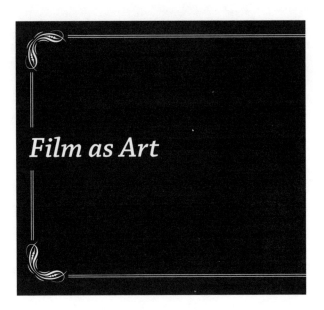

Film as Art

But What Kind of Art?

APRIL 20, 2007

David here:

We don't have to think of film as an art form. A historian can treat a movie as a document of its time and place. A war buff could scrutinize Eastwood's Iwo Jima movies for their accuracy, and a chess expert could sieve through *Looking for Bobby Fischer* to discover, move by move, what matches were dramatized. But most of the time we assume that cinema is an art of some sort.

Not necessarily *high art*. Cinema is often a popular art, or in philosopher Noël Carroll's phrase, a *mass art*. (See his *A Philosophy of Mass Art* [New York: Oxford University Press, 1998].) From this angle, there's no split between art and entertainment. Popular songs are undeniably music, and best-selling novels are instances of literature. Similarly, megaplex movies belong as fully to the art of film as do the most esoteric experiments. Whether those movies, or the experiments, are *good* cinema is another story, but cinema they remain.

So, at least, is our position in *Film Art: An Introduction*. We draw our examples from documentaries, animated films, avant-garde films, mainstream entertainment vehicles, and films aimed at narrower audiences. In other writing, Kristin has done research on high-art movements like German Expressionism and Soviet Montage (she wrote her dissertation on *Ivan the Terrible*), but she's also written about popular cinema from Doug Fairbanks to *The Lord of the Rings*. I've indulged my admiration for Hou Hsiao-hsien and Carl Theodor Dreyer, but also I've tried to tease out the aesthetics of Hong Kong action pictures and contemporary Hollywood blockbusters. Ozu Yasujiro gives us the best of both worlds: one of cinema's most accomplished artists, he was also a popular commercial filmmaker.

Still, people who look upon cinema as an art don't necessarily share the same notions of what kind of art it is. They have different conceptions of cinema's artistic dimensions, and we won't find unanimity of opinion among filmmakers, critics, academics, or audiences.

When we study film theory, this sort of question comes to the fore, and so today's blog will be a bit more theoretical than most. Don't let that scare you off, though; I'm trying for clarity, not murk.

Dimensions

People have tended to think of cinema as an art by means of rough analogies to the other arts. After all, film came along at a point when virtually all the other arts had been around for millennia. It's commonly said that film is the only art form whose historical origins we can determine. So it's been natural for people to compare this new medium with older arts.

Here are the comparisons that come to my mind:

- Film is a *photographic* art.
- Film is a *narrative* art.
- Film is a *performing* art.
- Film is a *pictorial* art.
- Film is an *audiovisual* art.

Let me say off the bat that I think that film is a synthetic medium, in the sense that all these features and more can be found in it. It's like opera, which is at once narrative, performative, musical, and even pictorial. I mark out these dimensions simply to show some emphases in people's thinking about cinema. As we'll see, these ideas can be mixed together in various ways.

Film as a Photographic Art

For many early filmmakers, such as the Lumière brothers, cinema was a means of capturing reality, recording the visible world. Movies were moving photographs. Naturally, this conception of cinema leads us to treat documentary as the central mode of filmmaking.

It's an appealing idea. G. W. Bush reading "My Pet Goat" wouldn't be as revelatory presented as a painting or a theater performance. On film we can see the event as it occurred and judge it as if we were in the same room. Even in fictional cinema, you can argue, the physicality of the actors, the tangibility of the setting, and the details—a train's pistons, wind rustling through grass—could not be rendered, or even imagined, so powerfully in a nonphotographic medium. In addition, consider Jackie Chan. His stunts are astonishing partly because we know he really did them and the camera photographed them. In an animated film, or a CGI-based one, a character's acrobatics or brushes with death aren't so thrilling.

The great film theorist André Bazin claimed that cinema's photographic basis made it very different from the more traditional arts. By recording the world in all its immediacy, giving us slices of actual space and true duration, film puts us in a position to discover our link to primordial experience. Other arts rely on conventions, Bazin thought, but cinema goes beyond convention to reacquaint us with the concrete reality that surrounds us but that we seldom notice.

I think that Bazin's idea lies behind our sense that long takes and a static camera are putting us in touch with reality and inviting us to notice details that we usually overlook in everyday life. Moreover, you can argue that in treating cinema as a photographic art the filmmaker surrenders a degree of control over what we see and how we see it. Bazin made this claim about the Italian neorealists and Jean Renoir: creation becomes a matter of an existential collaboration between humans and the concrete world around us.

An example I used in my book *Figures Traced in Light* pertains to a moment in Hou Hsiao-hsien's *Summer at Grandfather's*, when a tiny toy fan falls between railroad tracks as a locomotive roars past. The fan's blades stop, then spin in the opposite direction as the train thunders over it. The blades reverse again when the train has gone. (This detail might not be visible on video.) Did Hou know how the fan would behave? Isn't it just as likely he simply discovered it after the fact, making his shot a kind of experiment in the behavior of things? Conceived as a species of photography, cinema can yield visual discoveries that no other art can.

Interestingly, cinema didn't have to be photographic. Many early experiments with moving images were made with strips of drawings, as in Émile Reynaud's praxinoscope. You can argue that recording glimpses of the world photographically simply proved to be the easiest way to obtain a long string of slightly different images that could generate the illusion of movement. Some filmmakers, such as George Lucas, hold that filmmakers are no longer tied to photography, and that the digital revolution will allow cinema to finally realize itself as a painterly art. More on that below.

Film as a Narrative Art

This is at the core of Hollywood's explicit concerns. Producers, directors, crew, and of course screenwriters will agree that without a good story, the movie fails. Our indie and Indiewood filmmakers say they're trying to find fresh stories, the ones that "haven't been told yet." Overseas filmmakers competing with Hollywood tell us, "We have our own stories to tell." Even the most celebrated art-house filmmakers often say they're interested in character as revealed through action. Resnais, Rivette, Fassbinder, Haneke, and all the rest may have told unusual stories, but still they told 'em.

Likewise, many viewers will say that they go to the movies to experience a story. Reviewers online and in the popular press, if they do nothing else, are obliged to sketch out the film's plot, though they mustn't give away the ending. Even in academia, most discussions of films focus on what happens in the narrative.

When we consider film genres, we're usually concentrating on the narrative aspects of them. Most genres display typical characters and plot patterns. The backstage musical features aging stars and young hopefuls, caught up in the process of putting on a show. The horror film typically centers on a monster's attack on humans, who must fight back. One type of science fiction shows us an overweening scientist striving to go beyond "what is proper for humans to know." Both fans and scholars discuss other aspects of genre films, but narrative is often central to their concerns.

Historians have traced in great detail how filmmakers employed cinema as a narrative art, but we're making more discoveries all the time. How, for instance, have films signaled flashbacks? How do they let us know we're in a character's mind, or attached to his or her optical point of view? How have they structured their plots? Can we pick out distinct approaches to narrative—in various periods, or genres, or national cinemas? How have narrative conventions changed over the years? Some of the answers Kristin and I have proposed can be found elsewhere on this site, and in our books and articles.

Film as a Performing Art

In the West, since Plato and Aristotle, we've distinguished between verbal storytelling and dramatic presentation, or performance. Films may be stories, but they're not exactly told: they're enacted. At Oscar time, we're especially conscious of this analogy, for the Actor and Actress nominees usually garner the most public attention.

Hollywood acknowledged cinema as a performing art in the 1910s, when it created the star system. The star reminds us that film acting isn't exactly the same as theater acting, since an elusive charisma puts the performance across. John Wayne, Marilyn Monroe, Keanu Reeves, and many other "axioms of the cinema" aren't good actors by stage-bound standards, but once they show up on screen, you can't take your eyes off them. This notion intersects with the photographic premise: we say that the camera seems to love them.

You can argue that Andy Warhol revamped this idea. His Superstars weren't photogenic by ordinary standards, but their almost clinical narcissism and exhibitionism, captured by the camera, made them as mesmerizing as any matinee idols. Warhol films like *Paul Swann* create rather disturbing emotions by putting us in the presence of an awkward performer.

Reviewers place a premium on a movie's performance dimension. After they've told us a bit of the plot, they appraise the job the actors did. Some ambitious critics have written wonderful appreciative essays on acting, as in Andrew Sarris's *You Ain't Heard Nothin' Yet* and the collection *OK, You Mugs.*

Academic film studies has been slow to study acting systematically, partly because of a bias against considering cinema as a theatrical art, and partly because acting is very hard to analyze. But Charles Affron, James Naremore, Roberta Pearson, and Ben Brewster and Lea Jacobs have greatly helped us understand performance practices. They show, among other things, that it isn't just a matter of the face or the voice: a fluttered hand or a willowy stance can be as powerful as a frown or a line reading.

Film as a Pictorial Art

Progressive opinion in the silent era tended to deny that film was a performing art, since that would make it a form of theater. No, film had unique capacities. Cinema was essentially *moving pictures.*

It was a visual art that unfolded in time, so a movie was neither quite the same as a painting (frozen in time) or as a stage play (not pictures but three-dimensional reality). The coming of sound somewhat reduced the appeal of this line of argument, but to a very great extent, students of film technique still emphasize cinema as a visual art.

Theorists argued that the film frame was a pictorial field, not a proscenium stage. Action unfolded in the frame in ways that dynamized space. The choice of angle, camera distance, camera movement, and the like created a visual fluidity that had no equivalent on stage or in other graphic arts. Even cinematic staging was quite different from blocking in a theatrical space. Add to this the ability to join one strip of pictures to another via editing, and we have a unique pictorial medium.

The theorists of the silent era, like Rudolf Arnheim and the Russian montagists, gave us a vocabulary and an orientation to studying visual style, but their legacy hasn't been fully developed. Journalistic reviewers typically don't pay that much attention to the way movies look. Nor, surprisingly, do academics. Film studies departments seldom pursue research into visual style and structure.

Here the professors are out of sync with the people whose work they study. Manuals and film schools teach composition, lighting, cutting, camera placement, and the like. Professional filmmakers all over the world often think in pictures; they prepare shot lists and storyboards and care very much about the color values and editing patterns of the finished work. We can see their interest in visuals in DVD commentaries and supplements, and as viewers start to absorb bonus materials, perhaps their interest will be whetted too.

Needless to say, a number of avant-garde filmmakers, from Viking Eggeling and Walter Ruttmann to Maya Deren, Stan Brakhage, Ernie Gehr, James Benning, and Nathaniel Dorsky, have also thought of cinema as having the power to refresh, even redeem, our vision. But many of the most important directors aiming at broader audiences are also renowned for their visual styles. To mention just a few: Griffith, Feuillade, Sjöström, Keaton, De Mille, Murnau, Lang, Dreyer, Lubitsch, and Dovzhenko; Ford, Hitchcock, and von Sternberg; Renoir, Ozu, Mizoguchi, and Ophüls; early Bergman, Antonioni, Jancsó, Resnais, Angelopoulos, Tarr, Tarkovsky, Kieślowski, Kiarostami, and Mohsen Makhmalbaf; Scorsese, Spielberg, Michael Mann, and Tim Burton. Some, like Oshima, Sokurov, and Johnnie To, have been polystylistic, exploring many different pictorial pathways.

Film as an Audiovisual Art

In the 1920s, many theorists feared the coming of synchronized sound, since that would thrust film back toward theater. The "talkies" would sacrifice visual artistry to Broadway dialogue. This worry was mistaken, but I can sympathize. Probably the mandatory silence of early film pushed filmmakers to find means of visual expression. Would we have had Chaplin and the other clowns if actors could have spoken at the start?

Yet a great deal of sound cinema wasn't canned theater. Film became a synthetic medium blending imagery, the spoken word, sound effects, and music into something that was neither painting nor theater nor illustrated radio.

Although he's thought of as the premiere theorist of editing, Eisenstein favored this idea of audiovisual synthesis. He was fascinated by the ways in which images and music worked together, creating an idea or feeling that couldn't be expressed by either one. If shot A followed by shot B gave us something that wasn't present in either one, then why couldn't shot A and sound B yield the same results? He believed that Disney's 1930s films were the strongest efforts in this direction, as when a peacock fanned out his tail to a rippling melody. Eisenstein called it "synchronization of senses."

Eisenstein sometimes pushed this idea pretty far. His remarkable analysis of one sequence in *Alexander Nevsky* tried to show how the movement of the viewer's eye across a suite of shots actually mimicked the movement of the music. He made the case tough for himself because the shots contain almost no movement within them: Eisenstein claimed that we read the compositions from left to right, in time with the musical chords!

Not only Disney but many filmmakers of the 1930s experimented with audiovisual fusion—Kozintsev and Trauberg in *Alone*, Pudovkin in *Deserter*, Mamoulian in *Love Me Tonight*, Renoir in the final danse macabre of *The Rules of the Game*, and Busby Berkeley in his musicals. Welles made *Citizen Kane* a feast of audiovisual echoes, as when the wobbly descent of Susan's singing voice is matched by the flickering of a stage light that finally dies out.

With magnetic and multichannel recording in the 1950s, filmmakers could compose very complex sound mixes, and later improvements offered still more possibilities. After *Star Wars* and *Close Encounters of the Third Kind*, we expected a movie to be an immersive audiovisual experience, like the light show at a rock concert. Scorsese, especially in *Raging Bull* and *GoodFellas*, created powerful mergers of music, sound effects, camera movement, and character movement. So did the Hong Kong kung-fu films of the 1970s and early 1980s. The spellbinding languor of Wong Kar-wai's films stems largely, I think, from their synchronization of pulsing color, slow motion, drifting camerawork, and evocative music.

The avant-garde has pursued more elusive synchronizations of sense modes. The idea of synthesis was floated in the silent era, when experimenters like Oskar Fischinger used musical pieces to anchor their abstract imagery. This tendency has resurfaced in music videos, some of which (Michel Gondry's in particular) have clear links to the experimental tradition. So too do the shorts and features of Peter Greenaway, especially in his collaborations with composer Michael Nyman. In a film like *Prospero's*

Books, Greenaway seems to follow Eisenstein in imagining a Wagnerian synthesis of writing, image, and sound.

By contrast, Godard explores all manner of unpredictable junctures between image and sound, with the tracks teasing us but avoiding a complete coordination. Somewhat similar are the disjunctive image/sound juxtapositions in Peter Kubelka's *Unsere Afrikareise* and Bruce Connor's *Report*, or the inverse and retrograde organizations of Structural Film soundtracks like Michael Snow's *Wavelength* and J. J. Murphy's *Print Generation*.

Film academics have begun to analyze image/sound juxtapositions, studying the development of early talkies and more recent Dolby technology. Arguably, film researchers now pay more attention to music than they pay to imagery. By contrast, most journalistic critics ignore a film's soundtrack, except occasionally to comment on line readings and catchy tunes. As for ordinary audiences, perhaps DVDs and home theater technology have made people more aware of how movies can saturate our senses with audiovisual correspondences.

Three Waivers

1. Once I floated these distinctions in a seminar discussion, and a participant mentioned that cinema was also an *emotional* art. I'd agree that a lot of cinema aims at arousing feelings, but this idea can be found in all the dimensions I traced. Each conception of film favors different means of stirring up emotion.

For example, the photographic approach holds that recording and revealing the world is the most effective way to move spectators, while the narrative approach favors stories as the means to that end. The performance-based approach trusts that we'll react empathetically to the emotional states displayed by our fellow humans, but the visual-art approach says that cinema can arouse feeling by manipulating pictures in time and space, perhaps even pictures that don't show any people at all. Eisenstein argued that synchronization of senses was the most powerful form of emotional stimulation, creating in the viewer an "ecstasy" comparable to religious fervor. Beyond these general considerations, it would be worthwhile to tease out the different sorts of emotion that each perspective tends to emphasize.

2. Someone else might ask, what about other analogies? Filmmakers and critics have sometimes compared cinema to music or poetry. Shouldn't those arts be added to the list?

I think that these comparisons show up principally within the broad idea of film as a pictorial art. The French Impressionist directors of the silent era thought that they were making "visual music," and Brakhage's and Deren's conceptions of the "film lyric" were mainly pictorial. I'd suggest that filmmakers in the pictorial-art camp have looked to these adjacent arts for models of patterning (meter, rhythm, motif development) and imagery (metaphor and subjective states in lyric verse). Filmmakers are also attracted to the idea that music and poetry tend to be suggestive rather than explicit, conveying powerful feelings in elusive and open-ended ways.

Polemically, filmmakers often conjure up these musical and literary analogies to counter the mainstream cinema's emphasis on narrative and performance. If we think of film as lyric or rhapsody, story seems less important. The same thing goes, I think, for thinking of film as moving architecture or kinetic sculpture; the analogy again targets film's pictorial dimension and its non-narrative potential.

3. To think of film as having an affinity with another art form isn't to say that they're identical. Thinking of cinema as a performance-based art, for example, doesn't commit you to saying that film acting is the same as theatrical acting. Instead, thinking along these lines seems to create a first approximation, an initial comparison that lets you move on to notice differences. Once you consider film as a pictorial art, you can then ask in what ways it differs from other pictorial arts, or in what ways this particular movie transforms or reworks the techniques of painting. *Ballet mécanique*, which we analyze in *Film Art*, owes a lot to cubism, but its imagery isn't identical to what Picasso, Braque, and Gris came up with on canvas. All of these analogies seem to work best as frameworks for sensitizing us to both similarities and differences between film and other arts.

And ... So?

Each conception of film art harbors a good portion of truth. Each may fail to cover all of cinema, but for certain types of film, or particular movies, some are likely to be more helpful than others.

For example, it's useful to consider David Lynch as making audiovisual works, in which blinking lights or grooves in pine planks seem uncannily synchronized with throbs and hums and Julee Cruise vibrato. Very often story and acting seem to precipitate out of an enveloping pictorial/auditory atmosphere. This isn't to say that you couldn't study narrative or performance in Lynch films; it's just that taking up the audiovisual-mix perspective will throw certain aspects into sharper relief.

You could also argue that the Hollywood studio era blended many of these various appeals into a single strong tradition. Story was important, but so was performance. Visual style was often striking, but so too was an expressive soundtrack that went beyond simply recording the dialogue. Sound effects, musical scores, and verbal hooks between scenes created imaginative resonances with the image track. Contrariwise, we can see some avant-garde traditions as taking a purist tack. In several of his films, Brakhage reduces narrative, purges performance, and bans sound: we have to engage wholly and solely with a pictorial experience.

Just as we can distinguish film traditions along these dimensions, we can contrast writers and thinkers. Some critics are very good in pinning down performance qualities; others excel at plot dissection or visual analysis. Arnheim is sensitive to pictorial values but he has little to contribute to understanding storytelling.

Bazin and Eisenstein are attuned to several of the dimensions I've traced out. Bazin's interest in cinema's photographic basis also alerted him to pictorial possibilities, like deep focus and camera movement. Eisenstein, famous for his ideas on cinema's visual dimension, was as I've said interested in sound as well. He was no less concerned with film performance, which he conceived as expressive movement (to be synchronized with properties of the image and the soundtrack). But he voiced little interest in narrative or photography.

I warned you that this blog would be theoretical, but I hope the take-away message is clear. Cinema is teeming with artistic possibilities, and each of these frameworks can illuminate certain areas of choice and control. We don't need to pick a single creed to live by, but we deepen our understanding of film by being sensitive to as many as we can manage.

• •

The study of painting, literature, and music benefited from centuries of reflection on how each medium could be employed artistically. By contrast, thinking about film as a distinct art flourished from about 1910 to 1960—and during that brief period, the art's technological base was constantly changing (the inventions of sound, color, widescreen, television, video). During the 1960s, theorists began to consider film as a semiotic system, a system of culturally localized signs, with cinema seen as a vehicle of social and political signification. Calling something a *technique* suggests artistic choice and control; calling it a *code* emphasizes its place in a more impersonal system of signs and meaning.

By the 1980s, mainstream academic researchers were considering cinema primarily as a cultural arena teeming with conflicting notions of race, class, nation, gender, identity, and social processes. Films were read as symptoms of modernity, postmodernity, imperialism, and consumer culture. These frameworks continue to be central to film studies, and indeed to the humanities generally. As a result, the particularity of how cinema works as a unique art has often been ignored.

By playing down the artistic aspects of cinema, the socio-political-cultural frameworks have had little resonance with either practicing filmmakers or ordinary film lovers. Bernard Shaw's idea that every profession is a conspiracy against the laity was fulfilled as film scholars created a remarkably self-enclosed realm. Today talk about film proceeds on two tracks. Academics tend to concentrate on cinema as a cultural force, often appealing to abstract, not to say abstruse, theoretical doctrines. Journalistic and belletristic criticism treats film as an art, but without reflecting on what that concept entails. The two tracks almost never intersect.

Our own academic research explores film's capacities and history as an art form, while also noting how it has been shaped by social dynamics, production contexts, and adjacent arts. Thinking through cinema's artistic possibilities can be one bridge between academic inquiry and a wider readership of film lovers.

This Is Your Brain on Movies, Maybe

MARCH 7, 2007

David here:

Normally we say that suspense demands an uncertainty about how things will turn out. Watching Hitchcock's *Notorious* for the first time, you feel suspense at certain points—when the champagne is running out during the cocktail party, or when Devlin escorts the drugged Alicia out of Sebastian's house. That's because, we usually say, you don't know if the spying couple will succeed in their mission.

But later you watch *Notorious* a second time. Strangely, you feel suspense, moment by moment, all over again. You know perfectly well how things will turn out, so how can there be uncertainty? How can you feel suspense on the second, or twenty-second viewing?

I was reminded of this problem watching *United 93*, which presents a slightly different case of the same phenomenon. Although I was watching it for the first time, I knew the outcomes of the 9/11 events it portrays. I knew in advance that the passengers were going to struggle with the hijackers and deflect the plane from its target, at the cost of all their lives. Yet I felt what seemed to me to be authentic suspense at key moments. It was as if some part of me were hoping against hope that the disaster might be avoided. And perhaps the film's many admirers will feel something like that suspense on repeated viewings as well.

Psychologist Richard Gerrig in his book *Experiencing Narrative Worlds* calls this "anomalous suspense": feeling suspense when reading or viewing, although you know the outcome.

Anomalous Suspense: Some Theories

Anomalous suspense has been fairly important in the history of cinema. One of the most famous instances in the early years of feature film is the assassination of President Lincoln in Griffith's *The Birth of a Nation* (1915). Griffith prolongs the event with crosscutting and detail shots in a way that promotes suspense, even though we know that Booth will murder Lincoln. Anomalous suspense, of course, isn't specific to movies; we can feel this way reading a familiar book or watching a TV docudrama about historical events. Young children listening to the story of Little Red Riding Hood seem to be no less wrought up on the umpteenth version than on the first.

This is very odd. How can it happen?

One answer is simple: what you're feeling in a repeat viewing, or a viewing of dramatized historical events, isn't suspense at all. Robert Yanal has explained this position in chapter 8 of his *Paradoxes of Emotion and Fiction* (1999). He suggests that you're responding to other aspects of the story. Maybe in rewatching *Notorious* you're enjoying the unfolding romance, and you attribute your interest to suspense. And there are feelings akin to suspense that don't rely on uncertainty—dread, for instance, in facing inevitable doom. (This is my example, not Yanal's, but I think it's plausible.) Another possibility Yanal floats is that on repeat viewings, you have actually forgotten what happens next, or how the story ends.

Yanal's account doesn't fully satisfy me, largely because I think that most people know what suspense feels like and attest to feeling it on repeat viewings. I did feel some dread in watching *United 93*, but I think that was mixed with a genuine feeling of suspense—a momentary, if illogical uncertainty about the future course of events. In any case, I didn't forget what happened at the end; I expected it in quite a self-conscious way.

Richard Gerrig, the psychologist who gave anomalous suspense its name, offers a different solution. He posits that in general, when we reread a novel or rewatch a film, our cognitive system doesn't apply its prior knowledge of what will happen. Why? Because our minds evolved to deal with the real world, and there you never know exactly what will happen next. Every situation is unique, and no course of events is literally identical to an earlier one. "Our moment-by-moment processes evolved in response to the brute fact of nonrepetition" (*Experiencing Narrative Worlds*, 171). Somehow, this assumption that every act is unique became our default for understanding events, even fictional ones we've encountered before.

I think that Gerrig leaves this account somewhat vague, and its conception of a "unique" event has been criticized by Yanal. But I think that Gerrig's invocation of our evolutionary history is relevant.

Suspense as Morality, Probability, and Imagination

The most influential current theory of suspense in narrative is put forth by Noël Carroll. The original statement of it can be found in "Toward a Theory of Film Suspense" in his book *Theorizing the Moving Image*. Carroll proposes that suspense depends on our forming tacit questions about the story as it unfolds. Among other things, we ask how plausible certain outcomes are and how morally worthy they are. For Carroll, the reader or viewer feels suspense as a result of estimating, more or less intuitively, that the situation presents a morally undesirable outcome that is strongly probable.

When the plot indicates that an evil character will probably fail to achieve his or her end, there isn't much suspense. Likewise, when a good character is likely to succeed, there isn't much suspense. But we do feel suspense when it seems that an evil character is likely to succeed, or that a good character is likely to fail. Given the premises of the *Notorious* situation, the likelihood is very great that Alicia and Devlin will be caught by Sebastian and the Nazis, so we feel suspense.

What of anomalous suspense? Carroll would seem to have a problem here. If we know the outcome of a situation because we've seen the movie before, wouldn't our assessments of probability shift? On the second viewing of *Notorious*, we can confidently say that Alicia and Devlin's stratagems have a 100 percent chance of success. So then we ought not to feel any suspense.

Carroll's answer is that we can feel emotions in response to *thoughts* as well as beliefs. Standing at a viewing station on a mountaintop, safe behind the railing, I can look down and feel fear. I don't really *believe* I'll fall. If I did, I would back away fast. I *imagine* I'm going to fall; perhaps I even picture myself plunging into the void and, à la Björk, slamming against the rocks at the bottom. Just the thought of it makes my palms clammy on the rail.

Carroll points out that imagining things can arouse intense emotions, and his book *The Philosophy of Horror* uses this point to explain the appeal of horrific fictions. The same thing goes, more or less, for suspense. If the uncertainty at the root of suspense involves beliefs, then there ought to be a problem with repeat viewings. But if you merely *entertain the thought* that the story situation is uncertain, then you can feel suspense just as easily as if you entertained the thought that you were falling off the mountaintop.

In other words, the relation between morality and probability in a suspenseful situation is offered not to your beliefs but to your imagination. When you judge that in this story the good is unlikely to be rewarded, you react appropriately—regardless of what you know or believe about what happens next.

How are we encouraged to entertain such thoughts in our imagination? Carroll indicates that the film or piece of literature needs to focus our attention on the suspenseful factors at work, thus guiding us to the appropriate thoughts about the situation. There might, though, be more than attention at work here.

The Firewall

In *Consciousness and the Computational Mind* (1987), psychologist Ray Jackendoff asked why music doesn't wear out. When composers write tricky chord progressions or players execute startling rhythmic changes, why do those surprise or thrill us on rehearing? Similarly, you've seen this illusion many times, and you know that the two horizontal lines are of equal length. You can measure them.

 Yet your eyes tell you that the lines are of different lengths, and no knowledge can make you see them any other way. This illusion, in Jerry Fodor's phrase, is cognitively impenetrable.

 We can reexperience familiar music or fall prey to optical illusions because, in essence, our lower-level perceptual activities are *modular*. They are fast and split up into many parallel processes working at once. They're also fairly dumb, quite impervious to knowledge. Jackendoff suggests that our musical perception, like our faculties for language and vision, relies on "a number of autonomous units, each working in its own limited domain, with limited access to memory. For under this conception, expectation, suspense, satisfaction, and surprise can occur within the processor: in effect, the processor is always hearing the piece for the first time" (245).

"Early vision" is modular in a similar way, with different detection systems concentrating on specific features, such as shape, color, and movement. As students of cinema, we're familiar with the fact that vision can be cognitively impenetrable. We know that movies consist of single frames, but we can't see them in projection; we see a moving image. Early vision works fast and under very basic, hardwired assumptions about how the world is. That's because our visual system evolved to detect regularities in a certain kind of environment. That environment didn't include movies or cunningly designed optical illusions. So there might be a kind of firewall between parts of our perception and our knowledge or memory about the real world.

Daniel J. Levitin's lively book *This is Your Brain on Music* summarizes the neurological evidence for this firewall in our auditory system. When we listen to music, a great deal happens at very low levels. Meter, pitch, timbre, attack, and loudness are detected, dissected, and reconstructed across many brain areas. The processes run fast, in parallel, and we have very little voluntary control of them, let alone awareness of them. Of course higher-level processes, like knowledge about the piece, the composer, or the performer, feed into the whole activity. But that's inevitably running on top of the very fast uptake, disassembly, and reassembly of sensory information.

So here's my hunch: A great deal of what contributes to suspense in films derives from low-level, modular processes. They are cognitively impenetrable, and that creates a firewall between them and what we remember from previous viewings.

A suspense film often contains several very gross cues to our perceptual uptake. We get tension-filled music and ominous sound effects, such as low-bass throbbing. We get rapid cutting and swift camera movements. Often the shots are close-ups, as in *Notorious*'s wine-cellar scene and during the characters' final descent of the staircase. Close-ups concentrate our vision on one salient item, creating the attentional focus Carroll emphasizes. The shots are often cut together so fast that we barely have time to register the information in each one.

This isn't to say that the action itself has to be fast. The action in the Hitchcock scenes isn't rapid, but its stylistic treatment is. In typical suspense scenes, our "early vision" and "early audition," biased toward quick pickup, are given rapid-fire bursts of information while our slower, deliberative processes are put on hold. This is happening in the *Birth of a Nation* assassination scene, as well as in the frantic second half of *United 93*.

Further, what is shown can push our processing as well. Seeing people's facial expressions touches off empathy and emotional contagion, perhaps through mirror neurons, those neurons that fire when we perform an activity *or* when we see others perform it. This tendency may explain why we can, momentarily, feel a wisp of empathy for unsympathetic characters. When their expressions show fear, we detect and resonate to that even if we aren't rooting for them to succeed.

We may also be responding to some very basic scenarios for suspenseful action. Imagine dangling at a great height; "hanging" is the root of the word *suspense*. Or imagine hurtling toward an obstruction, or being stalked by an animal, or being advanced upon by a looming figure. As prototypes of impending danger, these events may in themselves trigger a minimal feeling of suspense. And such situations are part of filmic storytelling from its earliest years.

Maybe we're predisposed to find facial expressions and dangerous situations salient because of our evolutionary history. Creatures who were sensitive to such situations would have increased survival chances. Or maybe these predispositions are learned from a very young age. Either way, such responses don't require much deliberate thinking. They just trigger other responses that we can reflect upon later.

Stylistic emphasis and prototype situations surely help the attention-focusing that Carroll discusses. But I'm suggesting something stronger: Many of these cues don't merely guide our attention to the critical suspense-creating factors in the scene. These cues are arresting and arousing *in themselves*. They trigger responses that, in the right narrative situation, can generate suspense, regardless of whether we've seen the movie before.

Beyond these cues, of course we have to understand the story to some degree. Probably many of the aspects of storytelling that Carroll, Gerrig, and others (including me) have highlighted come into play. As Hitchcock famously pointed out, suspense sometimes depends on telling the viewer more than the character knows. We have to see the bomb under the table that the character doesn't know about. Suspense is also conjured up by Carroll's ratio of morality to probability, our real-world understanding of deadlines, and other higher-order aspects of comprehension. In addition, our knowledge of how stories are typically told probably shapes our uptake. We expect suspense to be a part of a film, and so we're alert for cues that facilitate it.

Involuntary Suspense

So I'm hypothesizing that part of the suspense we feel in rewatching a film depends on fast, mandatory, data-driven pickup. That activity responds to the salient information *without regard* to what we already know.

According to this argument, the sight of Eve Kendall dangling from Mount Rushmore will elicit some degree of suspense no matter how many times you've seen *North by Northwest*, and that feeling will be amplified by the cutting, the close-ups, the music, and so on. Your sensory system can't help but respond, just as it can't help seeing unequal-length lines in the pictorial illusion. For some part of you, every viewing of a movie is the first viewing.

This tendency may hold good for other emotions than suspense. In the psychological jargon I adopted in *Narration in the Fiction Film*, experiencing a narrative is likely to be both a bottom-up process and a top-down process. Suspense and other emotional effects in film may not depend only on conceptual judgments about uncertainty, likelihood, and so on. They may also depend on quick and dirty processes of perception that don't have much access to memory or deliberative thinking.

Film works on our embodied minds, and the "embodied" part includes a wondrous number of fast, involuntary brain activities. This process gives filmmakers enormous power, along with enormous responsibilities.

• •

There are plenty of academic discussions of cinematic perception and cognition. Although the theoretical literature is more subtle than I could convey in short compass, this blog essay was an effort to introduce those ideas by means of a puzzling phenomenon that every film viewer has encountered.

What emerges from these reflections is a common finding in research: what we call by a single name may not be a single thing. We use one word to describe suspense, and we feel it as a unified experience. But it probably has many different components, including direct sensory arousal (music, fast cutting), identification of emotional signals (facial expressions), responses to prototypical action scenarios (threat, falling, darkness), higher-level judgments (about moral desirability and causal likelihood), and expert assessments (about film conventions). Often one part of our film experience is actually a bundle of many factors, operating along different dimensions. We should be promiscuous, at least in our theories: we may need various sorts of explanations to understand how we react to movies.

The idea of "cognitively impenetrable" illusions refers to Jerry Fodor's classic *The Modularity of Mind* (1983). The modularity of "early vision"—the initial stages of visual processing—is exhaustively discussed in Zenon W. Pylyshyn's punningly titled *Seeing and Visualizing: It's Not What You Think* (2006).
• •

Movies Still Matter

MARCH 11, 2007

Kristin here:

I don't know whether I should be grateful when trade journals or major newspapers run columns bemoaning the decline of the cinema. On the one hand, these give me plenty of fodder for blogging. On the other, they promote a false impression that the movie industry and the art form in general are in far worse shape than they really are.

One recent case in point is Neal Gabler's "The movie magic is gone" story from February 25 (http://www.latimes.com/news/opinion/commentary /la-op-gabler25feb25,0,4482096.story), where he says that movies have lost their previous significance in American society and are less and less relevant to our lives.

Gabler makes some sweeping claims: Movie attendance is down because movies have lost the importance they once had in our culture. Our obsession with stars and celebrities has replaced our interest in the movies that create them. Niche marketing has replaced the old "communal appeal" of movies. The Internet intensifies that division of audiences into tiny groups and fosters a growing narcissism among consumers of popular culture. Audiences have become less passive, creating their own movies for outlets like YouTube. In video games, people's avatars make them stars in their own right, and the narratives of games replace those of movies.

Films will survive, Gabler concludes, but they face "a challenge to the basic psychological satisfactions that the movies have traditionally provided. Where the movies once supplied plots, there are alternative plots everywhere." This epochal challenge, he says, "may be a matter of meta-physics."

All this is news to me, and I have been paying fairly close attention to what has been going on in the moviemaking sphere over the past ten years—the period over which Gabler claims all this has been happening. Evidence suggests that all of his points are invalid.

1. Gabler states that "the American film industry has been in a slow downward spiral." Based on figures from Exhibitor Relations, a box-office tracking firm, attendance at theaters fell between 2005 (a particularly down year) and 2006. A Zogby survey found that 45 percent of Americans had decreased their moviegoing over the past five years, especially including the key 18-to-24-year-old audience. "Foreign receipts have been down, too, and even DVD sales are plateauing." Such a broad decline "suggests that something has fundamentally changed in our relationship to the movies."

Turning to a March 6 *Variety* article by Ian Mohr, "Box office, admissions rise in 2006" (http://www.variety.com/article/VR1117960597.html), we read a very different account of recent trends. According to the Motion Picture Association of America, admissions rose, "with 1.45 billion tickets sold in 2006—ending a three-year downward trend." Foreign markets improved as well, "where international box office set a record of $16.33 billion as it jumped 14 percent from the 2005 total." Within the United States, grosses rose 5.5 percent over 2005.

We should keep in mind that part of the perception of a recent decline comes from the fact that 2002 was a huge year for box-office totals, mainly stemming from the coincidence of releases of entries in what were then the four biggest franchises going: *Spider-Man*, *The Lord of the Rings*, *Harry Potter*, and *Star Wars*. There was almost bound to be a decline after that. Such films make so much money that the fluctuations in annual box-office receipts in part reflect the number of mega-blockbusters that appear in a given year.

Looking at the longer term, though, the biggest decline in U.S. moviegoing was in the 1950s, as television and other competing leisure activities chipped away at audiences. Even so, the movies survived, and from 1960 onward annual attendance hovered at just under a billion people. From 1992 on, a slow rise occurred, until by 1998 it reached roughly 1.5 billion and has hovered around that figure ever since, with a peak in 2002 at 1.63 billion. *Variety*'s figure of 1.45 billion for 2006 fits the pattern perfectly. In short, there has been no significant fall-off since the 1950s. (See the appendix in David's *The Way Hollywood Tells It* for a year-by-year break-down.) Mohr's article also states that industry observers expect 2007 to be especially high, given the *Harry Potter*, *Spider-Man*, and *Pirates of the Ca-ribbean* entries due out this year. About a year from now, expect pundits to be seeking reasons within the culture why moviegoing is up. I suspect they will find that we are looking for escapism. Safe enough. When aren't we?

Apart from theatrical attendance figures, let's not forget that more people are watching the same movies on DVDs and on bootleg copies that don't get into the official statistics.

2. *Gabler claims that movies are no longer "the democratic art" that they were in the 20th century.* During that century, even faced with the intro-duction of TV, "the movies still managed to occupy the center of Ameri-can life. . . . A Pauline Kael review in the *New Yorker* could once ignite an intellectual firestorm. . . . People don't talk about movies the way they once did."

Maybe the occasional Kael review created debate, as when she claimed that *Last Tango in Paris* was the "Rite of Spring" of the cinema. I think we all know by now that she was wrong. A lot of us even knew it at the time, and it's no wonder that people argued with her. I doubt that attempts to refute her claims there or in other reviews reflected much about the health of the general population's enthusiasm for movies.

More crucially, however, people do still talk about the movies, and lively debates go on. It's just that now much of the discussion happens on the Internet, on blogs and specialized movie sites, and in Yahoo! groups. (Who would have thought that David's entry on *Sátántango* [http://www.davidbordwell.net/blog/?p=31] would be popular? There turn out to be quite a few people out there passionately interested in Tarr's film.)

Some would see the health of movie fandom on the Internet as a sign that the cinema has become more democratic than ever. Now it's not just casual watercooler talk or a group of critics arguing among themselves. Anyone can get involved. The results range from vapid to insightful, but there's an immense amount of discussion going on.

3. *Interest in movies has eroded in part due to what Gabler has termed "know-ingness."* By this he means the delight people take in learning the latest gossip about celebrities. Movies have declined in importance because they exist now in part to feed tabloids and entertainment magazines.

"Knowingness" is basically a taste for infotainment. Movie infotain-ment had been around in a small way since before World War I in the form of fan magazines and gossip columns. It really took off beginning in the 1970s, with the rise of cable and the growth of big media companies that could promote their products—like movies—across multiple platforms. (I trace the rise of infotainment in chapter 4 of *The Frodo Franchise*.) It's not clear why one should assume that a greater consumption of infotainment leads to less interest in going to movies.

People in the film industry seem to assume the opposite. Studio publicity departments and stars' personal publicity managers feed the gossip outlets, in part to control what sorts of information get out but mainly because those outlets provide great swaths of free publicity. With the rise of new media, there are more infotainment outlets appearing all the time. Naturally this trend is obvious even to those of us who don't care about Britney's latest escapade. But I doubt that watching Britney coverage actually makes people less inclined to go to, say, *The Devil Wears Prada*, one of the mid-range surprise successes that helped boost 2006's box-office figures.

4. *Movies have lost their "communal appeal" in part because the public has splintered into smaller groups, and the industry targets more specialized niche markets.* According to Gabler, "the conservative impulse of our politics that has promoted the individual rather than the community has helped undermine movies' communitarian appeal."

Let's put aside the idea that conservative politics erode the desire for community. The extreme right wing has certainly put enough stress on community and has banded together all too effectively to promote their mutual interests lately. But is the industry truly marketing primarily to niche audiences?

Of course there are genre films. There always have been. Some appeal to limited audiences, as with the teen-oriented slasher movie. Yet despite the continued production of low-budget horror films, comedies, romances, and so on, Hollywood makes movies aimed at the "family" market because so many moviegoers fit into that category. Most of the successful blockbusters of recent years have consistently been rated PG or PG-13. According to *Variety*, 85 percent of the top 20 films of 2006 carried these ratings. *Pirates of the Caribbean, Spider-Man, Harry Potter*—these are not niche pictures, though distributors typically devise a series of marketing strategies for each film, with some appealing to teenage girls, others to older couples, and so on.

The result is that, despite the fact that niche-oriented films appear and draw in a limited demographic, there are certain "event" pictures every year that nearly everyone who goes to movies at all will see—more so than was probably the case in the classic studio era. Those films saturate our culture, however briefly, and surely they "enter the nation's conversation," as Gabler claims "older" films like *The Godfather*, *Titanic*, and *The Lord of the Rings* did. By the way, the last installment of *The Lord of the Rings* came out only a little over three years ago. Surely the vast cultural upheaval that the author posits can't have happened that quickly.

5. *The Internet exacerbates this niche effect by dividing users into tiny groups and creates a "narcissism" that "undermines the movies."*

See number 2 above. I don't know why participating in small group discussions on the Internet should breed narcissism any more than would a bunch of people standing around an office talking about the same thing. In fact, there are thousands of people on the Internet spending a lot of their own time and effort, many of them not getting paid for it, providing information and striving to interest others in the movies they admire.

The Internet allows like-minded people to find each other with blinding speed. Often fans will stress the fact that what they form are communities. They delight in knowing that many share their taste and want to interact with them. Some of these people no doubt have big egos and are showing off to whomever will pay attention. Narcissism, however, implies a solitary self-absorption that seems rare in online communities.

A great many of these communities form around interest in movies. In this way, the Internet has made movies more important in these people's lives, not less.

6. *Audiences have become active, creating their own entertainment for outlets like YouTube, and are hence less interested in passive movie viewing.* These are situations "in which the user is effectively made into a star and in which content is democratized."

No doubt more people are writing, composing, filming, and otherwise being creative because of the Internet. Some of this creativity and the consumption of it by Internet users takes up time they could be using watching movies.

Yet anyone who visits YouTube knows that a huge number of the clips and shorts posted there are movie scenes, trailers, and music videos based on movie scenes; little films re-edited out of shots taken from existing movies; and so on. In some cases the makers of these films have pored over the original and lovingly recrafted it in very clever ways. A lot of the creativity Gabler notes actually is inspired by mainstream movies. Some people post their films on YouTube because they are aspiring moviemakers hoping to get noticed. The movie industry as a whole is not at odds with YouTube and other sites of fan activity, despite the occasional removal of items deemed to constitute piracy.

7. *New media allow these active, narcissistic spectators to star in their own "alternative lives."* "Who needs Brad Pitt if you can be your own hero on a video game, make your own video on YouTube or feature yourself on Facebook?"

In discussing video games, Gabler perpetuates the myth that "video games generate more income than movies." This is far from being true, and hence his claim that video games are superseding movies is shaky. (I debunk this myth in chapter 8 of *The Frodo Franchise*.)

Even the spread of video games does not necessarily mean that fans are deserting movies. On the contrary, there is evidence that people who consume new media also consume the old medium of cinema. Mohr's *Variety* article reports on a recent study by Nielsen Entertainment/NRG: "Somewhat surprisingly, the same study revealed that the more home entertainment technology an American owns, the higher his rate of theater attendance outside the home. People with households containing four or more high-tech components or entertainment delivery systems— from DVD players to Netflix subscriptions, digital cable, videogame systems or high-def TV—see an average of three more films per year in theaters than people with less technology available in their homes."

Apart from the shaky factual basis of the column, what does the end-of-cinema genre tell us about how trends get interpreted by commentators?

As I pointed out in "World Rejects Hollywood Blockbusters!?" (pp. 3–11), some commentators explain perceived current trends in film by generalizing about the content of the movies themselves. Gabler is arguing for something different and more permanent—something that, if it were true, would be more depressing for those who love movies. He's not positing that movies have failed to cater to the national psyche. He's claiming that other forces, largely involving new media, have changed that national psyche in a way which moviemakers could never really cope with. Cinema as an art form cannot provide what these other media can, and spectators caught up in the options those media offer will never go back to loving movies, no matter what stories or stars Hollywood comes up with. By his lights, the movies are apparently doomed to a long, irreversible decline.

Hollywood has what I think is a more sensible view of new media.

Games, cell phones, websites, and all the platforms to come are ways of selling variants of the same material. Film plots are valuable not just as the basis for movies but because they are intellectual property that can be sold on DVD, pay-per-view, and soon, over the Internet. They can be adapted into video games, music videos, and even old media products like graphic novels and board games.

Not only Hollywood but the new media industries have already analyzed the changing situation and come up with new approaches to dealing with it. Consider IBM's *Navigating the Media Divide: Innovating and Enabling New Business Models* (http://www-935.ibm.com/services/us/index.wss /ibvstudy/gbs/a1026258?cntxt=a1000062). Those models include "walled communities," "traditional media," "new platform aggregation," and "content hyper-syndication," all of which, the authors predict, "will likely coexist for the mid term."

In other words, traditional media like the cinema aren't dying out. No art form that has been devised across the history of humanity has disappeared. Movies didn't kill theater, and TV didn't kill movies. It's highly significant that the main components of new media—computers, gaming consoles, personal music devices, cell phones, and the Internet— have all added features that allow us to watch movies on them.

The big movies still get more press coverage than the big video games partly because they usually are the source of the whole string of products. If a movie doesn't sell well, it's likely that its video game and its DVD and all its other ancillaries won't either. That is a key word, for many of the new media that Gabler mentions produce the ancillaries revolving around a movie. So far, very few movies are themselves ancillary to anything generated with new media. If you doubt that, examine Box Office Mojo's chart of films based on video games, which contains all of 22 entries made since 1989.

One final point. Film festivals are springing up like weeds around the world. Enthusiasts travel long distances to attend them. That's devotion to movies. From last year's Wisconsin Film Festival, add 26,000 tickets sold to that 1.5 billion attendance figure.

Movies still matter enormously to many people. New media have given them new ways to reach us, and us new ways to explore why they matter.

· ·

Virtually everything I said here still holds. There are now 28 video-game adaptations on Box Office Mojo's list, which perhaps signals a modest uptick in the influence of games on movies. Still, the big hits of the intervening years have been based on comics. (See "Superheroes for Sale," pp. 21–33.) That's a traditional, analog art form that predated new media and has been influencing movies at least since Winsor McCay animated *Little Nemo* in 1911.

The National Association of Theater Owners puts 2007 admissions at 1.4 billion, those for 2008 at 1.36 billion, and for 2009 at 1.41 billion (all very close to the 2000 figure of 1.38). 2009 saw a record box-office take, breaking $10 billion income for the studios for the first time. I don't recall a video game that has created anything like the furor around *Avatar* in late 2009 and early 2010.

In 2009, the Wisconsin Film Festival sold 32,645 tickets, up by more than 6,000.

As to broad appeal, Peter Krämer has written an insightful essay pointing out a common thread running through many blockbusters, "Would You Take Your Child to See this Film? The Cultural and Social Work of the Family-Adventure Movie," in Steve Neale and Murray Smith's anthology *Contemporary Hollywood Cinema* (Routledge, 1998).

If people updating their Facebook accounts and watching YouTube have not seriously eroded film attendance, where are they not spending their time? In Scott Rosenberg's *Say Everything: How Blogging Began, What It's Becoming, and Why It Matters* (Random House, 2009), he comes up with a simple answer based on polling: television. That's still bad news for the studios, which also produce TV shows, but not so much for the theater exhibitors.

• •

Storytelling and Style

Anatomy of the Action Picture

JANUARY 2007

David here:

For a long time Kristin and I have been interested in how films tell stories. We're fascinated by the principles that govern different storytelling traditions. For the sake of simplicity, we've called the principles *norms*.

The term implies a standard of craft competence, along with a dimension of collective decision-making. Norms are preferred alternatives within a tradition. A norm isn't a single and inflexible law; it's best seen as a roughly bounded set of options. Within any cluster of norms, there are always different ways to do something.

Film scholars occasionally object to the term *norm*. Doesn't the term suggest that we want to celebrate the normal and consign the non- or abnormal to some sort of lower status? But we're not suggesting that. Both Kristin and I have studied and praised filmmakers who do things differently. As historians we're simply studying principles of storytelling, as they've crystallized in norms that shape certain filmmaking trends. A researcher who studies norms of height in a population isn't implying that unusually tall or short people are second-class citizens.

Sometimes norms are just tacit, left to filmmakers to learn by example and intuition. My studies of art cinema and Hong Kong cinema provide examples of such cases. But sometimes filmmakers act in awareness of norms. More than other national cinemas, Hollywood has developed some fairly explicit rules for how stories can be told effectively. Moreover, a lot of Hollywood's storytelling rules aim at achieving a satisfying unity—the kind of plot we consider "tightly woven." This isn't to say that the rules are detailed or rigorous; sometimes they're loose and vague. And some principles at work seem never to be spelled out as rules.

Here are some of the questions that guide us:

Does actual Hollywood filmmaking follow the rules?

By examining the films, can we make vague guidelines more precise?

What other principles, even though they're not stated explicitly, contribute to Hollywood story making?

What are the variations within norms, the alternatives permitted or encouraged within a preferred set of practices?

Over the years, we've seen that our answers have occasionally been confirmed by practicing filmmakers. Some manuals of screenwriting have picked up on principles we've detected, turning them into explicit rules.[1]

Still, not all film scholars agree with our conclusions. A common objection is that U.S. mainstream movies aren't as tightly unified as the rules, or as our books, suggest. In particular, some scholars believe that the norms governing the contemporary action film don't aim at unity. Action movies, many suggest, are loose assemblies of chases, fights, explosions, stunts, and CGI effects, with little narrative coherence.

Granted, unity will always be a more-or-less quality; some plots are more tightly woven than others. Yet in *The Way Hollywood Tells It* I argue that if we analyze action-adventure films, we find more unity than we might expect. Hollywood action pictures are more tightly woven than they would need to be if all the makers or the audience cared about was splashy spectacle. (I contrasted U.S. films with Hong Kong ones, which favor much looser plotting.)

I didn't have the space in *The Way* to undertake a full analysis of any one action film, so I offer a case study here, centering on *Mission: Impossible III*. When I saw it last summer, it struck me as a fairly tight action picture, and rewatching it the other day, I started to count the ways.

Some Norms

Here are five principles of storytelling that Kristin and I consider crucial to most Hollywood films.

Goal orientation. The primary characters, protagonist and antagonist, both want something, or several somethings. The story progression is driven by characters' efforts to attain goals and by the way circumstances alter those goals. At the same time, characters' efforts to achieve goals create changes in the people themselves. Sometimes they realize that they're pursuing the wrong goal, or that they must become worthy of the goal. In *Storytelling in the New Hollywood* (1999), Kristin discusses such possibilities in relation to *Groundhog Day*.

The double plotline. Typically the goals govern at least two lines of action, and at least one of these involves heterosexual romantic love. A common pattern is a work/love pairing, where job problems affect and are affected by romantic relationships. Recent examples: *The Devil Wears Prada, The Good Shepherd, The Prestige*. In some cases one plotline is subordinate to the other, but both are very often present.

Here's a case of a norm that hasn't, so far as I know, been articulated by the filmmakers themselves. It seems simply to be taken for granted.

Discrete part-structure. The action revolves around goals: defining them, modifying them, and achieving or not achieving them. Hollywood films map the process onto several parts, each running 25–35 minutes (although climax sections tend to be shorter). The running times of these parts don't count credit sequences unless they carry story information, so the final crawl credits are typically not reckoned into the screen time of the film's narrative.

Since the mid-1970s, screenwriters have talked a lot about the idea of the three-act structure. In *Storytelling*, Kristin refined this cluster of rules. She suggested that we can analyze films more precisely by acknowledging that not all films have three acts. In features running around two hours, we typically find a four-part structure: Setup, Complicating Action, Development, and Climax. Usually there's a brief epilogue tacked on. Filmmakers working in the three-act paradigm in effect split the second act into two stretches around a midpoint.

Interestingly, Kristin's four-part structure is made explicit not only in manuals written after her book, but in the very architecture of Shane Black's *Kiss Kiss Bang Bang* (2005). The plot is split into four days, each given a title and each corresponding to one of the parts she identifies. Black's film ends with several epilogues; this convention is mocked in Harry's voice-over commentary, and one scene is labeled, "Epilogue."

Planting causes for future effects. Chekhov is said to have remarked that the gun on the wall in act 1 should go off in act 3. Likewise, Hollywood script carpentry lays in conditions that will prove important later. But it's not simply props that point forward: more common are what we call *dangling* *causes.* An unresolved action is presented near the end of one section that is picked up and pushed further in a later section. Every scene will tend to contain unresolved issues that demand settling further along.

Deadlines. It's surprising how often films in all genres set deadlines for the resolution of the plot. Screenwriters call it the "ticking clock," the time pressure that can rule any portion of the film but that is virtually mandatory at the Climax.

In *The Way Hollywood Tells It*, I trace these and other norms in detail through a particular example, Cameron Crowe's *Jerry Maguire*. What happens, though, when the mercurial Mr. Cruise makes a full-throttle action picture?

Mission: Impossible III   The Setup (00:32–31:34)[2]

A prologue establishes that the villain Owen Davian has captured Ethan Hunt and a woman we'll later realize is Ethan's wife, Julia. Davian demands to know where the Rabbit's Foot is, and he threatens to shoot Julia if Ethan doesn't say. As he fires, a brief title credit bursts up, and the rest of the film unfolds as an extended flashback.

You could argue that, given director J. J. Abrams's roots in TV, this prologue functions in the manner of the teaser that samples a later part of tonight's episode. But today many films employ this type of enframed flashback structure. The plot begins at a point of crisis and then whisks us back to show how things got to this pass. The resolution of the opening scene is postponed until the Climax. This strategy can be found at various points in the history of Hollywood. (See "Grandmaster Flashback," pp. 135–50.)

After the title credits, our protagonist Ethan is assigned two goals. First, during an engagement party, we learn that he and Julia Meade are planning to be married. He seems to have settled into an Agency desk job, concealed as a boring post in the Transportation Department.

Then he's yanked out of his home by a request from his colleague John Musgrave. Musgrave asks Ethan to lead a covert team to find Lindsey Farris, a young agent whom Ethan has mentored. She's disappeared, and master criminal Owen Davian is thought to be responsible.

Now the characteristic double plotline is established. Ethan wants a normal life with the woman he loves. "Family's everything," Musgrave remarks dryly. But Ethan also feels obliged to save Lindsey, whom he had trained for combat and released for duty, perhaps prematurely. So he's forced to lie to Julia and pretend to go to a professional convention. This sets up the work/romance tension we find so often in Hollywood films.

The M:I team is assembled, with the returning Luther Stickell joined by new members Declan and Zhen Lei. They and Ethan assault the Berlin factory where Lindsey is kept prisoner. As she's rescued, she tells Ethan she has information for him but there's no time for her to impart it. Deadlines keep the pressure on. Escaping in a helicopter, the team is chased by Damian's minions, while Ethan discovers that Lindsey's brain is carrying an explosive capsule. He tries to halt it by stopping her heart and using a defibrillator to bring her back, but the team runs out of time and she dies.

At home Ethan faces new problems. He's still in shock from Lindsey's death, which makes Julia apprehensive. At work, Ethan's supervisor, Brassel, criticizes Musgrave and Ethan, stating that his personal goal is to get Davian and they have thwarted his efforts. The Setup winds down when Ethan attends Lindsey's funeral, haunted by her question at the end of training: "Am I ready?"

Several important items are planted in this opening section. All the major characters are introduced. At the party we learn that Ethan can read lips, that Julia likes adventure (she's gone skydiving and hung from a helicopter), and that New Zealand's Lake Wanaka is a memorable place for both of them. The threat of an embedded brain capsule, the idea of letting someone die and be revived, and the fact that Julia works at a hospital will also become important in later parts.

Just as important, the action scene isn't just a gratuitous set-piece. It's central to achieving Ethan's goal, the rescue of Lindsey. The rescue's outcome—her death—motivates his hatred for Davian and drives a wedge into his relationship with Julia. From now on, as they say, it's personal.

The Setup runs about 31 minutes, with the key action of Lindsey's death taking place near the 25-minute mark, a sacred point in Hollywood dramaturgy. In addition, first parts often have a turning point about halfway through: here, that's when Ethan meets his team (at about 13 minutes).

Mission: Impossible III   The Complicating Action (31:34–62:05)

Lindsey's funeral could simply end the movie. She's beyond rescue, Davian has escaped, and Ethan is at a dead end. But dangling causes keep things going. We already glimpsed one in the factory assault, the urgent information that Lindsey started to recount to Ethan. Now, at the end of the funeral scene, he gets a call from a post office. A postcard is waiting for him. Dangling causes exemplify the famous linearity of classical construction: one scene hooks into the next.

The Complicating Action section serves to sharpen or alter the goals laid down in the Setup. The postcard remains a dangling cause, because Luther has to decipher the microdot that Lindsey has inserted under the stamp. In the meantime, Ethan learns from the techie Benji that Davian is seeking something called the Rabbit's Foot, "real end-of-the-world stuff." Davian is headed for the Vatican to make deals with arms buyers, and Ethan resolves to pursue him, without telling anyone at the Agency.

Meanwhile, Ethan's love affair with Julia is in jeopardy. Luther has warned that personal relationships don't mix with espionage, and his pessimism seems to be vindicated. When Ethan makes new excuses to leave on a trip, Julia worries that he's hiding something important from her. To reassure her, he marries her in the hospital where she works. Then it's off to Rome to kidnap Davian, leading to an even more elaborate set-piece. Using the twinning technology established in other *M:I* movies, Ethan and the others snatch Davian. Again, the action might seem to be at a standstill. Mission accomplished: the Agency boss Brassel congratulates Musgrave on Davian's capture. But fresh dangling causes emerge.

On the plane, Ethan questions their captive. Davian resists, vowing to make whomever Ethan cares about bleed—confirming Luther's warning that secret-agent work jeopardizes their loved ones. Further, Davian's gloating about Lindsey's death drives Ethan into a rage. Davian's a tough customer and may not reveal what the Rabbit's Foot is. What if he should escape? Davian threatens to kill Julia in front of Ethan, and we realize that this is no idle threat: the prologue showed exactly this situation. Somehow, we know, Davian will escape and turn the tables.

This Complicating Action is another longish section (about 31 minutes), with several new plants. Scenes with Julia establish that she's a doctor and that her relationship with Ethan still doesn't rest on full trust. Again, an elaborate action scene contributes to the plot. Not only does it show Ethan achieving his goal, it proves that, despite the death of Lindsey, he's still a skillful agent. This section also establishes an important minor character, Davian's female translator.

Mission: Impossible III   Development (62:05–93:56)

The Complicating Action often serves as a counter-setup, reversing the first phase of the plot. In the Setup of *M:I III*, Ethan's mission failed, Lindsey died, and Davian got off free. In the Complicating Action, circumstances have been reversed: Ethan succeeded, Lindsey was avenged, and Davian was taken in custody. What do Development sections do?

The Development can reverse the overall circumstances, creating new goals. It can sustain the situation. It can reveal backstory and deepen characterization. And it can simply delay resolution. The Development of *M:I III* does all of these things.

First, some massive reversals. A convoy is carrying Davian to Washington. On the bridge Luther finally cracks the microdot Lindsey had mailed Ethan. Her message accuses their boss, Brassel, of working in cahoots with Davian. At that instant a paramilitary force attacks the bridge and in an explosive firefight Davian is rescued. Ethan suffers a stunning setback, and not just from the concussive force of the assault.

He races to Julia's hospital to protect her, but too late: she's been kidnapped. As Ethan leaves the hospital, he's called by Davian. "Julia's life for the Rabbit's Foot." Davian gives him 48 hours to find it. A new goal has emerged, this time with a precise deadline. At this moment Ethan is captured by his own agency and is eventually immobilized, strapped to a gurney.

Ethan's capture blocks him from acting on Davian's command, and the situation is prolonged, delaying his progress toward rescuing Julia. The static situation is sustained by Brassel's address to Ethan, one that seems to confirm Lindsey's message. Talking like the conventionally obsessed villain, Brassel vows that he will "bleed on the flag" to get his way.

Again, the action seems at an impasse. When Brassel leaves, Ethan's contact Musgrave visits him and seems to chide him. But he mouths something quite different, and Ethan's lip-reading skills are now put to use. Musgrave says that he has intercepted Davian's call, and the Rabbit's Foot is in Shanghai. Musgrave also gives Ethan a weapon that enables him to escape from the Agency and head to China.

Ethan's new goal, that of getting the Rabbit's Foot, dominates the rest of the Development. From a structural standpoint, this subgoal is something of a delaying tactic, since Ethan's true goal is to rescue Julia. But this new goal ratchets up the work/love tension, since in pursuing the Rabbit's Foot, Ethan is betraying his professional duty. His choice to save Julia reveals his character: family is indeed everything. Ethan's new goal also motivates another action sequence, the incursion into a Shanghai skyscraper, and once more the pursuit and stunt work are driven by a deadline. "We have two hours before they kill my wife."

As the chase in Shanghai concludes, Ethan calls Davian, who orders him to the city's train yard. Ethan informs Musgrave about the rendezvous, and suspense is increased when Brassel questions Musgrave about the mission. Ethan leaves his team at the Shanghai train yard, so he faces

Davian alone. After a 31-minute Development, the climactic confrontation is imminent.

Mission: Impossible III   Climax (93:56–116:19)

Picked up in a stretch limo, Ethan is ordered to swallow the drink he's given. He passes out, dreaming of Julia. In flashes, we see him injected with the same sort of explosive capsule that killed Lindsey. Now we return to the situation presented in the prologue, with some repetition. Ethan is lashed to a chair facing Julia and Davian. Once again Davian demands to know where the Rabbit's Foot is, once more Ethan frantically bargains with him, and once again Davian threatens to shoot Julia, sitting bound and gagged across from Ethan.

Climax sections, as you'd expect, show the culmination and outcome of the plotlines running through the film. They also reveal information and clear up mysteries. Climaxes tend to be shorter than other sections, as this one is. As a denouement (literally, "untying"), the Climax may contain a final surprise as well.

Davian's confrontation with Ethan is crosscut with the arrival of the rest of the Mission: Impossible team in DC. They're greeted at the airport by Brassel's squad. This scene seems to function as a red herring, reassuring us that Brassel is indeed Davian's mole. It also deepens Ethan's plight, now that his team can't come to his rescue. Ethan doesn't know where the Rabbit's Foot is, so Davian shoots Julia and leaves. Ethan is shattered. (So are we, perhaps, because in the modern action picture even people we care about may die, as in *The Bourne Supremacy*.) After a long pause, Ethan's presumed ally John Musgrave enters. "It's complicated."

The familiar double-bluff of spy films locks in. Musgrave, not Brassel, is the mole. You could argue that this twist was planted near the end of the Development, when Musgrave turned away from Brassel and stared gravely offscreen as the camera lingered on him—the classic shot of a Suspect. Now Musgrave explains that the questioning of Ethan and the execution of "Julia" were methods of guaranteeing that he brought the genuine Rabbit's Foot. Musgrave peels the mask off the victim to reveal that it's not Julia but rather Davian's translator from the Vatican sequence.

Musgrave's goal is to find out what was in Lindsey's microdot message. In return Ethan demands proof that Julia is alive, and the Lake Wanaka motif comes to fruition as a way of identifying the voice on Musgrave's phone. Ethan escapes and, with the aid of Benji on his cell phone, sprints to save Julia. As he fights his way through Davian's lair, the fatal capsule

is triggered in his skull. Ethan falters and Davian begins to beat him. Another deadline: "You have maybe four minutes left."

Staggering, Ethan summons the strength to kill Davian, but to defuse the capsule, Julia must kill and revive Ethan. She's a doctor; there's a chance she can pull this off. As she's trying to save him, another wave of gunmen assaults her, and she puts them down with a forcefulness born of desperation. When Julia shoots Musgrave, the Rabbit's Foot rolls toward the camera. Julia's purported thirst for adventure pays off, and the parallel to Lindsey's gunplay in the Berlin factory is underscored. Lindsey was Ethan's action partner, Julia his romantic partner, but under the press of circumstance Julia has become both. The romantic line of action has been resolved. Ethan comes back to life. "You did that? Wow."

Mission: Impossible III   Epilogue (116:19–118:55)

The film could end here, and a Hong Kong film might do so. But Hollywood films like to wrap everything up with a scene or two assuring the audience that all is well. Not just a happy ending, then, but an emphatic resolution. Call it an epilogue.

First we reaffirm that the romantic line of action is tied up. Outside Davian's hideout Julia and Ethan walk across a bridge and he promises to tell her everything. He starts by describing the Impossible Missions Force, but she scoffs. The issue of their marriage is settled when she adds, "You can trust me."

Then we settle the professional line of action. Back at HQ, Brassel tells Ethan about a White House job that's available, but Ethan demurs. He just wants a honeymoon. The Rabbit's Foot is revealed as a MacGuffin, a mere pretext; we never learn what it really is. Julia is assimilated wholly into Ethan's world by meeting his entire team, including Benji, before the couple leave.

Implications

Clear and simple in outline, the classical film's dramaturgy can be manifested in intricate and subtle ways. Like the nineteenth-century well-made play, a film can fulfill principles of unity clumsily or adroitly. I'd put *M:I III* in the mid-range. It's not as cannily intricate as *Die Hard*, and not as well directed, in my opinion (though there are some fine stretches of cutting and composition). In all, the film is reasonably well wrought for its purposes. The point I'm proposing is that the action movie needn't be considered a mindless splatter of violent spectacle and CGI. It can have a cogent architecture.

There would be a lot more to say about unifying principles in *M:I III*, particularly at the level of the scene and the links between scenes. My analysis has emphasized overall narrative structure, not narration (the moment-by-moment flow of story information) or the world of the narrative (the characters and their surroundings). These aspects could be studied as well, but I wanted to make a prima facie case for the unity of construction at work here.

FAQs

Q. People go to see films like *M:I III* for action and spectacle. They don't care about plot; it often bores them. By attending to story factors, don't you deemphasize the genre's very reason for being?

A. First, the distinction between action and story seems to me untenable. Story goals can be fulfilled through action scenes and even what is called "spectacle." This happens throughout *M:I III*, in which the physical action furthers the overall plot. Action sequences create goals (saving Lindsey), eliminate characters (e.g., Lindsey), redefine goals (Davian's escape), and so on. Stories present constantly changing circumstances, and action sequences alter situations as effectively as conversation scenes do. As Murray Smith puts it, "The plot advances *through* spectacle."[3]

Of course action scenes are central to the genre, so we should expect them to be highlighted for special attention. The question is whether the action scenes are integrated into a larger pattern. I hold that very often they are. But if audiences don't care about plot, we ought to have a lot less plot than we do.

Try a thought experiment. Most action films aren't slam-bang action all the way through; they consist mostly of conversations and suspense scenes. So imagine a two-hour film containing 45 minutes of spectacular action. Why don't filmmakers simply release a movie containing only the action scenes? There are probably several reasons, but one reason is that the film works better for audiences, especially emotionally, when the plot ties the action scenes together. My analogy in *The Way Hollywood Tells It* is to the appeals of the star. Everybody likes stars, but nobody pays $8 to watch Sandra Bullock and Keanu Reeves sitting on a sofa together, Warhol-style, for 90 minutes. We like stars, but in stories, and in stories that move us.

Q. You claim that the action scenes play causal roles in advancing *M:I III*'s plot. But they're very long and elaborated, as in many action pictures. If the film were as tightly unified as you say, shouldn't they be shorter? Isn't the sheer fact of their duration proof that they overwhelm narrative principles?

A. Actually, a great many scenes of physical action depend on a basic narrative principle: overcoming obstacles. The action scenes in *M:I III* are little stories in themselves. Each one is governed by a goal, an effort to achieve it, a conflict with circumstances that block achievement, a redeployment of efforts in light of the obstacle, and so on . . . until the goal is definitely achieved or not. These mini-stories often operate under a deadline as well.

In the opening firefight of *M:I III*, Ethan tries to find Lindsey in the factory. After encountering some resistance, he does. Then he must get her out to the rest of the team. After conquering some obstacles, he does. Then the team sets off in a helicopter, but they're pursued. Then they have to save her from the exploding capsule, while also avoiding the villains' chopper. At the end, one goal is achieved—they escape—but the other isn't: Lindsey dies. If all that isn't narrative, what is?

The stretched-out duration of action sequences, I submit, involves not one-off attractions for their own sakes but micro-stories, short but twisting paths toward short-term goals, quick adjustments to a fast-changing situation. The gunplay, the escapes, the explosions, the bodies dangling from skyscrapers—all operate according to fundamental narrative principles of conflict, struggle, suspense, and resolution.

Q. Noting down all these structural patterns and unifying strategies focuses on the film as an object. What do these techniques do for *viewers*?

A. A great deal of our response is generated by a film's narration and its story world, not simply its structure, but we can at least say this: Structural unity of this or any other sort is a way of achieving *effects*. Thrills become more thrilling in a goal-oriented framework because then we care about who survives the chase or the plunge off a building. Connective scenes become more enjoyable when we spot recurring motifs or notice how characters are changing their beliefs and character traits. We don't always notice how the norms are shaping our response, but they do. That's one reason the norms are worth studying.

Another, perhaps more abstract, reason is that by studying norms we can make film history more intelligible. Norms of form and style come to be taken for granted by filmmakers, audiences, and scholars. We can usefully bring them to light. By studying norms as craft practices of filmmaking, we identify traditions and link the present to the past in an enlightening way.

At the same time, by studying norms as principles, rules, or rules of thumb, we become aware of alternatives, including the creative choices that move away from tradition. Sometimes we want to know why a film puzzles or intrigues or frustrates us, and it's often useful to trace those qualities to its refusal to play by the rules. Perhaps the reason we find some "art films" frustrating is that we can't identify character goals or clear-cut lines of cause and effect. (Have we internalized the Hollywood norms?) Studying norms of alternative traditions can enable us not only to understand their principles of construction but also to come to enjoy the distinctive experiences they offer.

Of course, films that play by the Hollywood rules can be fun too—as I think *M:I III* is.

Notes

1. See, for instance, Paul Joseph Gulino, *Screenwriting: The Sequence Approach* (New York: Continuum, 2004), 5–6, 12. Another example is the discussion of goals and deadlines in Karl Iglesias, *Writing for Emotional Impact* (Livermore, CA: Wingspan, 2005), 52, 100.

2. Timings come from the two-disc DVD release (Paramount, 2006).

3. Murray Smith, "Theses on the Philosophy of Hollywood History," in *Contemporary Hollywood Cinema*, ed. Steve Neale and Murray Smith (New York: Routledge, 1998), 13.

• •

This entry mentions film scholars' belief that in Hollywood films, narrative coherence is often undermined by "spectacle." I try to show here, as elsewhere, that the distinction between narrative and spectacle isn't so reliable. Very often features of what we intuitively call "spectacle" contribute to the narrative. A hard-core action movie like *Mission: Impossible III* can use its car crashes and gunfights to advance the plot and to give each set-piece a trajectory of overcoming obstacles and arriving at a clear-cut resolution. The same tactics can be found in the musical, which is often considered a genre that elevates spectacle and neglects story. In *Meet Me in St.*

Louis, the song "The Boy Next Door" gives us information about Esther's situation and state of mind. The song also poses the question of how the couple will get together, so it prepares for romantic complications. Even those kaleidoscopic dance sequences in Busby Berkeley films constitute a step in the story's progression (the show succeeds or fails), and some play out mini-narratives, as in the "Shanghai Lil" number of *Footlight Parade*.

In sum, the evidence inclines us to consider that narrative can incorporate all kinds of sound-and-image appeals in order to fulfill particular, and largely story-based, ends. That's not to say that popular cinema can't be episodic in structure. Kung-fu films, Bollywood romances from the 1950s, and South American musicals don't usually display the same degree of coherence we find in Hollywood. More generally, *commmedia dell'arte* and folk tales remind us that many of the world's storytelling traditions don't try for tight plotting. In the formative years of American cinema, filmmakers adapted conventions of the short story and the well-made play, and these have given American cinema an unusual concern for overarching goal orientation, deadlines, and the like. Hollywood's commitment to unity may be rare in the history of popular narrative.

By laying bare these principles of plot structure, aren't we confirming the belief that Hollywood is formulaic? Not necessarily. In any art, we enhance our appreciation by understanding how artists build upon traditional patterns—sonata form in music, columns and vaults in architecture. Once we've grasped those patterns, we're better able to point up skill and originality when we find it. Moreover, we shouldn't expect to find radical novelty in popular cinema. Hollywood filmmaking is closer to stable traditions like court verse or folk song, in which craftsmanship discovers fresh possibilities in familiar forms. Granted, *M:I III* isn't innovating on that level, but some films we discuss later, such as *The Power and the Glory* and *Inglourious Basterds*, are.

The distinctions among a film's story world, its narrative structure, and its narration are explained in more detail in "Three Dimensions of Film Narrative," in my collection *Poetics of Cinema* (New York: Routledge, 2008), 85–133.

Times Go by Turns

JUNE 21, 2008

Kristin here:

Last week during the Society for Cognitive Studies of the Moving Image conference here in Madison, I was talking with Prof. Birger Langkjær of the University of Copenhagen. He asked me some questions about the concept of "turning points" in film narrative as I had used it in my book *Storytelling in the New Hollywood* (1999). Specifically, he wondered if turning points invariably involve changes of which the protagonist or protagonists are aware. The protagonist's goals are usually what shape the plot, so can one have a turning point without him or her knowing about it?

I couldn't really give a definitive answer on the spot, partly because it's a complex subject and partly because I finished the book a decade ago. It seemed worth going back and trying to categorize the turning points in films I analyzed. Describing those turning points more specifically could be useful in itself, and it might help determine to what extent a protagonist's knowledge of what causes those turning points shapes the Development of the plot.

Characteristics of Turning Points

Most screenplay manuals treat turning points as the major events or changes that mark the end of an "act" of a movie. Syd Field, perhaps the most influential of all how-to manual authors, declared that all films, not just classical Hollywood ones, have three acts. (Field lays out his model in *Screenplay: The Foundations of Screenwriting*, originally published in 1979.) In a two-hour film, the first act will be about 30 minutes long, the second

60 minutes, and the third 30 minutes. Field believes that films have a significant event, a "midpoint," halfway through, but he doesn't consider it to be important enough to constitute a turning point.

I argued against this model in *Storytelling*, suggesting that upon analysis, most Hollywood films in fact have four large-scale parts of roughly equal length. The "three-act structure" has become so ingrained in thinking about film narratives that my claim is somewhat controversial. What has been overlooked is that I'm not claiming that all films have four acts. Rather, my claim is that in classical films large-scale parts tend to fall within the same average length range, roughly 25 to 35 minutes. If a film is two and a half hours rather than two hours, it will tend to have five parts; if three hours long, then six; and so on. And it's not that I think films must have this structure. From observation, I think they usually do. Apparently filmmakers figured out early on, back in the mid-1910s when features were becoming standard, that the action should optimally run for at most about half an hour without some really major change occurring.

Field originally called these changes "plot points," and he defined them as "an incident, or event, that hooks into the story and spins it around into another direction." Perhaps because of that shift in direction, these moments have come more commonly to be called "turning points." But what are they? Field's definition is pretty vague.

In *Storytelling* I wrote, "I am assuming that the turning points almost invariably relate to the characters' goals. A turning point may occur when a protagonist's goal jells and he or she articulates it. . . . Or a turning point may come when one goal is achieved and another replaces it." I also assumed that a major new premise often leads to a goal change (p. 29). "Almost invariably," because I don't assume that there are hard-and-fast rules. As with large-scale parts, my claims about other classical narrative guidelines aren't prescriptive in the way that screenplay manuals usually are. They are generalizations about patterns we can observe in the films.

To reiterate a few other things I said about turning points: They are not always the same as the moments of highest drama. Using *Jaws* as my example, I suggest that the moments of decision (not to hire Quint to kill the shark and later to hire him after all), rather than the big action scenes of the shark attacks, shape the causal chain (p. 33).

Not all turning points come exactly at the end of a large-scale part of the film (an "act" in most screenplay manuals). A turning point might come shortly before the end of a part, or it might come at the beginning of the new part (pp. 29–30). The final turning point that leads into the

Climax comes when "all the premises regarding the goals and the lines of action have been introduced" (p. 29).

Most screenplay manuals consider goals to be static. To me, "shifting or evolving goals are in fact the norm, at least in well-executed classical films" (p. 52). This doesn't mean that the goal changes at every turning point. Instead, the end of a large-scale part may lead to a continuation of the goal (or goals) but with a distinct change of tactics (p. 28).

One big advantage of talking about different types of turning points is that it allows the analyst to see how the different large-scale parts function. A well-done classical film doesn't just have exposition and a Climax with a bunch of stuff in the middle. (Field calls that long second act the "Confrontation.") I believe that once the Setup is over, there is a stretch of Complicating Action, which often acts as a sort of second Setup, creating a new situation that follows from the first turning point. The third part is the Development, which often consists of a series of delays and obstacles that essentially function to keep the complications from continuing to pile up until the whole plot becomes too convoluted. The Development also serves to keep the Climax from starting too soon. The third turning point is the last major premise or piece of information that needs to be set in place before the action can start moving toward its resolution in the Climax.

Types of Turning Points

Returning to some of the examples I used in *Storytelling*, let's see what sorts of changes their turning points involve. In most of these cases, the protagonist is aware of what is happening, but there are some exceptions or nuances.

1. *An accomplishment, later to be reversed*

TOP HAT: End of Setup, Jerry and Dale fall in love, but she soon conceives the mistaken idea that he is married to her best friend (p. 28).

TOOTSIE: End of Setup, Michael gets a job, but the results will throw his life increasingly into chaos (p. 60).

PARENTHOOD: End of Complicating Action, the parents seem to be making progress in solving their problems (p. 268).

2a. *Apparent failure, reiteration of goal*

THE MIRACLE WORKER: End of Development, parents remove Helen from cabin; Anne states goal again (p. 28).

THE SILENCE OF THE LAMBS: Turning point comes at beginning of

Development; Chilton makes Lecter a counteroffer, removing him from the FBI's charge. The FBI's tactic has failed, but soon Clarice visits Lecter to pursue her questioning (p. 123).

Here's a case where we don't see Clarice learning about Chilton's treacherous undermining of the FBI's efforts. A few scenes later she simply shows up to visit Lecter, and we realize that she has not given up her goal of getting information from him. Clearly a turning point can occur without the main character's knowledge, but he or she will usually learn about it shortly thereafter.

GROUNDHOG DAY: End of Development, failure to save the old man. No reiteration of goal, which is implicitly that Phil will continue to improve himself (p. 147).

2b. *Failure, new goal*

AMADEUS: End of Complicating Action, Salieri declares that he is now God's enemy and will ruin Mozart (p. 195).

Amadeus is what I call a "parallel protagonist" film, where two characters are equally important and have separate goals. Here Salieri is aware of his own decision, but Mozart never learns that his colleague hates him so. Parallel protagonists have separate goals, but they need not be aware of each other's goals. The same would be true in a film with more than two protagonists, to the extent that they have separate goals.

2c. *Failure, lack of goal*

GROUNDHOG DAY: End of Complicating Action, suicidal despair (p. 144).

AMADEUS: End of Setup, Salieri humiliated by Mozart, conceives strong resentment but no specific goal (p. 191).

PARENTHOOD: End of Development, the parents are all resigned to their failures (pp. 275–76).

3. *Major new premise, reiteration of strategy*

WITNESS: End of Complicating Action, Book receives Amish clothes from Rachel, who also returns his gun; her actions emphasize his contradictory role in the community just before Carter tells him to stay hidden (p. 29).

THE WRONG MAN: End of Complicating Action, Manny is freed on bail; he has the chance to try and prove his innocence (p. 39).

TERMINATOR 2: End of Development, Sarah, Terminator, and John steal chip from Cyberdine, continue in their attempt to destroy it (p. 42).

AMADEUS: End of second Development, Constanza leaves Mozart, allowing Salieri the access that will permit him to fulfill his goal of killing his rival (p. 205).

4. *Protagonist/important character makes a decision that changes or modifies goal*

LITTLE SHOP OF HORRORS (1986): End of Complicating Action, Seymour agrees to kill someone to obtain blood for Audrey II (p. 29).

THE GODFATHER: End of Development, Michael says family will go legit, asks Kay to marry him (p. 30).

CASABLANCA: End of Complicating Action, Rick rejects Ilsa's account of her relationship with Victor (p. 32).

THE PRODUCERS: End of Setup, Leo decides to join Max in committing fraud (p. 38).

TOOTSIE: End of Complicating Action, Michael decides to start improvising Dorothy's lines, setting up "her" success (p. 64).

BACK TO THE FUTURE: End of Development, Marty decides to leave a message for Doc warning him about the Libyan attack, thus preventing Doc's death (p. 94).

DESPERATELY SEEKING SUSAN: End of Setup, Roberta apparently decides to pursue Susan and change her boring life (p. 166).

Major decisions often furnish turning points, and by definition the protagonist is aware of what is happening.

5. *Major revelation, new goal or move into Climax*

WITNESS: End of Setup, Book is told the killer is a cop, changes tactics, flees (p. 28).

WITNESS: End of Development, Book learns partner has been killed, realizes he must act (p. 29).

THE BODYGUARD: End of Development, revelation of Nikki as villain, attack on house, death of Nikki (p. 31).

TERMINATOR 2: End of Setup, John discovers the Terminator must obey him, sets goals of protection without killing and of rescuing Sarah from the asylum (p. 41).

TERMINATOR 2: End of Complicating Action, Sarah realizes that the war can be prevented, conceives goal of killing Dyson (p. 42).

TOOTSIE: End of Development, Michael's agent tells him he must get out of playing Dorothy without being charged with fraud (p. 69).

THE SILENCE OF THE LAMBS: End of Setup, Clarice finds the body in the warehouse and realizes that Lecter is willing to help her (p. 115).

THE SILENCE OF THE LAMBS: End of Development, Clarice and Ardelia realize "he knew her," the clue that will lead to the solution (p. 126).

ALIEN: End of Development, revelation that the "company" and Ash are prepared to sacrifice the crew; will lead to decision by survivors to abandon the ship and save themselves (p. 299).

Such revelations usually involve the protagonist knowing what is happening, but I believe there are exceptional cases where the viewer learns something that the protagonist does not. This kind of revelation often involves either villains turning out to be allies or apparent allies turning out to be villains.

Take the case of *Demolition Man*. At 54 minutes into the film, about 9 minutes before the end of the Complicating Action, the audience learns that the apparently benevolent Dr. Cocteau (Nigel Hawthorne), who has developed the new pacifist society of Los Angeles, is a ruthless villain. This moment isn't the turning point that ends the Complicating Action; I take that to be the escape of the "Scraps," the rebels who oppose Cocteau, from their underground prison. Most of those nine minutes consist of the hero, John (Sylvester Stallone), meeting Cocteau and going out to dinner with him. John shows signs of strongly disliking the new society, and he refuses to kill the rebels when they escape. Still, there is no sign that he considers Cocteau a villain. Rather, John thinks of himself as a misfit and expresses a desire to leave the new Los Angeles. The turning point that ends the complication depends on his assumption that Cocteau is on his side, even if John considers the leader's bland society to be unattractive.

The Development portion is full of typical delays: the scene of John visiting Lenina Huxley's (Sandra Bullock) apartment, where she invites him to have virtual sex; and the following scene of John exploring the odd, modernistic apartment assigned to him. At 74 minutes in, or about six minutes before the end of the Development, John begins to learn of Cocteau's true nature. He confronts Cocteau in the latter's office and nearly shoots him. The scene in which John tells the members of the police department who remain loyal to him that they will invade the underground prison to capture Cocteau's violent agent, Simon Phoenix (Wesley Snipes), marks the end of the Development, with a new, specific goal determining the action of the Climax.

For a significant portion of *Demolition Man*'s narrative, the protagonist remains ignorant of something that the audience has been shown. Even so, John displays a dislike of Cocteau and what he has done to Los Angeles society. Classical films seem disinclined to show their heroes as thoroughly deluded. John's underlying decency and common sense make him ready to distrust a leader whom everyone else, including Lenina, admires.

6. *Enough information accumulates to cause the formulation of goals*
BACK TO THE FUTURE: End of Complicating Action, goals of synchronizing with lightning storm, getting Marty's father and mother together at dance (p. 90).
DESPERATELY SEEKING SUSAN: End of Complicating Action, information about gangsters and growing attraction to Dez lead to convergence of Roberta's goals (p. 170).
PARENTHOOD: End of Setup, in this case with multiple goals formed for four separate plotlines, ending with Gil's declaration to his boss that he needs to spend more time with his troubled son.

7. *A disaster, accidental or deliberate, changes the characters' situations/ goals*
THE WRONG MAN: End of Setup, Manny is mistakenly arrested (p. 39).
JURASSIC PARK: End of Complicating Action, Nedry shuts down the electricity grid of the park, freeing the dinosaurs (p. 32).
JAWS: End of Complicating Action; the attack involving his son makes Brody force the mayor to accept his original, thwarted tactic of hiring Quint (p. 34).
ALIEN: End of Setup, facehugger attaches itself to Kane. The goal conceived shortly thereafter is to investigate it and save him (p. 292).
ALIEN: End of Complicating Action, alien bursts from Kane's stomach; goal becomes to save the crew and ship (p. 295).
DESPERATELY SEEKING SUSAN: End of Development, Roberta's arrest leads to a low point, and she opts to turn to Dez for help (p. 172).
AMADEUS: End of first Development, death of Leopold, which Salieri later exploits in his plot against Mozart (p. 201).
THE HUNT FOR RED OCTOBER: End of Complicating Action, Ramius realizes he has a saboteur aboard and needs Ryan's help; Ryan starts planning actively to help him (p. 233).

8. *Protagonist's tactics are blocked or he/she is forced to use the wrong tactics*
JAWS: End of Setup, Brody's desire to hire Quint is rejected (p. 23).
BACK TO THE FUTURE: End of Setup, Doc sets time machine's date; after new large-scale section begins, attack by Libyans accidentally sends Marty back to 1955 (p. 85).

GROUNDHOG DAY: End of Setup, Phil is trapped in repeating time, his goal of becoming a network weather forecaster destroyed. He soon opts for irresponsible self-indulgence (p. 139).

9. *Characters working at cross-purposes resolve their differences*
JAWS: End of Development, the three main characters bond, allowing them to cooperate to kill the shark (p. 35).
THE HUNT FOR RED OCTOBER: End of Development, with Captain Mancuso's help, Ramius and Ryan make contact with each other and start working together (p. 237).

10. *A supernatural premise determines a character's behavior*
LIAR, LIAR: End of Setup, Max wishes that his father would have a day during which he is unable to tell a lie. Also end of Complicating Action, Max fails to cancel the wish (p. 38).

11. *The protagonist/major character succeeds in one goal, allowing him/her to pursue another*
LIAR, LIAR: End of Development, Fletcher wins his court case, freeing him to try and regain his wife and son (p. 39).
THE HUNT FOR RED OCTOBER: End of Setup, Ramius learns that the silent feature of his new submarine works; he apparently intends some sort of attack on the United States but is in fact plotting an elaborate ruse to defect (p. 225).

These examples suggest that protagonists usually do know about the major events that form turning points, or they learn about them shortly after they occur. The main exception would seem to be when there are two major parallel characters, one of whom is to some extent villainous. This happens in *Amadeus*, where one of the characters is duped. This reminds me of *The Producers*, where Max and Leo leave the theater early, convinced that they have succeeded in their goal of creating a box-office disaster. Lingering in the theater, the narration allows us to see the transition from audience disgust to fascination. Only after audience members enter the bar where Max and Leo are celebrating do the two partners realize what has happened ("I never in a million years thought I'd ever love a show called *Springtime for Hitler!*"). To understand the irony or humor in such situations, the film spectator must at least briefly know more than the main characters do.

The examples also confirm that character goals seldom endure unchanged across the length of a film. Revelations, decisions, disasters, supernatural events, and other kinds of causes frequently involve major shifts in characters' goals or at least in the tactics they employ in pursuing them. Even in what seems like a fairly straightforward thriller like *Alien*, the crew's assumptions that they must loyally protect their spaceship are completely reversed at the end of the Development, and the narrative turns into an attack on corporate greed and ruthlessness. Whatever one thinks of classical Hollywood films, they are usually more complex than the three-act model allows for.

Note

My title comes from Robert Southwell's poem of the same name.

• •

I mentioned *Amadeus*'s "second Development" here. In cases where a film has more than four large-scale parts, it has two of one of the four types. *Amadeus*, the only five-part film I analyze in detail in *Storytelling*, has two Development sections. So do *The Sound of Music* and *The Godfather*. *Titanic* is unusual in having a double Climax—the hour devoted to the ship's sinking—with the first half dealing with the upper-class characters and the second focusing more on the steerage passengers.

Blogger Jim Emerson made some insightful comments on this entry on *Scanners* (http://blogs.suntimes.com/scanners/2008/07/tell_me_a_story_act_ii.html).

• •

Grandmaster Flashback

JANUARY 27, 2009

David here:

Would that the Fox Movie Channel were as committed to classic cinema as that other basic-cable staple, Turner Classic Movies, is. It's curious that a studio with a magnificent DVD publishing program (the Ford boxed set, the Murnau/Borzage one) is so lackluster in its broadcast offerings. Fox was one of the greatest and most distinctive studios, and its vaults harbor many treasures, including glossy program pictures that would still be of interest to historians and fans. Where, for instance, is *Caravan* (1934), by the émigré director Erik Charell who made *The Congress Dances* (1931)? *Caravan*'s elaborate long takes would be eye candy for Ophüls-besotted cinephiles.

Occasionally, though, the Fox schedulers bring out an unexpected treat, such as the sci-fi musical comedy *Just Imagine* (1930). Last month, the main attraction for me was *The Power and the Glory* (1933), directed by William K. Howard from a script by Preston Sturges.

This was an elusive rarity in my salad days. As a teenager I read about how it prefigured *Citizen Kane* by presenting the life of a tycoon in a series of daring flashbacks. I think I first saw it in the late 1960s at a William K. Everson screening at the New School for Social Research. I caught up with it again in 1979, at the Thalia in New York City, on a double bill with *The Great McGinty* (1940). In my files, along with my scrawls on ring-binder paper, is James Harvey's brisk program note, which includes lines like this: "One of Sturges' achievements was to make movies about ordinary people that never ever make us think of the word 'ordinary.'" I was finally able to look closely at *The Power and the Glory* while doing research for *The Classical Hollywood Cinema* (1985). The UCLA archive kindly let me see a 16mm print on a flatbed viewer.

So after a lapse of twenty-eight years I revisited *P&G* on the Fox channel last month. It does indeed prefigure *Kane*, but I now realize that for all its innovations it belongs to a rich tradition of flashback movies, and it can be correlated with a shorter-term cycle of them. Rewatching it also teased me to think about flashbacks in general, and to research them a little.

A Trick, an Old Story

On our subject for today, the indispensible book is Maureen Turim's *Flashbacks in Film: Memory and History* (Routledge, 1989). We may think of the flashback as a modern technique, but Turim shows that flashbacks have been a mainstay of filmic storytelling since the 1910s.

Although the term *flashback* can be found as early as 1916, for some years it had multiple meanings. Some 1920s writers used it to refer to any interruption of one strand of action by another. At a horse race, after a shot of the horses, the film might "flash back" to the crowd watching. (See "Jargon of the Studio," *New York Times*, October 21, 1923, X5.) In this sense, the term took on the same meaning as then-current terms like "cut-back" and "switch-back." There was also the connotation of speed, as "flash" was commonly used to denote any short shot.

But around 1920 we also find the term being used in our modern sense. You can find it in popular fiction; one short story has its female protagonist remembering something "in a confused flashback" ("A Philistine in Arcady," by Elliott Field). F. Scott Fitzgerald writes in *The Beautiful and Damned* of 1922: "Anthony had a start of memory, so vivid that before his closed eyes there formed a picture, distinct as a flashback on a screen." At about the same time writers on theater began to adopt the term and credit it to film. A historian of drama writes in 1921 of a play that rearranges story order: "The movies had not yet invented the flashback, whereby a thing past may be repeated as a story or a dream in the present."

Within film circles, there were signs of an exasperation with the device. One 1921 writer calls the flashback a "murderous assault on the imagination." Turim quotes a *New York Times* review of *His Children's Children* (1923): "For once a flash-back, as it is made in this photoplay, is interesting. It was put on to show how the older Kayne came to say his prayers." In the same year, a critic discusses Elmer Rice's *On Trial*, an influential 1911 stage play. Rice employs "a dramatic technique which up to its time was probably unique, though since then the ever recurrent 'flash back' of the movies has made the trick an old story."

During the 1930s, although some critics and filmmakers employed older terms like "switch-back" and "retrospect," *flashback* seems to have become the standard label. It denoted any shot or scene that breaks into present-time action to show us something that happened in the past. It probably speaks to the intuitive and informal nature of filmmaking that writers and directors didn't feel a need to name a technique that they had been using confidently for two decades.

The early flashback films pretty much set the pattern for what would come later. Turim shows that all the options we find today have their precedents in the 1910s and 1920s. Adapting her typology a little bit, we can distinguish between character-based flashbacks and "external" ones.

A character-based flashback may be presented as purely subjective, a person's private memory, as in *Letter to Three Wives* or *The Pawnbroker* or *Across the Universe*. There's also the flashback that represents one character's recounting of past events to another character, a sort of visual illustration of what is told. This flashback is often based on testimony in a trial or investigation (*Mortal Thoughts*, *The Usual Suspects*), but it may simply involve a conversation, as in *Leave Her to Heaven*, *Titanic*, or *Slumdog Millionaire*. It can also be triggered by a letter or diary, as happens with the doubly embedded journals in *The Prestige*.

The alternative is to break with character altogether and present a purely objective or "external" flashback. Here an impersonal narrating authority simply takes us back in time, without justifying the new scene as character memory or as illustration of dialogue. The external flashback was rare in classic studio cinema but was common in the 1900s and 1910s and has returned in contemporary cinema. Nowadays the film begins at a point of crisis before a title appears signaling the shift to an earlier period. Recent examples are *Michael Clayton* ("Three Days Earlier"), *Iron Man* ("36 Hours Before"), and *Vantage Point* ("23 Minutes Earlier").

In current movies, flashbacks can fall between these two possibilities. Are the flashbacks in *The Good Shepherd* the hero's recollections (cued by him staring blankly into space) or more objective and external, simply juxtaposing his numb, colorless life with the past disintegration of his family? The point would be relevant if we were trying to assess how much self-knowledge he gains across the present-time action of the film.

Rationales for the Flashback

What purposes does a flashback fulfill? Why would any storyteller want to arrange events out of chronological order? Structurally, the answers come down to our old friends causality and parallelism.

Most obviously, a flashback can explain why one character acts as she or he does. Classic instances would be Hitchcock's trauma films like *Spellbound* and *Marnie*. A flashback can also provide information about events that were suppressed or obscured; this is the usual function of the climactic flashback in a detective story, filling in the gaps in our knowledge of a crime.

By juxtaposing two incidents or characters, flashbacks can enhance parallels as well. The flashbacks in *The Godfather: Part II* are positioned to highlight the contrasts between Michael Corleone's plotting and his father's rise to power in the community. *Citizen Kane*'s flashbacks are famous for juxtaposing events in the hero's life to bring out ironies or dramatic contrasts.

Of course, flashbacks need not explain or clarify things; they can make things more complicated too. We tend to think of the "lying flashback" as a modern invention (a certain Hitchcock film has become the prototype), but Turim shows that *The Goose Woman* (1925) and *Footloose Widows* (1926) did the same thing, although not with the same surprise effect. Kristin points out to me that an even earlier example is *The Confession* (1920), in which a witness at a trial supplies two different versions of a killing we have already (sort of) seen.

At the limit, flashbacks can block our ability to understand characters and plot actions. This is perhaps best illustrated by *Last Year at Marienbad*, but the dynamic is already there in Jean Epstein's *La Glace à trois faces* ("The Three-Sided Mirror," 1927).

At bottom, flashbacks fulfill a broader purpose: breaking up the story's chronological order. You can begin the film at a climactic moment; once the viewers are hooked, they will wait for you to move back to set things up. You can create mystery about an event that the plot has skipped over and then answer the question through a flashback. You can establish parallels between past and present that might not emerge so clearly if the events were presented in 1-2-3 order. Consequently, you can justify the switch in time by setting up characters as recalling the past, or as recounting it to others.

Having a character remember or recount the past might seem to make the flashback more "realistic," but flashbacks usually violate plausibility. Even "subjective" flashbacks usually present objective (and reliable) information. More oddly, both memory-flashbacks and telling-flashbacks usually show things that the character didn't, and couldn't, witness.

I don't suggest that recollections and recountings are merely alibis for time-juggling. They bring other appeals into the storytelling mix, such as allegiance with characters, pretexts for point-of-view experimentation, and so on. Still, the basic purpose of nonchronological plotting, I think, is to pattern information across the film's unfolding so as to shape our state of knowledge and our emotional response in particular ways. Scene by scene and moment by moment, flashbacks play a role in pricking our curiosity about what came before, promoting suspense about what will happen next, and enhancing surprise at any moment.

A Trend Becomes a Tradition

When *The Power and the Glory* was released in August 1933, it was part of a cycle of flashback films. *The Trial of Mary Dugan* (1929), *The Trial of Vivienne Ware* (1932), and other courtroom films rendered testimony in flashbacks. A film of the era might also wedge a brief or extended flashback into an ongoing plot. The most influential instance was probably *Smilin' Through* (1931), which is notable for using a crane shot through a garden to link present and past.

Also well established was the extended-insert model. Here we start with a critical situation that triggers a flashback (either subjective or external), and this occupies most of the movie. Digging around, I found these instances, but I haven't seen all of them; some don't apparently survive.

> *Behind the Door* (1919): An old sea salt recalls life in World War I and, back in the present, punishes the man responsible for his wife's death. A ripoff of Victor Sjöström's *Terje Vigen* (1917)?
>
> *An Old Sweetheart of Mine* (1923): A husband goes through a trunk in an attic and finds a memento that reminds him of his childhood sweetheart. The pair grow up and marry, facing tribulations. At the end, back in the present, she comes to the attic with their kids.
>
> *His Master's Voice* (1925): Rex the dog is welcomed home from the war. An extended flashback shows his heroic service for the cause, and back in the present he is rewarded with a parade.
>
> *Silence* (1926): A condemned man explains the events that led up to the crime. Back in the present, on his way to be executed, he is saved.
>
> *Forever After* (1926): On a World War I battlefield, a soldier recalls what brought him there.
>
> *The Woman on Trial* (1927): A defendant recalls her past.

The Last Command (1928): One of the most famous flashback films of the period. An
old movie extra recalls his life in service of the czar.

Mammy (1930): A bum reflects on the circumstances leading him to a life on the road.

Such is Life (1931): A ghoulish item. A fiendish scientist confronts a young man with the
corpse of the woman he loves. A flashback to their romance ensues.

The Sin of Madelon Claudet (1931): A young wife bored with her husband is told the
story of a neighbor woman who couldn't settle down.

Two Seconds (1932): A man about to be executed remembers, in the two seconds
before death, what led him here. This is a more mainstream reworking of a premise
of Paul Fejos's experimental *Last Moment* (1928), which is evidently lost.

An interesting variant of this format is *Beyond Victory*, a 1931 RKO release. The plot presents four soldiers on the battlefield, each one recalling
his courtship of the woman he loves back home. The principle of assembling flashbacks from several characters was at this point pried free of the
courtroom setting, and multiple-viewpoint flashbacks became important
for investigation plots like *Affairs of a Gentleman* (1934), *Through Different
Eyes* (1942), *The Grand Central Murder* (1942), and of course *Citizen Kane*,
itself a sort of mystery tale.

Why this burst of flashback movies? It's a good question for research.
One place to look would be literary culture. The technique of flashback
goes back to Homer, and it recurs throughout the history of both oral and
written narrative. Literary modernism, however, made writers highly conscious of the possibility of scrambling the order of events. From middle-
brow items like *The Bridge of San Luis Rey* (1927) to high-cultural works by
Dos Passos and Faulkner, elaborate flashbacks became organizing principles for entire novels. It's likely that Sturges, a Manhattanite of wide
literary culture, was keenly aware of this trend in conceiving *The Power
and the Glory*.

It's likely that he noticed similar developments in another mass medium. By 1931, when Katharine Seymour and J. T. W. Martin published
How to Write for Radio (New York: Longmans, Green & Co.), they could
devote considerable discussion to frame stories and flashbacks in radio
drama (pp. 115–137). Especially interesting for Sturges's film, radio pro-
grams were letting the voice of the announcer or the storyteller drift in
and out of the action that was taking place in the past.

Filmmakers apparently picked up on the technique. The year 1933 saw
several flashback films besides *The Power and the Glory*. In the didactic ex-
ploitation item *Suspicious Mothers*, a woman recounts her wayward path
to redemption. *Mr. Broadway* offers an extensive embedded story using

footage from another film (a common practice in the earliest days). *Terror Aboard* begins with the discovery of corpses on a foundering yacht, followed by an extensive flashback tracing what led up the calamity. A borderline case is the what-if movie *Turn Back the Clock* (1933). Ever-annoying Lee Tracy plays a small businessman run down by a car. Under anesthesia, he reimagines his life as it might have been had he married the girl he once courted. Call it a rough draft for the "hypothetical flashbacks" that Resnais was to exploit in his great *La Guerre est finie*.

The point of this cascade of titles is that in writing *The Power and the Glory*, Sturges was working with a set of conventions already in wide circulation. His inventiveness stands out in two respects: the handling of voice-over and the ordering of the flashbacks.

Narratage, Anyone?

The Power and the Glory begins with what became a commonplace opening gesture of film, fiction, and nonfiction biography: the death of the protagonist. We are at the funeral of Thomas Garner, railroad tycoon. His best friend and assistant Henry slips out of the service. After visiting the company office, Henry returns home. Sitting in the parlor with him, his wife castigates Garner as a wicked man. "It's a good thing he killed himself." So we have the classic setup of anomalous suspense: we know the outcome but become curious about what led up to it.

Henry's defense of Garner launches a series of flashbacks. As a boyhood friend, Henry can take us to three stages of the great man's life: adolescence, young manhood, and late middle age. Scenes from these time periods are linked by returns to the narrating situation, when Henry's wife will break in with further criticisms of Garner.

Sturges boasted in a letter to his father: "I have invented an entirely new method of telling stories." He wrote that the result combined silent film, sound film, and "the storytelling economy and the richness of characterization of a novel." At the time, the Paramount publicists trumpeted that the film employed a new storytelling technique labeled *narratage*, a wedding of "narrating" and "montage." One publicity item called it "the greatest advance in film entertainment since talking pictures were introduced." Hyperbole aside, what did Sturges have in mind?

There is evidence that some screenwriters were rethinking their craft after the arrival of sound filming. Exhibit A is Tamar Lane's book *The New Technique of Screen Writing* (McGraw-Hill, 1936). Lane suggests that the talking picture's promise will be fulfilled best by a "composite" construction blending various media. From the stage come dialogue technique and sharp compression of action building to a strong climax. From the novel come a sense of spaciousness, the proliferation of characters, a wider time frame, and multiple lines of action. Cinema contributes its own unique qualities as well, such as the control of tempo and a "pictorial charm" (p. 28) unattainable on the stage or page.

Vague as Lane's proposal is, it suggests a way to think about the development of Hollywood screenwriting at the time. Many critics and theorists believed that the solution to the problem of talkies was to minimize speech; this is still a common conception of how creative directors dealt with sound. But Lane acknowledged that most films would probably rely on dialogue. The task was to find engaging ways to present it. Several films had already explored some possibilities, the most notorious probably being *Strange Interlude* (1932). In this MGM prestige product, the soliloquies spoken by characters in O'Neill's play are rendered as subjective voice-over. The result, unfortunately, creates a broken tempo and overstressed acting. A conversation halts, and through changes of facial expression, the performer signals that what we're now hearing is purely mental.

The Power and the Glory responds to the challenge of making talk interesting in a more innovative way. For one thing, there is the sheer pervasiveness of the voice-over narration. We're so used to seeing films in which the voice-over commentary weaves in and out of a scene's dialogue that we forget that this was once a rarity. Most flashback films in the early sound era had used the voice-over to lead into a past scene, but in *The Power and the Glory*, Henry describes what we see as we see it.

Most daringly, in one scene Henry's voice-over substitutes for the dialogue entirely. Young Tom and Sally are striding up a mountainside, and he's summoning up the nerve to propose marriage. What we hear, however, is Henry at once commenting on the action and speaking the lines spoken by the couple, whose voices are never heard. This scene, often commented upon by critics then and now, seems to have exemplified what Sturges late in life recalled "narratage" to be. Describing that technique in his autobiography, he wrote: "The narrator's, or author's, voice spoke the dialogue while the actors only moved their lips" (p. 272).

So one of Sturges's innovations was to use the voice-over not only to link scenes but to comment on the action as it played out. In her pioneering book *Invisible Storytellers: Voice-Over Narration in American Fiction Film* (Univesity of California Press, 1988), Sarah Kozloff has argued that the pervasiveness of Henry's narration has no real precedent in Hollywood, and few successors until 1939 (pp. 31–33). (There's one successor in Sacha Guitry's *Roman d'un tricheur*, 1936.) The novelty of the device may have led Sturges and Howard toward redundancies that we find a little labored today. The transitions into the past from the frame story are given rather emphatically, with Henry's voice-over aided by camera movements that drift away from the couple. (Compare the crisp shifts in *Midnight Mary*, below.) Henry's comments during the action are sometimes accentuated by diagonal veils that drift briefly over the shot (see below), as if assuring us that this speech isn't coming from the scene we see.

The "montage" bit of "narratage" also invokes the idea of a series of sequences guided by the voice-over narrator. The concept might also have encompassed the most famous innovation of *The Power and the Glory*: Sturges's decision to make Henry's flashbacks *non*-chronological.

Even today, most flashback films adhere to 1-2-3 order in presenting their embedded, past-tense action. But Sturges noticed that in real life people often recount events out of order, backing and filling or free-associating. So he conceived *The Power and the Glory* as a series of blocks. Each block contains several scenes from either boyhood, youth, or middle age. Within each block, the scenes proceed chronologically, but the narration skips around among the blocks.

For example, a block of boyhood scenes gives way to a set showing Garner, now in middle age, ordering around his board of directors. The next cluster of flashbacks returns to Garner's youth and his courtship of his first wife, Sally. Then we are carried back to his middle age, with scenes showing Garner alienated from Sally and his son Tommy but also attracted to the young woman Eve. And from there we return to Garner's early married life with Eve.

To keep things straight, Sturges respects chronology along another dimension. Not only do the scenes within each block follow normal order, but the plotlines developing across the three phases of Garner's life are given 1-2-3 treatment. In one block of flashbacks, we see Tom and Sally courting. When we return to that stage of their lives in another block, they are happily married. The next time we see Garner as a young man, he is improving himself by attending college. Garner's later romance with Eve develops in a similar step-by-step fashion across the blocks devoted to middle age.

A major effect of the shuffling of periods is ironic contrast. Maureen Turim points out that juxtaposing different phases of Garner's life points up changes and disparities. In his youth, Tom watches the birth of his son with awe; in the next scene, we are reminded what a wastrel young Tommy turned out to be.

The alignment of time frames also nuances character development. As Sally ages, she turns into something of a nag, quarreling with her husband and pampering Tommy. But in the next sequence we see her young, ambitiously pushing Tom to succeed and willing to undergo sacrifice by taking up his job as a railroad trackwalker. The next scenes show Tom in class and in a bar while Sally walks the desolate tracks in a blizzard. She has given up a lot for her husband. In the next scene, set in middle age, Garner confesses his love to Eve but says he could never leave Sally, and the juxtaposition with Sally's solitary trackwalking suggests that he recognizes her sacrifice. And in the following scene, when Sally comes to Garner's office, she admits that she has become disagreeable and asks if they couldn't take a trip to reignite their love. The juxtaposition of scenes has turned a caricatural shrew into a woman who is a more complex mixture of devotion, disenchantment, and self-awareness.

Other characters aren't given this degree of shading—Tommy is pretty much a wastrel, Eve a vamp—but another married couple deepens the central parallel. Meek Henry is dominated by his wife, but by the end she is chastened by what she learns of Garner's real motives. Critic Andy Horton, in his helpful introduction to Sturges's published screenplay, indicates that this couple adds a note of contentment to what is otherwise a pretty sordid melodrama of adultery.

The innovative flashbacks and voice-overs are an important part of the film's appeal, but director William K. Howard supplied some craftsmanship of his own. Particularly striking are some silhouette effects, low angles, and deep-focus compositions (see next page) that underscore the parallels between Sally's suicide and Garner's impending death.

The original screenplay suggests that Sturges intended to push his innovations further. About halfway through, he starts to break down the time-blocks. In the script, Sally visits Garner while he's working on a bridge. The next scene shows their son Tommy already grown and spoiled, being taken back into his father's good graces. Then the script returns to the bridge, where Sally tells Tom she's pregnant. The interruption of the bridge scene would have reminded us of how badly their child turned out.

The script jumps back to the birth of the baby. In the film the birth scene plays out in its entirety, but in the screenplay Sturges cuts it off by the

scene (retained in the film) showing Garner's marriage to Eve. The final moments of the birth scene, when Garner prays ("Thou art the power and the glory"), become in the script the very end of the film. Coming after Tom's death at the hand of his son, this epilogue is a bitter pill, rendered all the harder to take by providing no return to Henry and his wife.

The greater fragmentation of the script's second part, along with Garner's death as a sort of murder-suicide and the failure to return to the narrating frame, is striking. It's as if Sturges felt he could take more chances, counting on his viewers' familiarity with current flashback conventions and on his film's firmly established time-shuttling method. But if, as sources report, Sturges's script was initially filmed exactly as written, then it seems likely that the film's June 1933 preview provoked the changes we find in the finished product. "The first half of the picture," he remarked in a letter, "went magnificently, but the storytelling method was a little too wild for the average audience to grasp and the latter half of the picture went wrong in several spots. We have been busy correcting this and the arguments and conferences have been endless."

Even the compromised film proved difficult for audiences. Tamar Lane, proponent of the "composite" form suitable for the sound cinema, felt that the "retrospects" in *The Power and the Glory* were too numerous and protracted. Nonetheless, he praised it for its "radical and original cinema handling" (p. 34). That handling rested upon tradition—a tradition that in turn encouraged innovations. Once flashbacks had become solid conventions, Sturges could risk pushing them in fresh directions.

Mary and Nora

Finally, two more flashy flashback movies from 1933.

Midnight Mary (MGM, William Wellman) works a twist on the courtroom template. The defendant Mary Martin is introduced jauntily read-

ing a magazine while the prosecutor demands that the jury find her guilty of murder. This also sets up a nice little motif of shots highlighting Loretta Young's lustrous eyes. The motif pays off with a soft-focus shot of her in jail just before the climax.

As the opening scene ends, Mary is led to a clerk's office to wait for the verdict. There's an automatic dose of suspense (will she be found guilty?), but there's also considerable curiosity: Whom has she killed? How was she caught?

These questions won't be answered for some time. Lounging in the clerk's office, Mary runs her eye across the annual reports filling his shelves. The flashbacks, which constitute most of the film, are introduced as close-ups of the volumes' spines—1919, 1923, 1926, 1927, and so on up to the present. They serve as neatly motivated equivalents of those clichéd calendar pages that ripple through montage sequences of the 1930s.

The flashbacks are presented as subjective ones; Mary doesn't recount her life to the clerk but simply reviews it in her mind. Unlike the flashbacks in *The Power and the Glory*, they are chronological and without strategic gaps. Nothing is skipped over to be revealed later. As usual, though, once Mary's recollections have triggered the rearrangement of story order, the flashbacks are filmed as any ordinary scenes would be, including bits of action that she isn't present to witness. The film is a good example of using the extended-flashback convention chiefly to delay the resolution of the climactic action. Told in chronological order, Mary's tale of woe would have had much less suspense.

Transitions between present and past are areas open to innovation, and

early sound filmmakers took advantage of them. In *Midnight Mary*, the long flashback closes with gangsters pounding on the door of Mary's boudoir; this sound continues across the dissolve to the present, with Mary roused from her reverie by a knock on the clerk's office door. Earlier, one transition into the past begins with Mary blowing cigarette smoke toward the bound volumes on the shelf.

Dissolve to a close-up of one book as smoke wafts over it.

Dissolve to a shot of Mary's gangster boyfriend blowing cigarette smoke out before he sets up a robbery.

At one point the narration supplies a surprise by abruptly shifting into the present. Once Mary has become a prostitute, she is slumped over a barroom table in sorrow, while her pal Bunny consoles her. In a tight shot, Bunny (Una Merkel, always welcome) leans over and says, "Oh, what's the diff, Mary? A girl's gotta live, ain't she?"

Cut directly to the present, with Mary murmuring, "Not necessarily, Bunny. The jury's still out on that."

Mary's reply casts Bunny's question about needing to live in a new light, since Mary is facing execution, while her use of the stereotyped phrase, "The jury's still out," now with a double meaning, reminds us of the present-tense crisis. It is a more crisp and concise link than the transitions we get in *The Power and the Glory*. But then, Wellman has no need for continuous voice-over, which gives the Sturges/Howard film its more measured pace.

Filmmakers were concerned with finding storytelling techniques appropriate to the sound film, and these unpredictable links between sequences became characteristic of the new medium. Similar links had appeared in silent films, but they gained smoothness and extra dimensions of meaning when the images were blended with dialogue or music.

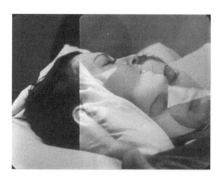

The hooks between scenes are perhaps the least outrageous stretches of *The Sin of Nora Moran*, a Majestic release that, thanks to a gorgeous restoration and a DVD release, has earned a reputation as the nuttiest B-film of the 1930s.

It is a flashback frenzy, boxes within boxes. A district attorney tells the governor's wife to burn the apparently incriminating love letters she's found. In explaining why, the DA introduces a flashback (or is it a cutaway?) to Nora in prison. We then move into Nora's mind and see her hard life, the low point occurring when she's raped by a lion tamer.

Now we start shuttling between the DA telling us about Nora and Nora remembering, or dreaming up, traumatic events. At some points, characters in her flashbacks tell her that what she's experiencing is not real. In one hazy sequence, her circus pal Sadie materializes in her cell to remind Nora that she killed a man. (Actually, she didn't.) At other points Nora's flashbacks include moments in which she says that if she does something differently, *it* will change—*it* being the outcome of the story. At this point another character will point out that they can't change the outcome because it has already happened . . . of course, since this is a flashback.

By the end, after the governor has had his own flashback to the end of his affair with Nora and after she appears as a floating head, things have gotten out of hand. The rules, if there are any, keep changing. And the whole farrago is propelled by furious montage sequences built out of footage scavenged from other films.

Publicity and critical response around *The Sin of Nora Moran* implied that the movie followed the "narratage" method. There was surely some influence. Scenes contain fairly continuous voice-over commentary, and director Phil Goldstone occasionally drops in the diagonal veil used in *The Power and the Glory*. But on the whole this delirious Poverty Row item falls outside the strict contours of Sturges's experiment. *Nora Moran* blurs the line separating flashbacks and fantasy scenes, and it illustrates how easily we can lose track of what time zone we're in. Watching it, I had a flashback of my own—to Joseph Cornell's *Rose Hobart*, another compilation revealing that Hollywood conventions are only a few steps from phantasmagoria.

Unwittingly, *Nora Moran*'s peculiarities point forward to the flashback's golden age, the 1940s and early 1950s. Then we would get contradictory flashbacks, flashbacks within flashbacks within flashbacks, flashbacks from the point of view of a corpse (*Sunset Boulevard*) or an Oscar statuette (*Susan Slept Here*). Filmmakers knew they had found a good thing, and they weren't going to let it go.

Notes

The original screenplay of *The Power and the Glory* is included in Andrew Horton, ed., *Three More Screenplays by Preston Sturges* (Berkeley: University of California Press, 1998). Sturges's reflections from the late 1950s are to be found in *Preston Sturges by Preston Sturges: His Life in His Words*, ed. Sandy Sturges (New York: Simon and Schuster, 1990). The quotations from Sturges's letters and from publicity about "narratage" can be found in Diane Jacobs, *Christmas in July: The Life and Art of Preston Sturges* (Berkeley: University of California Press, 1992), 123–129; and James Curtis, *Between Flops: A Biography of Preston Sturges* (New York: Harcourt Brace Jovanovich, 1982), 87.

My citatations of literary uses of the term come from Elliott Field, "A Philistine in Arcady," *The Black Cat*, July 1919, 33; Fitzgerald's *The Beautiful and Damned* (1922), available here: http://books.google.com/books?id= 7slL1znfyF4C&printsec=frontcover&source=gbs_v2_summary_r&cad=0#v=onepage&q&f=false, 433; Samuel A. Eliot Jr., ed., *Little Theater Classics*, vol. 3 (Boston: Little, Brown, 1921), 120; *The Outlook*, May 11, 1921, 49; review of *His Children's Children*, quoted in Turim, 29; commentary on *On Trial*, in the *New York Times*, March 25, 1923, X2.

For more on the history of flashback construction, apart from Maureen Turim's *Flashbacks in Film*, see Barry Salt's *Film Style and Technology: History and Analysis*, 2nd ed. (London: Starword, 1992), especially 101–102, 139–141. There are discussions of the technique throughout David Bordwell, Janet Staiger, and Kristin Thompson, *The Classical Hollywood Cinema: Film Style and Mode of Production to 1960* (New York: Columbia University Press, 1985), especially 42–44.

• •

Ever since my adolescent years reading Faulkner and mystery stories, I've been captivated by nonlinear plots. Film research has enabled me to indulge this impulse to the fullest. The flashback is a fascinating storytelling technique partly because its effects are so striking. Events presented out of chronological order can have a sharply different impact than events following 1-2-3 sequence. Moreover, the flashback in cinema differs crucially from its use in other media. Language provides overt markers of tense and aspect, which can signal a shift to an earlier period. Cinema needs other indications, such as the audiovisual transitions I mention, and these offer great opportunities for enriching the fabric of the film—creating recurring motifs or moments when stylistic patterning becomes sharply noticeable.

Even the most mundane flashbacks are worth thinking about. As this essay points out, in most films that show a character recounting the past, that character isn't in a position to witness all the events she tells. Her flashback serves primarily to justify the reordering of the plot actions, and that reordering is what counts. Plausibility is sacrificed to effect on the audience. Once more our filmmakers are intuitive psychologists.

In addition, this blog entry illustrates the value of the Internet for historical research. It would have been impossible for me to chart the changing uses of the term *flashback* without Google, Amazon book search, and digital archives of various magazines and newspapers. Similarly, my keyword search of film databases yielded titles and plot synopses I probably couldn't have detected by other means. My survey is only a first approximation, but even these few soundings allow us to pursue questions about how filmmakers described their craft.

One of Turner Classic Movies' valuable rediscoveries, *A Man to Remember* (1938), employs external flashbacks, a rare option in the studio years (though familiar to us now in films like *Pulp Fiction*). See my blog entry on the film (http://www .davidbordwell.net/blog/?p=514). Many flashbacks are introduced or concluded with transitional "hooks," a narrative strategy I discuss in an online essay (http:// www.davidbordwell.net/essays/hook.php). *The Way Hollywood Tells It* proposes a quick survey of some flashback strategies employed in current mainstream movies.

Originality and Origin Stories

NOVEMBER 7, 2006

Kristin here:

In the November 6 issue of *Newsweek* (also online at http://www.newsweek
.com/2006/11/05/back-to-the-future.html), Devin Gordon comments on
the recent trend in franchise series to throw in a prequel covering an earlier period in the main character's life. "So-called origin stories—how fill-
in-the-blank became fill-in-the-blank—are all the rage."

At first David and I wondered whether Gordon, like so many film journalists, would go for an easy answer. There are at least two such answers
in the context of popular films, and especially blockbuster franchise films.
One, their stories reflect something about the current psyche of the nation. Two, they are symptoms of Hollywood running out of creativity and
backbone and going for the tried and true.

The public-psyche theory may sound profound at first, but it's basically
a quick way to write a story without needing to examine film history or
how the film industry works. There may be all sorts of reasons why a given
kind of movie is made at a certain time. We all know about genre cycles.
But society is vast and multifaceted, and it isn't hard for the critic to make
any given film seem to "reflect" some aspect of it. Might the vogue for
origins stories mirror a widespread desire to return to a more innocent
era before 9/11? Bingo, you've got your hook and can make your deadline.
(Problem: most big films these days are negotiated, greenlit, planned, and
in production for years before they appear, thus presumably reflecting not
our own zeitgeist but one that has come and gone.)

As for Hollywood running out of creativity, there are probably plenty of people in Tinseltown with great scripts and the desire to make them. We're living in an age, though, when the big studios are owned by conglomerates. More than ever, the studio decision makers and the investors who buy their stocks keep an eye on the bottom line. *Variety*'s October 23 front-page story, "Less Dream, More Factory" (http://www.variety.com /article/VR1117952384.html?categoryid=13&cs=1), is on the layoffs and other cost-cutting measures that the big studios face. So producers now must focus on exploiting the most popular characters and story premises for their tentpole projects.

Gordon recognizes this and puts his finger on a major reason for the vogue for "origin stories." The studios have to prolong their most lucrative franchises, which are essentially their owners' big brands. Yet those franchises can grow formulaic. One way to renew their energy can be to leap back in time.

Gordon opines, too, that "ironically, playing it safe financially also provides studios with the cover to take creative chances." He points to the fact that Peter Webber, who is directing *Young Hannibal*, has only the indie hit *Girl with a Pearl Earring* to his credit. Similarly, art-house darling Christopher Nolan gave one big franchise a new respectability and audience with *Batman Begins* and will try to continue with *The Dark Knight*.

Linking origin stories to the hiring of such filmmakers is perhaps a bit of a stretch. The new Bond film, *Casino Royale*, the earliest in the order of Ian Fleming's original novels, shows a younger agent. Many of the flashier high-tech props of recent entries in the series are apparently gone, with a grittier feel to the film. Yet it was directed by Martin Campbell, who also had made an earlier entry, *GoldenEye*, as well as both the Zorro films.

It's true that recently Hollywood studios have shown a strange propensity to hire independent or foreign directors to helm entries in franchises. In the wake of his hit *Once Were Warriors*, New Zealand's Lee Tamahori was imported and made *Die Another Day* and *xXx: State of the Union*. Warner Bros. brought in Mexican director Alfonso Cuarón (*Y tu mamá también*) to make the third Harry Potter film, presumably because many critics had dubbed the first two, by Chris Columbus, too bland. Perhaps the studios simply see franchises as needing shaking up at intervals. Yet this is part of a larger trend of indie directors suddenly boosted to blockbuster assignments, as when Doug Liman went from *Go* to *The Bourne Identity* and *Mr. and Mrs. Smith*.

An "origin story," in the sense that Gordon is using the phrase, is a type of prequel that jumps back far enough to show the protagonist distinctly younger and different from the way he is in the original film or series. It then explains how he changed into that protagonist.

Hong Kong filmmakers are adept at prequels of this sort. *God of Gamblers: The Early Years*, shows us the source of the protagonist's lucky ring and his taste for gold-wrapped chocolate, both of which are major motifs in the original *God of Gamblers*. The case of *A Better Tomorrow* is more complicated. John Woo and Tsui Hark had intended it to be a stand-alone film, and they made the mistake of killing off the most charismatic character. The film was such a hit, largely on the basis of Chow Yun Fat's performance as Mark, that *A Better Tomorrow II* gave Mark a twin brother, Ken, and put Chow back in action. That film's success led to a prequel to the first film. *A Better Tomorrow III* traces how the Mark character acquired his fighting skills and his signature costume and habits.

Origin stories are not entirely new to Hollywood, either. As far back as 1974, *The Godfather: Part II* wove in flashbacks to a time well before the first film's action, tracing Don Corleone's rise. In 1979, there was *Butch and Sundance: The Early Days*.

Origin stories can be thought of as expansions of a basic convention of mainstream storytelling: the flashback to crucial formative moments in a character's life. In that sense, perhaps the quintessential origin story is *Citizen Kane*. Today, when everything is potentially franchisable, such an early-days sequence can create a series. The prologue of *Indiana Jones and the Last Crusade* shows young Jones launching upon an adventure that prefigures the man he will become. (In an inside joke, River Phoenix even acquires Harrison Ford's chin scar.) That sequence in turn spawned *The Chronicles of Young Indiana Jones* TV series ("Before the world discovered Indiana, Indiana discovered the world") and four cable movies.

As a term, "origin stories" was coined by students of mythology, who use it to refer to various ethnic groups' accounts of the origin of the world. In that case, it didn't have anything to do with what we now call prequels.

Then the term got taken up in discussions of comic books to identify the sort of thing that Gordon is talking about. Before television, comic books were the ultimate franchise form of the twentieth century. In comic franchises, particularly those centering on superheroes, a book or short series of books might be devoted to an origin story. (Dave Carter's blog has a lengthy entry on comic-book origin stories, giving examples, at http://yetanothercomicsblog.blogspot.com/2005/01/origin-stories.html.) It's not surprising that one of the main origin films, *Batman Begins*, came from the comics.

Gordon does not mention another reason why studios might want to continue a franchise by jumping back to the hero's origins: actors can age too much to continue a role. It's been over 14 years since *The Silence of the Lambs*, and Anthony Hopkins could probably not be convincing in another turn as Lecter. Possibly we'll get a chance to see whether a 60-something (or 70-something at the rate things are going) Harrison Ford can bring audiences in for the on-again-off-again Indiana Jones continuation. Or actors may exit the franchise, as Jodie Foster did before *Hannibal*. Or grow up too quickly, as the Harry Potter kids are doing before our eyes. Or die, as Richard Harris did in the same series, forcing Warner to substitute Michael Gambon as Dumbledore.

But origin stories don't have these problems. Just get new actors. One thing tentpole franchise films have taught us is that as strongly identified with a character a star may become, if the character and premises are even stronger, a new actor will be accepted. It's happened with Batman, Superman, Bond, and almost did—and could yet—with Spider-Man.

Such stories, however, have their dangers as well. If the audience is devoted to the character as he (and it's mostly *he* so far) is, will they care about seeing him as a very different person? If Hannibal Lecter is the middle-aged psychopath we love to hate, do we want to learn that he was once a vulnerable, suffering youth?

• •

Big franchise tentpoles remain the anchors of the studios' annual outputs. Christopher Nolan succeeded mightily in sustaining the Batman series with *The Dark Knight*. Daniel Craig similarly caught the public's fancy as a younger Bond. Origin stories are extending the X-Men franchise and even becoming part of the titles, with *X-Men Origins: Wolverine* the first of a planned series.

The release of *Indiana Jones and the Kingdom of the Crystal Skull* (which we blogged about here: http://www.davidbordwell.net/blog/?p=2379) appeared four years before Ford's seventieth birthday and, despite complaints from critics and fans, was a considerable success. *Young Hannibal*, however, justified the skepticism of my closing paragraph by failing to attract audiences. (Its release title, *Hannibal Rising*, probably made matters worse.) After three successful Spider-Man movies, in early 2010 Sony announced that it would reboot the series with a new director and cast, sending the hero back to high school, at a point where he had already discovered his superhuman powers.

• •

Good Actors Spell Good Acting

NOVEMBER 24, 2006

Kristin here:

I suppose all movie lovers have favorite quotations that become part of their everyday conversation. Norman Bates's "One by one you drop the formalities" fits a surprising number of situations. The film-studies professors here in Madison often communicate with each other using lines from Howard Hawks films, especially *Rio Bravo*. "Let's take a turn around the town," "We'll remember you said that," and, of course, "It's nice to see a smart kid for a change." Any time David or I get a particularly small royalty check, we echo Hildy Johnson's sour "Buy yourself an annuity."

One of our favorite everyday-life quotations comes not from a movie but from the endlessly hilarious *SCTV* series. It's a skit in which Steve Roman (played by John Candy) promotes his new TV show, *Juan Cortez, Courtroom Judge*. He explains part of its appeal: "It's got good actors, and that spells good acting" (fifth season, episode 110, for you *SCTV* buffs).

Almost invariably we use this line when we come across one of those films that receive highly positive reviews largely because of one great performance. You know the kind: Charlize Theron in *Monster*, Halle Berry in *Monster's Ball*, Hilary Swank in *Boys Don't Cry*, and more recently Forest Whitaker in *The Last King of Scotland* and Helen Mirren in *The Queen*.

Usually I avoid such films, because the reviews tend to plant the idea that they are primarily actors' vehicles. I enjoy good acting as much as the next person, but I want the rest of the film to be interesting as well.

Are there any film classics that are truly great solely for the acting? It's hard to think of any. Maybe *The Gold Rush*, which is stylistically fairly pedestrian but which is redeemed by Chaplin's inspired performance. Maybe *Duck Soup*, also quite undistinguished for much of anything other than the Marx Brothers cutting loose without being saddled with the sort of plots involving young, singing lovers that MGM would soon foist upon them. Maybe a few others. Usually, though, we tend not to think of a performance, however dazzling, as adding up to a great film.

Still, when I think of some of the finest performances ever put on film, I think of Falconetti in *La Passion de Jeanne d'Arc* by Carl Dreyer. There her luminous portrayal of determination and religious devotion is embedded in an equally extraordinary film, with its minimalist sets by Hermann Warm, its insistently tight framings on faces, and its vertiginous camera movements. Similarly, Nicolai Cherkasov as Ivan the Terrible in Eisenstein's film poses against the shapes of the settings, moves to the music of Prokofiev, and casts great shadows on the walls. Buster Keaton, though not as popular in his day as Chaplin, had an instinctive feel for both the flat space of the screen and the depth of the represented image, and his films are exciting in themselves and not simply as backgrounds to his clowning.

We're now well into the time of year when the studios bring out the films they hope will garner Oscar nominations and wins. Journalists covering film, reviewers and feature writers alike, can get some copy out of speculating about the Oscars. That speculation seems to start earlier and earlier each year, like Christmas shopping. Given that the public is a lot more interested in acting than cinematography or screenwriting, perhaps it's not surprising that reviewers focus so much on star turns. But in doing so, do they slight other aspects of those films? Do they unfairly scare off those of us who are wary of Oscar bait?

I decided to do my part for the good of the blog and see *The Queen*. I'm not a huge fan of Stephen Frears, but *My Beautiful Laundrette* is a good film, with an early sympathetic, non-sensationalized view of homosexuality in London. *Mary Reilly* is not exactly a masterpiece, but it's worth watching and has been underrated. Its failure may have been due in part to the fact that most reviewers focused in on whether Julia Roberts could handle a dramatic role in a thriller and then found her wanting.

Anyway, *The Queen* turned out to be an entertaining, well-made film. Yes, Helen Mirren is remarkable as Queen Elizabeth II, and she may well win an Oscar for her performance. Yet equally interesting is the fact that Frears almost entirely avoids the "intensified continuity" style that David has analyzed in *The Way Hollywood Tells It*.

The film is basically pretty simple, moving back and forth between the royal family and the newly elected Tony Blair surrounded by his wife and staff. The royals react to the death of ex-Princess Diana with stony silence despite the huge outpouring of public grief. As is clear from the indifference and even hostility toward Diana that the members of the family's older generations voice in private, they do not feel a comparable grief. But Blair strives to maneuver the Queen into going public and expressing a sense of loss.

Frears set out to contrast the two worlds stylistically. The scenes with the royals are shot in a classical, non-intensified style: distant shots to establish space, two-shots for face-to-face conversations, over-the-shoulder shot/reverse shots as the dialogue unfolds. The framing seldom goes in for the tight close-up but stays in medium shot or medium close-up. The cutting is slow relative to the current norm, as befits both the subject and the style. One reason people are so impressed with Mirren's performance may be that it is not made up of a bunch of different shots stitched together. She has shots that allow her to develop a reaction or attitude slowly.

And best of all, the camera doesn't glide toward or around the characters. It stays put unless it needs to perform one of its traditional roles: reframing to keep characters balanced, and following the characters as they move from one room to another or walk along a country track. The lighting is suitably subdued and directional, another reversion to a more classical age.

A great deal is currently being made of Steven Soderbergh's reversion to 1940s Hollywood style in *The Good German*. Frears isn't quite as systematic, perhaps, but the royal-family scenes in *The Queen* look very 1950s to me.

In contrast, the Tony Blair scenes were shot with a handheld camera, to convey the bustle of his staff and the more casual situation. Even so, the camera movement is not obtrusive, and Frears still doesn't constantly cut in for the tight close-up. Here, too, he keeps his camera back a bit, framing groups as they talk. The lighting tends to be brighter and more diffuse than in the scenes with the royals. The contrast works well, and yet Frears never pushes it in our faces and asks us to be impressed.

The narrative seems a little thin, mostly because, unlike most classical films, *The Queen* has only one plotline. There's no subsidiary crisis, no romance, no other conflict. It's just the royals versus the liberal prime minister's team until one side cracks. Even the potential conflict that could have easily arisen from Blair's wife's anti-royalty position never goes anywhere. She's mainly there as a sounding board for him. And if the plot is thin, it is also refreshingly elegant in its simplicity.

One remarkable aspect of the plot is that none of the characters is treated as a villain. Blair's position is held up as the wise one, yet the film goes to great lengths to suggest that the Queen and her family have reasons for behaving the way they do. Not excuses, but reasons. Fittingly, the film concludes with the Queen and her new prime minister walking out into the palace gardens for a stroll and a chat.

At the end, I didn't feel that I had sat through a great performance. I had seen a good, entertaining, somewhat unusual, and skillfully made film that had a great performance in it. Indeed, it has a second from Michael Sheen as Blair, and the supporting players are fine as well.

But good directors spell good directing, and good cinematographers spell . . . you get the idea. It would be nice to see more rounded reviews. *Variety*'s reviewers, it must be said, seem to have a mandate to mention style, since every review comments at least briefly on the film's techniques. But most critics give you no sense of the film as a whole—its narrative construction (apart from a plot synopsis) or its stylistic texture.

· ·

Alas, film reviewers have not paid much attention to my suggestions. In the intervening years, have I been wrong to skip *Doubt*, *The Reader*, *Rachel Getting Married*, and *The Wrestler*?

I went to *There Will Be Blood* not because the reviews touted Daniel Day-Lewis's performance, though it was truly amazing and made me pity all the actors competing with him for the Oscar. I went because Paul Thomas Anderson is one of the best, most consistently inventive directors now working in the United States. I went to *Eastern Promises* not simply for Viggo Mortensen's virtuoso acting but because it's a David Cronenberg film. I saw *Milk* because it had Gus Van Sant's name on the credits, though as always I admired Sean Penn's performance. I must say that with established auteurs like these, some reviewers do feel obligated to mention something beyond the acting. When Tarantino signs a film, reviewers don't tend to spend the whole review praising Christoph Waltz's multi-lingual acting in *Inglourious Basterds*, though they rightly mention it.

These films all contained performances that got nominated for and in some cases won Oscars. Other auteur vehicles like *No Country for Old Men* and *The Curious Case of Benjamin Button* can boast the same. That's partly because stars like to work with good directors, knowing that they spell good directing.

By Annie Standards

DECEMBER 10, 2006

Kristin here:

Among the new films I've seen in the past couple of years, I find that a significant proportion are animated. I don't think that's because I prefer animated films but because these days they are among the best work being created by the mainstream industry.

Why would that be? There are probably a lot of reasons, but let me offer a few. Animated films, whether executed with CGI or drawings, demand meticulous planning in a way that live-action films don't. David has written about directors' heavy dependence on coverage in contemporary shooting ("Cutting Remarks: On *The Good German*, Classical Style, and the Police Tactical Unit," http://www.davidbordwell.net/blog?p=91). Coverage means that many filmmakers don't really know until they get into the editing room how many shots a scene will contain, which angles will be used, when the cuts will come, and other fairly crucial components of the final style. This is true even despite the fact that filmmakers increasingly have storyboarded their films (mainly for big action scenes) or created animatics (a.k.a. pre-visualization or pre-viz) using relatively simple computer animation.

People planning animated films don't have the luxury of lots of coverage, and that's probably a good thing. Storyboards for animated films mean a lot more, because it's a big deal to depart from them. Every shot and cut has to be thought out in advance, because whole teams of people have to create images that fit together—and they don't create coverage. (For a look at how Pixar plans and executes the editing in its films, see our entry "A Glimpse into the Pixar Kitchen," http://www.davidbordwell.net /blog/?p=2205.) There aren't many directors in Hollywood who think their scenes out that carefully. Steven Spielberg, yes, and maybe a few others.

A similar thing happens with the soundtrack. In animated films, the voices are recorded before the creation of the images. That's been true since sync sound was innovated in the late 1920s. Prerecording means that images of moving lips can be matched to the dialogue far more precisely than if actors watched finished images and tried to speak at exactly the right time to mesh with their characters' mouths. The lengthy fiddling possible with ADR isn't an option. Most stars are used to recording their entire performances within a few days, picking up their fees, and moving on to more time-consuming live-action shooting.

In *The Way Hollywood Tells It* and *Film Art*, David has briefly discussed the modern vogue for muted tones, usually brown and blue, of many modern features. (Remember what a big deal it was when *Dick Tracy* used bright, comic-book colors in its sets?) The old vibrant hues of the Technicolor days are largely absent, at least from dramas and thrillers. Not so in animated films. Most animated films are full of bright colors. (Some tales, like *Tim Burton's Corpse Bride* and *Happy Feet*, call for the minimization of color, but they're exceptional.) Think of *Monsters, Inc.*, and just about any modern action, mystery, or thriller film, like *Se7en*. Yes, *Se7en* is dark in its subject matter, but the drab style begins well before the nastiness starts in Fincher's film. For those of us who like some variety in our moviegoing, an animated film can be visually pleasing in ways that few other films are.

Makers of animated films aren't obligated to drag in sex scenes or to undress the lead actress. Maybe such scenes in live-action films really do draw in some viewers, but they can be hokey and definitely slow down the action. (Remember Ben Affleck rubbing animal crackers on Liv Tyler's bare midriff in *Armageddon*?) Animated films tend to have romance, and sometimes even mildly raunchy innuendo, but it doesn't slow down the plot. The romances in *Flushed Away* and *Cars* are very much like the ones in Hollywood comedies of the 1930s and 1940s, flowing along with the narrative in a more logical way.

Animated films don't have to be tailored to the egos and ambitions of their stars to the degree that many live-action features are. Indeed, often stars bring projects to studios or produce their own films. The growing number of stars providing voices for mice and penguins and spiders don't have that sort of investment, emotional or financial.

Some of the best directors working today are in animation. Pixar's John Lasseter hasn't let us down in any of his Pixar films, whether he personally directs them or supervises others. Nick Park's shorts and features, especially *Creature Comforts* and *The Wrong Trousers*, are works of genius, and other director/animators at Aardman aren't bad either. Then there's Hayao Miyazaki (*Spirited Away*, to mention only one). There aren't many live-action directors working in commercial cinema today with such track records.

Despite all this, studio executives and commentators continue to debate whether there are now too many CGI films coming out. Indeed, the November 24 issue of *Screen International* says, "Much has been made this year of the seeming over-saturation of studios' computer-generated titles, with critics and analysts pointing to growing movie-goer apathy." Of course most people don't notice any difference between CGI 3-D films and those made with claymation (Parks) or puppets (Burton), so *SI*'s article talks about the successes and failures among the family-friendly animated films of 2006, including the 2-D *Curious George*.

This debate over a possible saturation of the market with CGI films seems bizarre. As a proportion among the total number of films made, CGI's box-office successes seem fairly high compared to live-action films. Yet one doesn't see execs and pundits mulling over whether audiences are tired of the latter. (See "Too Many Toons?," http://www.davidbordwell .net/blog/?p=338.)

Certainly success or failure isn't based on quality. *Wallace & Gromit: The Curse of the Were-Rabbit*, last year's winner of the Oscar as Best Animated Feature, was a commercial disappointment (in the United States, not elsewhere). *Monster House* got a lot of highly favorable reviews, but similarly had a mediocre reception from ticket buyers.

This week the nominations for the Annie Awards, given out by the International Animated Film Society, were announced. The Best Animated Feature competition is among *Cars*, *Happy Feet*, *Monster House*, *Open Season*, and *Over the Hedge*. But in the "what's the logic behind that?!" world of awards, *Cars* and *Flushed Away* got the highest number of individual nominations, nine each, followed by *Over the Hedge* with eight.

I'll confess right now that I've only seen three CGI-animated films this year, because, as I say, I'm not an animation specialist. I go to animated films for specific reasons. One, *Cars* is a Pixar film. Two, *Flushed Away* is an Aardman film. Three, *Happy Feet* is directed by George (*Road Warrior*) Miller.

On the other hand, *Over the Hedge* was advertised as being "from the creators of *Shrek*." *Shrek* is an entertaining film, but I think it has been overrated. Besides, a check through the main credits of *Over the Hedge* reveals no one who had worked on *Shrek*. "Creators" here must mean Dreamworks. That, by itself, is not enough to draw me in.

Of the three I've seen, I would rate *Cars* the best, *Flushed Away* a not-too-distant second, and *Happy Feet* a distinct third. So how come *Flushed Away* didn't get nominated for Best Animated Feature?

A cynic might point out that on a list of the ten highest-grossing animated features of 2006, by year's end the five nominees will end up among the top six. *Ice Age: The Meltdown*, currently at number two, received four nominations, but not one for best feature. *Flushed Away* is at number nine and likely to remain so. I'm sure that's not the only factor, but as with many other awards nominations, hits tend to maintain a high profile through the year. I suspect that *Cars* will end up becoming the fourth Pixar film to win the Annie for Best Animated Feature during the seven-year period since *Toy Story*, the first totally CGI feature, won.

Quality apart, though, why do industry people doubt the wide appeal of CGI animation? Why do they think rising above an indeterminate number of such features per year causes CGI-fatigue among moviegoers? They certainly go on releasing far more live-action films than could possibly all become hits.

As I suggested in an earlier entry on *Flushed Away* ("Flushed Away for Real?," http://www.davidbordwell.net/blog/?p=129), most of the companies releasing animated films don't know how to market them very well. Let me offer a couple of suggestions as to why everyone but Pixar often seems so clueless.

First, although animated features seem like the ideal family-friendly product, they're quite different from the family-friendly live-action film. Every studio wants films that appeal "to all ages" (i.e., to everyone but small kids), preferably with a PG-13 rating. Think *Pirates of the Caribbean: Dead Man's Chest*, *The Lord of the Rings: The Return of the King*, and *Titanic*, in ascending order the three top international grossers of all time (in unadjusted dollars).

With most animated features, however, there's a big gap in that family audience: teenagers. Animated films ("cartoons") are still perceived as largely for children. Sure, savvy filmmakers like the people at Pixar and Aardman are putting more sophisticated references and jokes into their films, things that are more entertaining to adults than to children. The assumption is that parents who take their kids to the movies might be more likely to pick a film if they think they'll have something to engage their attention, as opposed to sitting tolerantly waiting for the thing to be over.

This, by the way, is another reason why some animated films are among the best products of the mainstream film industry these days. They've got a wit and visual sophistication that is sorely lacking in many live-action films. (That's certainly not true of all of them. I thought *Madagascar* and the first *Ice Age* had simple plots that would be engaging mainly to small children.)

So the grown-up humor may please the adults, many of whom, like me, go to them without children in tow. Kids, of course, will watch just about anything animated that's put in front of them. But suppose a bunch of high-school kids on a Saturday are trying to decide which film to attend. Would any of them suggest *Cars* or *Happy Feet*? Maybe I'm behind the times, but I find it hard to imagine. Most teenagers among themselves, after all, would do anything to avoid seeming not to be grown-up, and watching cartoons is just too childish. (Even the CGI film most obviously aimed at teens, *Final Fantasy*, was a flop.) This is not to say that teenagers don't see or enjoy *Cars* and *Happy Feet*, but I'm guessing they probably go with their families on holidays or see them at home on DVD.

The second big problem that stymies the industry when it comes to promoting animated features is that they usually can't be branded by director or star, the way "regular" films are. Pixar, as usual, is the exception. John Lasseter is sort of the Steven Spielberg of animation—one of the few directors with wide popular name-recognition. Pixar quickly became a brand in the world of animation, even more than Disney was at that point. Now they're under the same roof. But Dreamworks really isn't a high-profile brand, and the newer Sony Pictures Animation certainly isn't. Their films succeed and become franchises in a hit or miss way. "From the people who brought you *Shrek*" is a feeble way of branding a film. Mostly I think distributors market animated films to kids and hope the adults will be there, too. Maybe they don't even think about the teenage audience, considering it a lost cause.

More and more famous actors are doing voices for animated films, but that's far from the same thing as appearing in a live-action one. Hugh Jackman was a big selling point for the *X-Men* movies, but who would go to see *Flushed Away* mainly because he voices the lead character?

So what can the studios do to integrate CGI and other types of animated films into their flow of regular releases, comparable to live-action films?

One solution is obvious: make the characters into stars. Disney created the prototype with Mickey Mouse. Buzz Lightyear and Woody would be stars with or without Tim Allen's and Tom Hanks's voices. Shrek is a star. Wallace and Gromit are beloved stars outside the United States. It might have occurred to Paramount to lead up to its release of *The Curse of the Were-Rabbit* by circulating a package of the three earlier shorts, in order to familiarize Americans with the duo. (That was done in European theaters years ago.) Roger Ebert's review of the feature opined that "Wallace and Gromit are arguably the two most delightful characters in the history of animation" (http://rogerebert.suntimes.com/apps/pbcs.dll/article?AID=/20051006/REVIEWS/50929001/1023). A pity the American public has not yet been given much of a chance to discover that.

Another possibility is doing what Hollywood is starting to do for live-action films: publicize award nominations other than the Oscars. More awards ceremonies are being broadcast on TV as time goes by, and audiences seemingly love these contests. Why not tout an animated film's garnering of Annie nominations?

Of course companies use Oscar nominations in their ads, but under Academy rules, only three animated features can be nominated in any year unless sixteen or more such features are released that year. Then the number of nominations jumps to five, but so far that hasn't happened. It may finally happen this year, if all sixteen features currently under consideration qualify under Academy rules.

One might object that the general public doesn't know or care about the Annies. But it's a vicious circle. They don't know about them because the industry doesn't bother to publicize them, and the industry doesn't publicize them . . . well, you can see where this is going. If the industry promoted the Annies as signs of quality animation, the public might know and possibly care about them. They've learned to be interested in the Golden Globes, because those have been increasingly covered by the infotainment section of the media. And the infotainment industry largely covers the "news" that the industry's publicity departments want it to, star scandals excepted.

And then there's the Internet, where fans often do a better job (and for free) of publicizing films than their distributors do. Case in point, Elizabeth Krumbach's site, *WallaceAndGromit.net* (http://wallaceandgromit.net/). I can't get into online publicity here, or this entry would balloon out of control. Still, there seems an obvious link between people who spend time on the Internet and those who are interested in CGI animation.

Note: Information on the Annie Awards is available at http://www
.annieawards.org.

• •

After this entry was posted, Jason Mittell, who teaches at Middlebury College,
pointed out to me other factors closely related to the thorough storyboarding of
animated films and to the prerecording of dialogue.

Live-action projects often go into the shooting phase with the script still being
tinkered with. The main writers are long gone, script doctors have taken over, and
stars may request, nay demand, changes in their dialogue. But for animated films,
the script, like the editing, is usually in finished form at the move from pre-production
to production.

Jason also points out that makers of animated films carefully differentiate the
characters by distinctive dialogue and voices. In contrast, do planners of live-action
films think much about the combination of vocal tones that the actors will bring to
the project? It's indicative of the difference, I think, that the Annies have a category
for best vocal performance and the Oscars don't. Ian McKellen was nominated
for an Annie in that category for his contribution of the Toad's dialogue in *Flushed
Away*—tailored to the role and totally different from his usual voice. As Jason concludes, "Live-action filmmakers should try to emulate Pixar's pre-production strategies to raise the quality bar."

Some updates. *Cars*, as I predicted, won the Annie as Best Animated Feature,
though it lost the Oscar to *Happy Feet*. (The online version of this entry concludes
with a brief review of *Happy Feet*.)

Two films have joined the three top-grossers I mentioned. *Avatar* and *The Dark
Knight* now belong to the exclusive club of films whose box-office takings are over
a billion dollars worldwide (as ever, in unadjusted dollars). Both also carry PG-13
ratings.

The number of films eligible to be nominated for an Oscar as best animated film
did not top sixteen until 2009, when twenty films qualified. For the first time five films
were nominated. That caused something of a stir in the infotainment sphere, but
perhaps now commentators will accept that animated films play a more prominent
and regular role among the total number of movies released to theaters.

Many mainstream animated features continue to appeal to adults as well as
children. *Coraline*, *Fantastic Mr. Fox*, *Up*, *Monsters vs. Aliens*, and *Cloudy with a
Chance of Meatballs* all do. Perhaps animation has even become cool enough that
teenagers will be attracted. Although *Fantastic Mr. Fox* is based on a children's
book, Wes Anderson's participation as director may signal that animation is becoming cool.

Alas, no one has yet tried to bring Aardman films back into the American market.

A Matter of Loaf and Death, shown on the BBC for Christmas 2008, maintains the high standards of the three earlier Wallace and Gromit shorts, but to buy it when it first came out I had to preorder the DVD from England. The British disc was released on March 23, 2009, the American one on September 22 of that year. Had it not been nominated for an Oscar, I wonder how many Americans would even know it exists.

. . . .

Unsteadicam Chronicles

AUGUST 17, 2007

David here:

A specter is haunting contemporary cinema: the shaky shot.

Viewers have been protesting for some years now. I recall friends asking me why the images were so bumpy in Woody Allen's *Husbands and Wives* and Lars von Trier's *Dancer in the Dark*. *The Bourne Ultimatum*, this summer's wildest excursion into Unsteadicam, has put the matter back on the agenda.

If you drop in at Roger Ebert's website (http://rogerebert.suntimes .com/apps/pbcs.dll/article?AID=/20070816/COMMENTARY/70816001), you'll find many annoyed comments from readers about what one calls the "Queasy-Cam." The writers make shrewd points about the purpose and effects of director Paul Greengrass's technique. I'll try to add some historical perspective and a little analysis.

From Whose Bourne No Traveling Shot Returneth

First, what exactly are we talking about? Some viewers and critics think the jarring quality of the movie proceeds from rapid editing. The cutting in *Bourne Ultimatum* is indeed very fast; there are about 3,200 shots in 105 minutes, yielding an average of about 2 seconds per shot. But there are other fast-cut films that don't yield the same dizzy effects, such as *Sky Captain and the World of Tomorrow* (1.6 seconds average), *Batman Begins* (1.9 seconds), *Idiocracy* (1.9 seconds), and the *Transporter* movies (less than 2 seconds).

As for the series, *The Bourne Identity*, directed by Doug Liman, was edited a tad slower, averaging 3 seconds per shot. The second entry, *The Bourne Supremacy*, also signed by Greengrass, was as fast-cut as *The Bourne Ultimatum*, coming in at 1.9 seconds. People noticed the rough texture of the second one, but it didn't arouse the protests that this last installment does. Something else is up.

Partly, it's not the pace of the editing but the spasmodic quality of it. Cuts here seem abrasive because they interrupt actions and camera movements. Pans, zooms, and movements of the actors are seldom allowed to come to rest before the shot changes. This creates a strong sense of jerkiness and visual imbalance.

Still, a lot of the film's effect has to be laid at the handheld camera. The technique in itself, however, shouldn't shock us. The handheld aesthetic has been with us a long time. There were silent-era experiments with the technique by E. A. Dupont (*Variety*, 1925) and Abel Gance (*Napoleon*, 1927). It recurred sporadically after that, but in mainstream cinema handheld shooting became common in 1960s films as different as *The Miracle Worker*, *Seven Days in May*, *Dr. Strangelove*, and the dramas of John Cassavetes. Today, many films from Asia and Europe as well as the United States rely on the device all the way through. The trend is so widespread that it's been satirized: in the Danish comedy *Clash of Egos* (2006), when an ordinary workman gets a chance to direct a movie, he insists that the camera be put on a tripod, and the cinematographer complains that he hasn't done that since film school. Directors nowadays tell us that they are in search of *energy*, a moment-by-moment spiking of audience interest. You can get it through fast cutting, arcing camera movements, sudden frame-entrances, the nervousness of the handheld shot, or all of the above.

Roughhouse

I think the upsetting qualities of the visuals in *The Bourne Ultimatum* derive principally from the particular way the handheld camera is used. Several of Ebert's writers complain that the camerawork made them nauseated, and there seems little doubt that the shots are bouncier and jerkier than in much handheld work. Adding to the effect is the fact that Greengrass often doesn't try to center or contain the main action. Sometimes, as in a fight scene, the camera is just too close to the action to show everything, so it tries to grab what it can. At other times Greengrass pans away from the subject, or shoves it to the edge of the 2.40:1 frame. In the standard technique of over-the-shoulder reverse angles, we see one character's shoulders in the foreground and the primary character's face

clearly. Greengrass likes to let a neck or shoulder overwhelm the composition as a dark mass, so that only a bit of the face, perhaps even just a single eye, is tucked into a corner of the shot. This visual idea was already on offer in *The Bourne Supremacy* (as illustrated above).

In *The Way Hollywood Tells It*, I described contemporary films as employing "intensified continuity," an amplification and exaggeration of traditional methods of staging, shooting, and cutting. What Greengrass has done is to roughen up intensified continuity, making its conventions a little less easy to take in. Normally, for instance, rack-focus smoothly guides our attention from one plane to another. But in *The Bourne Ultimatum*, when Jason bursts into a corridor close to the camera, the camera tries but fails to rack focus on his pursuer darting off in the distance. Likewise, most directors fill their scenes with close-ups, and so does Greengrass, but he lets the main figure bounce around the frame or go blurry or slip briefly out of view.

Essentially, intensified continuity is about using brief shots to maintain the audience's interest but also making each shot yield a single point,

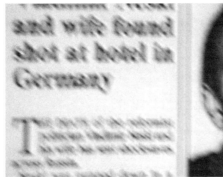

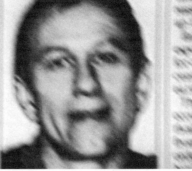

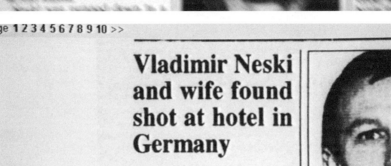

Vladimir Neski and wife found shot at hotel in Germany

THE DEATH of the reformist

a dab of information. Got it? On to the next shot. Greengrass's camera technique makes the shot's point a little harder to get at first sight. Instead of a glance, he gives us a glimpse.

Although this strategy is more aggressive in this third Bourne installment, we can find it as well in *Supremacy*. An agent pulls a document out of a carry-on bag, and for an instant we can see the government seal. In the next shot the agent bobs in and out of the frame, as if the camera can't anticipate his next move. Later the camera jerks across a computer display and suddenly focuses, evoking the jumpy saccadic flicks with which we scan our world (above).

Greengrass claims that his creative choices were influenced by the cinéma-vérité documentary school and cites as well *The Battle of Algiers*, which helped popularize the handheld look in the 1960s. Yet he adds that the style is subjective: "Your p.o.v. is limited to the eye of the character, instead of the camera being a godlike instrument choreographed to be in the right place at the right time" (http://www.variety.com/article /VR1117969675.html). But our point of view isn't confined to what Bourne or anybody else sees and knows. The whole movie relies on crosscutting to create an omniscient awareness of various CIA maneuvers to trap him. And if Bourne really saw his enemies in the flashes we get, he couldn't wreck them so thoroughly.

The Bourne Ultimatum belongs to a trend of rough-edged stylization sometimes called run-and-gun. The film has been described as bare-bones but it's actually quite flashy. All the crashing zooms (accompanied by whams on the soundtrack), jittery shots, drifting framings, uncompleted pans, freeze-frame flashbacks, and other extroverted devices call attention to themselves. You can find earlier instances in Oliver Stone's *Natural Born Killers* and *U-Turn*, along with stretches in Michael Mann's latest films. In milder form you find the style on display in TV crime shows, as well as in the notorious docudrama *The Road to 9/11*.

The most extreme practitioner of this style is probably Tony Scott. From *Spy Game* through *Man on Fire*, *Domino*, and *Déjà Vu*, he has taken the run-and-gun aesthetic in delirious directions. His framing is often restless, as if groping for the right composition. In one shot from *Domino*, the camera starts a bit too far to the right, shifts left to frame Charles a little better, zooms back hesitantly, then finally stabilizes itself as he addresses the Motor Vehicles worker (see next page).

A single shot may give us not only changes of focus but jumps in exposure, lighting, and color; sometimes it's hard to say whether we have one shot or several. The result is a series of visual jolts, as in *Man on Fire* (p. 173).

Scott, trained as a painter, pushes toward a mannered, decorative abstraction, aided by long-lens compositions and a burning, high-contrast palette. For *Supremacy*, Greengrass adopted a toned-down version of Scott's approach, whereas in *Ultimatum*, he favors drab surroundings and steely colors. Still, both men's approaches to run-and-gun are frankly artificial, and both remain within the premises of intensified continuity. Of the Waterloo Station sequence Greengrass says, "It has got a sense of energy."

The Bourne Coverup

There's one more function of *Bourne*'s style I want to consider. Hong Kong cinematographers have a saying. *The handheld camera covers three mistakes: bad acting, bad set design, and bad directing.* It's worth considering, as some of Ebert's correspondents do, what Greengrass's style may serve to camouflage.

One suggests that because the cutting doesn't let the viewer reconstruct the fights blow by blow, anybody can seem to be a superhero if the filming

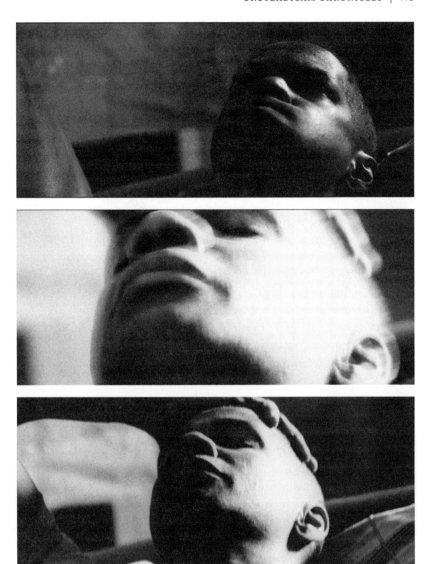

is flurried enough. Just as important, the director who is just (apparently) snatching shots doesn't have to worry about building up performances slowly; he or she can simply give us the most minimal, stereotyped signals in facial close-ups. Lengthier shots let the actor develop the character's re-actions in detail, and force us to follow them. Classic studio cinema, with its more distant framings and longer takes, lets you follow the evolution of a feeling or idea through the actor's blocking and behavior. The villain in the average Charlie Chan movie displays more psychological continuity than the nasty agents in *The Bourne Ultimatum*.

Moreover, run-and-gun technique doesn't demand that you develop an ongoing sense of the figures within a spatial whole. The bodies, fragmented and smeared across the frame, don't dwell within these locales. They exist in an architectural vacuum. In *United 93*, the technique could work because we're all minimally familiar with the geography of a passenger jet. But in *The Bourne Ultimatum*, could anybody reconstruct any of these stations, streets, or apartment blocks on the strength of what we see? *Of course!* some will say. *That's the point. Jason himself is dizzyingly preoccupied by the immediacy of the action, and so are we.* Yet Jason must know the layout in detail, if he's able to pursue others and escape so efficiently. Moreover, we can justify any fuzziness in any piece of storytelling as reflecting a confused protagonist. This rationale puts us close to Poe's suggestion that we shouldn't confuse obscurity of expression with the expression of obscurity.

The run-and-gun style is indeed visceral, but let's be aware of how it achieves its impact. The clean, hard-edged technique of classic Hong Kong films allows extravagant action to affect us viscerally; by following the action effortlessly, we can feel its bodily impact. We're shown bodies in sleek, efficient movement that gets amplified by cogent framing and smooth matches on action. But in the fancy run-and-gun style, cinematography and sound do most of the work. Instead of arousing us through kinetic figures, the film makes bouncy and blurry movement do the job. Rather than exciting us by what we see, Greengrass tries to arouse us by how he shows it. The resulting visual texture is so of a piece, so persistently hammering, that to give it flow and high points, Greengrass must rely on sound effects and music. As a friend points out, we understand that Bourne is wielding a razor at one point chiefly because we hear its whoosh.

What else does the handheld style conceal? Since the 1980s, in many action pictures the cutting has become so fast, and often capricious, that we can't clearly see the physical action that's being executed. That complaint is justified in *The Bourne Ultimatum*, certainly, but here the style also seeks to make the stunts seem less preposterous. Instead of showing cars crashing and flipping balletically, Greengrass barely lets us see the crash. The conventions of the action film are smudged in *The Bourne Identity*, as if a sketchy rendering makes them seem less outlandish. In a Hong Kong film, Bourne in striding flight, grabbing objects to use as weapons without missing a beat, would be presented crisply, showing him executing feats of resourceful grace. But many viewers seem to find this sort of choreography outlandish or cartoony. So when Bourne plucks up pieces of laundry and wraps them around his hands when he vaults a glass-strewn wall, Greengrass's shot-snatching conceals the flamboyance of the stunt.

Finally, I'd argue that the style camouflages something else: plot problems. I'm not talking about the hero's indestructibility, which is a given in this genre. John McClane in *Live Free or Die Hard* survives about as much mayhem as does Jason Bourne. But there are some howlers here that, because of the rapid pace and the just-barely-visible action, are somewhat muffled. By whisking the action past us and forcing us to keep up, the film doesn't allow us to dwell on its holes and thin patches.

The plot, praised by so many, is actually a very simple one: find Guy A, but when he's killed, locate the clues that will lead you to Guy B, and so on, until you get to Mr. Big. The mechanics of how the clues are pursued remain obscure. Why would an all-powerful CIA operation house its key players in offices that can easily be watched from a neighboring building? How does Bourne get into Noah Vosen's office, past all the security? Is the revelation of Bourne's identity and his training regimen really much of a surprise? The wrap-up, showing the bad guys exposed by the press and punished by government investigation, seemed risible, not only because of the current inability of either the press or Congress to right any wrongs, but because I had no idea to whom Pamela Landy has faxed the incriminating documents. "You can't make stuff like this up," remarks one sinister agency boss, but many, many films have done so.

I'm not against handheld styles as such, and even Late Tony Scott Rococo can have its virtues. Yet I find the style as practiced by Greengrass to be pretty incoherent and nowhere near as engaging as most critics claim. It just seems too easy. But then, I think that certain standards of filmmaking craftsmanship have pretty much vanished, and the run-and-gun trend is one more symptom of that. Given the praise heaped on *The Bourne Ultimatum*, however, things are unlikely to change. Next time you head to the movies, you might want to bring your Dramamine.

• •

This has proven one of the most enduringly popular of our entries. I think that's less due to the persuasiveness of my arguments than to people's continued admiration of the Bourne films and a wide curiosity about the run-and-gun style. After yet another viewing, I stand by what I said here, but for a fuller and less sour discussion, you might read my two follow-up posts (http://www.davidbordwell.net /blog/?p=1230, and http://www.davidbordwell.net/blog/?p=1285). The latter gives the film some points for ingeniously meshing its time scheme with that of the previous installment in the trilogy.

The Bourne films suggest one way styles change. Once "intensified continuity" had brought together a powerful set of schemas, directors could revise them in fresh, sometimes eccentric ways. I argue that a good model of the eccentric dimension is provided by Tony Scott. Greengrass took a different option, emphasizing quick uptake. Committed to the quick-cutting option, he made each brief shot merely gesture toward each dramatic point. His allusive visuals were supplemented by the strongly conventional nature of the plots. The sketchy shot works best when whatever we glimpse—pursuer or pursued, a pistol or a syringe—is something we've seen in the genre many times before.

I discuss "intensified continuity" not only in *The Way Hollywood Tells It* but also in a blog entry (http://www.davidbordwell.net/blog/?p=859). For my arguments about Hong Kong action style, see *Planet Hong Kong: Popular Cinema and the Art of Entertainment* (Harvard University Press, 2000). Perhaps out of an accommodation to the international action-movie market, some Hong Kong directors have adopted the run-and-gun style, as in Soi Cheang's *Dog Bite Dog* (2006).

• •

Pausing and Chortling: A Tribute to Bob Clampett

FEBRUARY 28, 2008

The Great Piggy Bank Robbery

Kristin here:

During my first year as a PhD candidate at the University of Wisconsin–Madison, the great animator Bob Clampett paid a visit to our campus. I actually got to sit next to him at lunch, and he was a charming, amusing man. Unfortunately I didn't really know at the time what a genius he was, and, to my regret, I neglected to ask for his autograph.

Today Clampett is less well known to the general public than is Chuck Jones or Tex Avery. Jones and the other main creators of the classic Warner Bros. cartoons reportedly resented Clampett's attempts to promote his own reputation by claiming sole credit for major achievements, such as "inventing" Bugs Bunny. When Jones put together *The Bugs Bunny/Road Runner Movie* (1979), he did not include any Clampett-supervised cartoons. Clampett never wrote his memoirs. Jones did and left Clampett out.

These three major directors had their own distinctive approaches. Jones was on the whole more cerebral and often opted for beautiful visuals, perhaps most obviously evident in *What's Opera, Doc?* Avery had a penchant for bad puns, often assembling whole cartoons around them. Clampett went for craziness and breakneck speed. The Wikipedia entry on him (http://en.wikipedia.org/wiki/Bob_Clampett) has this to say: "His characters are easily the most rubbery and wacky of all the Warner directors'."

Wackiness was built into the name of one of Warner's two animated series, "Looney Tunes." Daffy Duck's name characterizes him, but modern audiences may not be aware that "Bugs" also was a slang term for "crazy." Along with Porky Pig, those were the characters that Clampett used most often.

I'm not going to sum up Clampett's career here. There is already quite a bit of excellent material on him available on the Internet. For an overview of his career and style, see Adrian Danks's "It Can Happen Here! The World of Bob Clampett," *Senses of Cinema* (http://archive.sensesofcinema .com/contents/directors/05/clampett.html). Michael Barrier's epic 1970 interview with Clampett (http://www.michaelbarrier.com/Funnyworld /Clampett/interview_bob_clampett.htm), with comments and corrections, is available on his website. That website contains many other shorter pieces on Clampett (most notably http://www.michaelbarrier.com/Essays /Milt_Gray/Gray_on_Clampett.htm and http://www.michaelbarrier.com /Feed-back/feedback_clampett.htm). Danks and the Wikipedia entry both give enough bibliographical sources to direct enthusiasts to additional information.

My purpose here is more modest. I simply want to point out how to find even more hilarity in Clampett's cartoons beyond simply watching them.

David and I are in the process of revising our second textbook, *Film History: An Introduction*. The other day I was working on the section that deals with Hollywood animation in the 1930-to-1945 period. We're adding more color to the book for its third edition, so I decided that *Draftee Daffy*, which we describe briefly, should have its own color plate.

As I watched the film on DVD, I paused on a number of possible frames to use, and I found myself laughing out loud at almost every one—something that doesn't often happen during the revision of a textbook. Some of the character movements in Clampett's films are so fast that they come across as a flurry of images too fleeting to register. Frozen, they reveal some of the extraordinary means that the director and his animators used to achieve those effects of speed. Clampett was also adept at highly exaggerated reactions and hilarious distortions of the animal body. Watching these cartoons with a finger on the pause button can enhance amusement and teach you a lot about normally hidden aspects of the art of animation.

David has written about the artistry of Walt Disney's films in "Uncle Walt the Artist" (http://www.davidbordwell.net/blog/?p=247). He points

out that a quick movement may be accomplished by adding extra limbs, as when in *Melody Time* Johnny Appleseed gathers an armload of falling apples, and multiple arms and hands convey the speed of his gestures—as do a pair of phantom heads in the uppermost frame of the three David reproduces.

Such multiple images work without our noticing them. It's not an obvious sort of technique to use. As David wrote, "Through trial and error Disney's animators learned that rather strange single images will look exactly right on the screen; these men were practical perceptual psychologists."

The same was true in the Warner animation department. In *The Big Snooze* (1946), Clampett's last cartoon for the studio, he includes a scene of Bugs rapidly tying Elmer to some railroad tracks (previous page). In a couple of frames, Bugs sprouts extra arms and hands. In *The Great Piggy Bank Robbery* (1946), phantom images of Daffy accompany his firing a machine gun (previous page).

But Clampett's single images were often far stranger than the ones in the *Melody Time* example. In this one from *Draftee Daffy*, for example, the extra figures of Daffy as he frantically builds a wall between himself and his nemesis (the little man from the draft board) are purple. I suppose that's because multiple black figures of Daffy would blend together, but it's still a bit weird. As an animator, how do you decide on a color?

Maybe it's because purple is a subdued color that won't call attention to the extra ducks and yet will contrast well with the black. It's also the same color as the floor, so that might create an extra reason why we won't notice them as standing out from the overall composition as it flashes past.

If you know those purple ducks are there, you can just barely see them during normal projection. If you don't know that, then you're likely to miss them.

Clampett often draws upon a standard animation device, "stretch," to convey a sense of speed—although his characters may cross a room in as little as two or three frames. A shot of Daffy jumping for joy in *The Great Piggy Bank Robbery* is a fairly straightforward example of stretch; in a later scene, Daffy rapidly turning around holding a phone uses the opposite technique, "squash."

When a character is about to launch into a rapid movement,

Clampett employs squash with a perspective effect stretching the character toward the viewer, as in *The Big Snooze* when Bugs instructs Elmer to "run this way." (Bugs isn't the only one who gets into drag in these cartoons.)

I've picked some of my favorite Clampett films, but many frames worth pausing on are to be found in others. With the Looney Tunes DVD sets still coming out, in five volumes to date, one can hunt out the Clampett films—though annoyingly, the indexes list neither the date nor the supervising animator, and there seems to be little logic involved in which films go on which discs. (There are also occasional jumps where something has presumably been censored.) It's best to get thoroughly familiar with these films by simply viewing them. Then, pick up that remote and begin your search. You'll discover that Clampett was one of the most imaginative of those "practical perceptual psychologists."

The Great Piggy Bank Robbery

The illustrations here are from color cartoons, so seeing them in the original entry (http://www.davidbordwell.net/blog/?p=1991) would be helpful—though watching the cartoons themselves would be better. A sixth volume of the Looney Tunes Golden Collection has appeared, announced as the final one. This extras-laden series should not be confused with the Spotlight boxed sets of Warner Bros. cartoons, a cheaper series with few supplements and considerable duplication of items on the Golden discs.

Films

A Behemoth from the Dead Zone

JANUARY 25, 2008

David here:

The first quarter of the year is the biggest slump time for movie theaters.[1] Holiday fatigue, thin budgets, bad weather, the Super Bowl, and the distractions of the awards season depress admissions. If people go to the movies, they tend to catch up on Oscar nominees, and studios don't want to release high-end films that might suffer from the competition. Granted, there are two desirable weekends in the first quarter, those around Martin Luther King's birthday and Presidents' Day. Studios typically aim their highest-profile winter releases (e.g., *Black Hawk Down*, 2001) for those weekends. But screens need fresh product every week, so most of what gets released at this time of the year might charitably be called second-tier.

Ambitious filmmakers fight to keep out of this zone of death. You could argue that the January release slot of *Idiocracy* told Mike Judge exactly what Fox thought of that ripe exercise in misanthropy. *Zodiac*, one of the best films of 2007, opened on March 1, and even ecstatic reviews couldn't push it toward Oscar nominations.

Yet this is a flush period for those of us who like to explore low-budget genre pieces. I have to admit I enjoy checking on those quickie action fests and romantic comedies that float up early in the year. They're today's equivalent of the old studios' program pictures, those routine releases that allowed theaters to change bills often. In their budgets, relative to blockbusters, today's program pix are often the modern equivalent of the studios' B films.

More important, these winter orphans are often more experimental, imaginative, and peculiar than the summer blockbusters. On low budgets, people take chances. Some examples, not all good but still intriguing, would be *Wild Things* (1998), *Dark City* (1998), *Romeo Must Die* (2000), *Reindeer Games* (2000), *Monkeybone* (2001), *Equilibrium* (2002), *Spun* (2003), *Torque* (2004), *The Butterfly Effect* (2004), *Constantine* (2005), *Running Scared* (2006), *Crank* (2006), and *Smokin' Aces* (2007). The mutant B can be found in other seasons too—one of my favorites in this vein, *Cellular* (2004), was released in September—but they're abundant in the year's early months.

By all odds, *Cloverfield* ought to have been another low-end release. A monster movie with unknown players, running a spare 72 minutes sans credits, budgeted at a reputed $25 million, it's a paradigm of the winter throwaway. Except that it pulled in $46 million over a four-day weekend and became the highest-grossing film (in unadjusted dollars) ever to be released in January. Here the B in "B movie" stands for blockbuster.

I enjoyed *Cloverfield*. It starts with a sharp premise, but as ever, execution is everything. I see it as a nifty digital update of some classic Hollywood conventions.

If You Find This Tape, You Probably Know More about This than I Do

Everybody knows by now that *Cloverfield* is essentially "Godzilla Meets Handicam." A covey of twentysomethings are partying when a monster attacks Manhattan, and they try to escape. One, Rob, gets a phone call from his off-again lover Beth, who's trapped in a high-rise. He vows to rescue her. He brings along some friends, one of whom documents their search with a video camera. It's a shooting-gallery plot. One by one, the characters are eliminated until we're down to two, and then . . .

Cloverfield exemplifies what narrative theorists call "restricted narration." In the narrowest case of restricted narration, the film confines the audience's range of knowledge to what one character knows. Or, when the characters are clustered in the same space, we're restricted to what they collectively know. In other words, you deny the viewer a wider-ranging body of story information. By contrast, the usual Godzilla installment is presented from an omniscient perspective, skipping among scenes of scientists, journalists, government officials, Godzilla's free-range ramblings, and other lines of action. Instead, *Cloverfield* imagines what Godzilla's attack would look and feel like on the ground, as observed by one group of victims.

Horror and science-fiction films have used both unrestricted and restricted narration. A film like *Cat People* (1942) crosscuts what happens to Irena (the putative monster) with scenes involving other characters. *Jurassic Park* and *The Host* likewise trace out several plot strands among a variety of characters. The advantage of giving the audience so much information is that viewers can feel apprehension and suspense about what the characters don't know is happening. Our superior knowledge can make us worry about those poor victims oblivious to their fate.

But these genres have relied on restricted narration as well. *Invasion of the Body Snatchers* (1956) is a good example; we are at Miles's side in almost every scene, learning of the gradual takeover of his town as he does. *Night of the Living Dead* (1968), *Signs* (2002), and *War of the Worlds* (2005) do much the same with a confined group, attaching us to one or the other momentarily but never straying from their situation.

The advantages of restricted narration are pretty apparent. You can build up uncertainty if we know no more than the characters being attacked by a monster. You can also delay full revelation of the creature, a big deal in these genres, by giving us only the glimpses of it that our characters get. In addition, by focusing on the characters' responses to their peril, you have a chance to build audience involvement. We can feel empathy and loss if we've come to know the people more intimately than we know the anonymous hordes stomped by Godzilla. Finally, if you need to give more wide-ranging information about what's happening outside the characters' immediate situation, you can always have them encounter newspaper reports, radio bulletins, and TV coverage of action occurring elsewhere.

People sometimes think that theoretical distinctions like this over-intellectualize things. Do filmmakers really think along these lines? Yes. Matt Reeves, the director of *Cloverfield*, remarks: "The point of view was so restricted, it felt really fresh. It was one of the things that attracted me [to this project]. You are with this group of people and then this event happens and they do their best to understand it and survive it, and that's all they know" (http://www.zap2it.com/movies/zap-story-cloverfieldsmonsterconcept,0,492802.story).

For Your Eyes Only

Restricted narration doesn't demand optical point-of-view shots. There aren't that many in *Invasion of the Body Snatchers* or the other examples I've indicated. Still, for quite a while and across a range of genres, filmmakers have imagined entire films recording a character's optical/auditory experience directly, in "first person," so to speak.

Again, it's useful to recognize two variants of this narrational strat-

egy. One we can call *immediate*—experiencing the action as if we stand in the character's shoes. In the late 1920s, the great documentary filmmaker Joris Ivens tried to make what he called his *I-film*, which would record exactly what a character saw when riding a bike, drinking a glass of beer, and the like. He was dismayed to find that bouncing and swiveling the camera as if it were a human eye ignored the fact that in real life, our perceptual systems correct for the instabilities of sensation. Ivens abandoned the project, but evidently he couldn't get the notion out of his head; he called his autobiography *The Camera and I*.[2]

Hollywood's most strict and most notorious example of directly subjective narration is Robert Montgomery's *Lady in the Lake* (1947). Its strangeness reminds us that this approach has inherent drawbacks. How do you show the viewer what your protagonist looks like? (Have him pass in front of mirrors.) How do you skip over the boring bits? (Have your hero knocked unconscious from time to time.) How do you hide the inevitable cuts? (Try your best.) Even Montgomery had to treat the subjective sequences as long flashbacks, sandwiched within scenes of the hero in his office in the present telling us what he did next.

Because of these problems, a sustained first-person immediate narration is pretty rare. The best compromise, exploited by Hitchcock in many pictures and especially in *Rear Window* (1954), is to confine us to a single character's experience by alternating "objective" shots of the character's action with optical point-of-view shots of what he or she sees.

What I'm calling "immediate optical point of view" is just that: sights (and sounds) picked up directly, without a recording mechanism between the story action and the character's experience. But we can also have *mediated* first-person point of view. The character uses a recording technology to give us the story events.

In a brilliant essay on the documentary *Kon-Tiki* (1950), André Bazin shows that our knowledge of how Thor Heyerdahl filmed his raft voyage lends an unparalleled authenticity to the action. Heyerdahl and his crew weren't experienced photographers and seem to have taken along the 16mm camera as an afterthought, but the very amateurishness of the enterprise guaranteed its realism. The imperfections, often the result of hazardous conditions, were themselves testimony to the adventure. When the men had to fight storms, they had no time to film; so Bazin is able to argue, with his inimitable sense of paradox, that the absence of footage during the storm is further proof of the authenticity. If we were given such footage, we might wonder if it were staged afterward. "How much more moving is this flotsam, snatched from the tempest, than would have been the faultless and complete report offered by an organized film. . . . The missing documents are the negative imprints of the expedition."[3]

What about fictional events? In the 1960s we started to see fiction films that presented themselves as recordings of the events as the camera operator experienced them. One early example is Stanton Kaye's *Georg* (1964). The first shot follows some infantrymen into battle, but then the framing wobbles and the camera falls to earth. We see a tipped angle on a fallen solider and another infantryman approaches. He bends toward us;

the frame starts to wobble, and we are lifted up. On the soundtrack we hear, "I found my camera then."

The emergence of portable equipment and cinéma-vérité documentary seems to have pushed filmmakers to pursue this narrational mode in fiction. One result was the pseudo-documentary, which usually doesn't present the story as a single person's experience but rather as a compilation of first-person observations. Peter Watkins's *The War Game* (1967) presents itself as a documentary shot during a nuclear war, and it contains many of the visual devices that would come to be associated with the mediated format—not only the flailing camera but the face-on interview and the chaotic presentation of violent action. There's also the pseudo-memoir film, pioneered in *David Holzman's Diary* (1967). Later examples of the pseudo-documentary are Norman Mailer's *Maidstone* (1971) and the combat movie *84 Charlie MoPic* (1989).[4]

As lightweight 16mm cameras made filming easier, directors adapted that look and feel to fictional storytelling. The arrival of ultra-portable digital cameras and cell phones has launched a similar cycle. Brian De Palma's *Redacted* (2007), yet another war film, has exploited the technology for docudrama. A digital equivalent of *David Holzman's Diary*, apart from webcam and YouTube material, is Christoffer Boe's *Offscreen* (2006).

Interestingly, Orson Welles pioneered both the immediate and the mediated subjective formats. One of his earliest projects for RKO was an adaptation of *Heart of Darkness*, in which the camera was to represent the narrator Marlowe's optical perspective throughout.[5] Welles had more success with the mediated alternative, though in audio form. His "War of the Worlds" radio broadcast mimicked the flow of programming and interrupted it with reports of the aliens' attack. The device was updated for television in the 1983 drama *Special Bulletin*.

Sticking to the Rules

Cloverfield, then, draws on a tradition of using technologically mediated point of view to restrict our knowledge. Like *The Blair Witch Project* (1999), it does this with a horror tale. But it's also a Hollywood movie, and it follows the norms of that moviemaking mode. So the task of Reeves, producer J. J. Abrams, and the other creators is to fit the premise of video recording to the demands of classical narrative structure and narration. How is this done?

First, exposition. The film is framed as a government SD video card (watermarked "DO NOT DUPLICATE"), the remains of a tape recovered from an area "formerly known as Central Park." This is a modern version of the discovered-manuscript convention familiar from the nineteenth-century novel. When the tape starts, showing Rob with Beth in happy times, its read-out date of April plays the role of an omniscient opening title. In the course of the film, the read-outs (which come and go at strategic moments) will tell us when we're in the earlier phase of their love affair and when we're seeing the traumatic events of May.

Likewise, the need for exposition about characters and relationships at the start of the film is given through a basic premise. Jason wants to record Rob's going-away party and he presses Rob's friend Hud into service as the cameraman. Off the bat, Hud picks out our main characters in video portraits addressed to Rob. What follows indicates that Hud will be amazingly prescient: his camera dwells on the characters who will be important in the ensuing action.

Next, overall structure. The *Cloverfield* tape conforms to the overarching principles of plotting outlined in earlier entries (pp. 113–34). A 72-minute film won't have four large-scale parts, most likely two or three. As a first approximation, I think that *Cloverfield* breaks into the following:

A Setup lasting about 30 minutes. We are introduced to all the characters before the monster attacks. Upon the attack, our protagonists flee to the bridge, where Jason dies. Near the end of this portion, Rob gets a call from Beth, and he formulates the dual goals of the film: to escape from the creature, and to rescue Beth. Along the way, Hud declares he's going to record it all: "People are gonna know how it all went down. . . . It's gonna be important."

A Development section lasting about 22 minutes. This is principally a series of delays. Rob, Hud, Lily, and Marlena encounter obstacles. Marlena falls by the wayside. They are given a deadline: at 0600 they must meet the last helicopters leaving Manhattan.

A Climax lasting about 20 minutes. The group rescues Beth and meets the choppers, but the one carrying Rob, Hud, and Beth falls afoul of the beast. They crash in Central Park, and Hud is killed, his camera recording his death at the jaws of the monster. Huddled under a bridge, Rob and Beth record a final video testimonial before an explosion cuts them off.

An Epilogue of one shot lasting less than a minute. Rob and Beth are shown in happier times on the Ferris wheel at Coney Island—a shot left over from the earlier use of the tape in April.

Next, local structure and texture. It takes a lot of artifice to make something look this artless. The imagery is rich and vivid, the sharpest home video you ever saw. The sound is pure shock-and-awe, bone-rattling, with a full surround ambience one never finds on a handicam.[6] Moreover, Hud is remarkably lucky in catching the turning points of the action. All the characters' intimate dramas are captured, and Hud happens to be on hand when the head of Miss Liberty hurtles down the street.

Bazin points out that in fictional films the ellipses are cunning gaps, not portions left out because of the physical conditions of the shoot (as in

Kon-Tiki). In *Cloverfield*, the cunning gaps are motivated as constrained by the physical circumstances of filming. When Hud doesn't show something, it's usually because it's what the genre considers too gory, so the worst stretches take place in darkness, or offscreen, or strategically shielded by a prop when the camera is set down. Mostly, though, Hud just shows us the interesting stuff. He turns on the camera just before something big happens, or he captures a disquieting image like that of the empty Central Park carriage.

At least once, the semi-documentary premise does yield something evocative of the *Kon-Tiki* film. Hud has to leap from one building to another, many stories above the street. He turns the camera on himself: "If this is the last thing you see, then I died." He hops across, still running the camera, but when a rocket goes off nearby, a sudden cut registers his flinch. For an instant out of sheer reflex, he turned off the camera.

Overall, Hud's tape respects the flow of classical film style. Unlike the *Lady in the Lake* approach, the mediated POV format doesn't have a problem with cuts; any jump or gap is explained as a moment when the operator switched off the camera. Most of Hud's "in-camera" cuts are conventional ones, skipping over a few inconsequential stretches of time. There are as well plenty of hooks between scenes. Hud says: "I'll walk in the tunnels." Cut to characters walking in the tunnels. More interestingly, visible cuts are rare, which again respects the purported conditions of filming. *Cloverfield* has much longer takes than any recent Hollywood film I know. I counted only about 180 shots, yielding an average of 24 seconds per shot (in a genre in which today's films average 2–5 seconds per shot).

The Digital Palimpsest

We could find plenty of other ways in which *Cloverfield* adapts the handicam premise to the Hollywood storytelling idiom. There are the product placements that just happen to be part of these dim yuppies' milieu. There are the character types, notably the sultry Marlena and the hero's weak friend who's comically a little slow. There's the developing motif of the to-camera addresses, with Rob's and Beth's final monologues to the camera counterbalancing the party testimonials in the opening. There's the final romantic exchange: "I love you." "I love you." The very last shot even includes a detail that invites us to re-view the entire movie, at the theater or on DVD. But let me close by noting how some specific features of digital-video hardware get used imaginatively.

I've already mentioned how the viewfinder date readout allows us to keep the time structure clear. There's also the use of a night-vision camera feature to light up those spidery parasites shucked off by the big guy. Which scares you more—to glimpse the pinpoint eyes of critters skittering around you in the dark, or to see them up close in a sickly green light?

More teasing is the fact, set up in the first part, that this video is being recorded over an old tape of Rob's. That's what turns the opening sequence of Rob and Beth in May into a prologue: the tape wasn't rewound completely for recording the party. Later, at intervals, fragments of that April footage reappear, apparently through Hud's inadvertently advancing the tape. The snippets function as flashbacks, showing Rob and Beth going to Coney Island and juxtaposing their enjoyable day with this horrendous night.

Cleverly, on the tape that's recording the May disaster something always prepares the audience for the shift. For instance, when Jason hands the camera over, we hear Hud say, "I don't even know how to work this thing." Cut to an April shot of Beth on the subway, suggesting that he's advanced fast forward without shooting. Likewise, when Rob says, "I had a tape in there," we cut to another April shot of Beth. As a final fillip, the footage taken in May halts before the full tape ends, so we get the Epilogue showing Rob and Beth on the Ferris wheel in April, emerging like figures in a palimpsest.

No less clever, but more poignant, is the use of the fallen-camera convention. It appears once when Beth has to be extricated from her bed. Hud sets the camera down by a concrete block in her bedroom, which conceals her agony. More poignant is the shot when the camera, dropped from Hud's hand, lies in the grass, and the autofocus device oscillates endlessly, straining to hold on his lifeless face.

In sum, the filmmakers have found imaginative ways of fulfilling traditional purposes. *Cloverfield* shows that the look and feel of digital video can refresh genre conventions and storytelling norms. So why not for the sequel show the behemoth's attack from still other characters' perspectives? This would mobilize the current conventions of the narrative replay and the companion film (e.g., Eastwood's Iwo Jima diptych). Reeves says: "The fun of this movie was that it might not have been the only movie being made that night, there might be another movie! In today's day and age of people filming their lives on their iPhones and Handycams, uploading it to YouTube . . ." (http://cloverfield-2-movie-trailer.blogspot.com/2009/01/cloverfield-2-movie.html).

So the Dead Zone of January through March yields another hopeful monster.

Notes

1. The only period that rivals this slow winter stretch is mid-August to October, when genre fare gets pushed out to pick up on late-summer business.

2. Joris Ivens, *The Camera and I* (New York: International Publishers, 1969), 42.

3. André Bazin, "Cinema and Exploration," *What Is Cinema?*, vol. 1, trans. and ed. Hugh Gray (Berkeley: University of California Press, 1967), 162.

4. Not all pseudo-documentaries present themselves as records of a person's observation. Milton Moses Ginsberg's *Coming Apart* (1969) presents itself as an objective record, by a hidden camera, of a psychiatrist's dealings with his patients. Like a surveillance camera, it doesn't purport to embody anybody's point of view.

5. Jonathan Rosenbaum, *Discovering Orson Welles* (Berkeley: University of California Press, 2007), 28–48.

6. For discussions of contemporary sound practices in this genre, see William Whittington's *Sound Design in Science Fiction* (Austin: University of Texas Press, 2007).

• •

This entry tries to show that an idea-driven approach to Internet writing can bridge academic concerns and the interests of a wider audience. If you can show how a current release relies on concepts from narrative theory like restricted narration, mediated point of view, and canonical script structure, you can induce readers to think about the broader principles of storytelling informing the movies they see. It also helps when filmmakers like Matt Reeves acknowledge that they use these concepts in their craft. Once more, a middle-level, film-as-art approach can illuminate the creative process; theory meets practice.

When we review a current film, we get reactions on the blogosphere. Several fans indicated that they learned something from the post. Some asked me to comment on the social and cultural implications of *Cloverfield*'s references to 9/11. As I said at the time, and as I still believe, genre cinema has dealt more vividly with the traumas and questioning around this horrendous event than the more portentous dramas like *United 93*, *World Trade Center*, and the TV show *The Road to 9/11*.

The two most intriguing post-9/11 films I know are by Spielberg. *War of the Worlds* gives a really concrete sense of what a hysterical America under attack might be like, warts and all. Spielberg's underrated *The Terminal* suggests, despite its Frank Capra optimism, that the new security state is run by bureaucrats with fixed agendas and staffed by overworked people of color, some themselves exiles and immigrants. I think that *Cloverfield* adds its own dynamic sense of how easily a national disaster can shatter the entitlement culture of upwardly mobile twentysomethings. Genre films carry well-established patterns and triggers for feelings, and a shrewd filmmaker can exploit the conventions in order to suggest attitudes toward current events. We see this prospect in the changing face of Westerns and war films during earlier phases of Hollywood history.

Since this essay was published, there have been other low-budget dark-horse releases that caught the public's fancy in the first quarter. *Paul Blart: Mall Cop* and *Taken* (both released in January 2009) are recent instances. But Hollywood's first-quarter release strategies are already changing. I was able to add to the original post a reference to Steven Zeitchik's *Hollywood Reporter* article of January 28, 2008 (http://www.hollywoodreporter.com/hr/content_display/film /news/e3i5eded68f1bef1eeaf954eac430dc518a). Zeitchik pointed out that a few high-end releases have done well between January and April; a big film looks bigger when there is less competition. He indicates that executives, who need a strong first weekend, sometimes turn away from the heavy packing of the May–August period and spread a few major releases through the less-trafficked months. Successful examples would be *Dr. Seuss' Horton Hears a Who!* (March 2008), *Monsters vs. Aliens* (March 2009), *The Book of Eli* (January 2010), *Shutter Island* (February 2010), and *Alice in Wonderland* (March 2010)—this last the most lucrative film ever released in the first quarter. So I must hope that programming the Dead Zone with tonier fare won't crowd out the gimmicky, low-end genre pieces that bring me in.

Cronenberg's Violent Reversals

OCTOBER 18, 2007

Kristin here:

A Pair of Films

I haven't read nearly all the reviews of *Eastern Promises*, but sampling eight or so, I have noticed that quite a few critics briefly note a similarity between David Cronenberg's new film and his previous one, *A History of Violence*. There are obvious links. In both, Viggo Mortensen plays the lead, a man with a secret—or a bunch of them. Both involve crime syndicates run by families. Both contain scenes of graphic, brutal violence.

Reviewer John Beifuss calls *Eastern Promises* "a sort of companion piece to Cronenberg's previous feature, 'A History of Violence' (2005)," adding that "'Eastern Promises' opens in a modest barber shop that recalls the small-town diner that was the site of unexpected brutality in 'Violence'" (http://www.commercialappeal.com/news/2007/sep/21/another-masterful-shocker-from-cronenberg/). Beth Accomando comments, "In some ways, Nikolai has much in common with Mortensen's character in A History of Violence, who hides one persona beneath another" (in a review for KPBS no longer on the Internet).

J. Hoberman goes a little further in defining the parallels. "*Eastern Promises* is very much a companion to *A History of Violence*. Both are crime thrillers that allow Viggo Mortensen to play a morally ambiguous and severely divided, if not schizoid, action-hero savior; both are commissioned works that permit hired-gun Cronenberg to make a genre film that is actually something else" (http://www.villagevoice.com/2007-09-04/film/still

-cronenberg/). (For more reviews, see Rotten Tomatoes' page on the film, http://www.rottentomatoes.com/m/eastern_promises/.)

It would be hard to discuss the similarities between the films without giving away too much of the plot, and clearly that's why reviewers have said so little on the subject. So I should make it very clear that I'm writing a brief analysis, not a review. *A History of Violence* and especially *Eastern Promises* fundamentally depend on the withholding of information. I urge you to see both films before reading the rest of this entry.

What I'm interested in here is the extent to which the second film manages to be a mirror-image reversal of the first. It's a remarkable formal accomplishment, I think, for a director to make two consecutive films with different plots, characters, settings, and narrational strategies that are such exact reversals of each other. *Eastern Promises* isn't a sequel, yet it forms a pair with *A History of Violence*. It's like those trilogies that are united by theme rather than by being parts of the same story (e.g., Ingmar Bergman's *Through a Glass Darkly*, *Winter Light*, and *The Silence*, or Philip Glass's three biographical operas, *Einstein on the Beach*, *Satyagraha*, and *Akhnaton*). Whether or not this pairing was intended by Cronenberg, one could easily imagine him working again in the same vein.

Basically you've got a central character with two sides to him, the criminal and the good. In *A History of Violence*, the protagonist is leading an ordinary domestic life that is threatened by a revelation of his criminal past. He barely manages to suppress the threat to his family that results when his former associates re-establish contact with him, and he can suppress it only by using more violence and revealing to his family what he had been.

In *Eastern Promises*, the hero does the opposite. He is voluntarily leading a criminal life undercover in order to fight the Russian mafia gang he works for. By meeting and falling in love with Anna, he is given a chance to lead a normal life with her but manages to suppress his longing for that in order to continue his struggle. Even his boss in whatever crime-fighting organization he secretly works for offers him an out, saying that the Russian embassy has requested he be taken off the case. Nikolai insists on continuing his activities, since he now has had a promotion that will allow him to penetrate to the very heart of the criminal gang he has been fighting.

There are contrasts and parallels that encourage a comparison of the two films. The modest diner that Tom Stall runs in *A History of Violence* could not be more unlike the sumptuous Russian restaurant that is the front for Semyon's *vory v zakone* activities. The much-lauded fight scene in the public baths in *Eastern Promises* is a more visceral version of a battle late in *A History of Violence* when Tom, about to be executed at his brother's order, manages to kill all five of the men holding him captive.

The black, forbidding car that Nikolai drives echoes that of the vengeful thug Fogarty in *A History of Violence*; both cars glide to ominous stops on the street outside the dwellings of their presumed victims. Each film ends on a close view of the protagonist seated at a table: Tom fearfully yet hopefully searching the faces of his family for signs of acceptance, and Nikolai sitting in the Russian restaurant he now runs, thinking in sorrow of Tatiana and presumably of his missed life with Anna. Even the meals that Tom returns home to and that Anna's family sit down to at the end are similar: roast beef and vegetables.

Ultimately the contrasts in the two films are what make the ending of *Eastern Promises* even more affecting than that of *A History of Violence*. Tom Stall has used deceit to walk away from his violent life and make a new and normal one. By the end the revelation of the deceit has damaged that normal life considerably, but there are indications that the damage will gradually, though not wholly, fade through re-established love and trust. Nikolai, on the other hand, has gone down the far more difficult road: walking away from a potentially normal life to continue to use deceit and violence to fight the vicious organization that preys upon normal people. When Anna's mother warns her away from her contact with the criminals, saying, "This isn't our world. We are ordinary people," Stepan responds that Tatiana was an ordinary person, too.

One thing that distinguishes the films is that we never learn whether Nikolai was already a real criminal earlier in his life, one whom the British authorities successfully recruited to help them run an underground operation against the *vory v zakone* in London. Were his tattoos really given him in Russian prisons, or are they an elaborate disguise created in England? We don't know if Nikolai had a normal life before and gave it up to play out this ruse or if this undercover job is his redemption for past evils.

Tatiana's Voice

One specific device intrigued me the first time I saw the film: the voice of Tatiana, the girl who dies early in the film giving birth. That voice is heard at intervals, speaking passages from the diary that Anna finds in her purse and tries to get translated. What is the source of this voice-over? Against seeming logic, the voice-over becomes associated with people reading or translating the diary only fairly late in the film. The early instances occur over scenes where no one present could know the contents of the diary.

On my second viewing of the film, I took notes on the contexts in which the voice is heard, and I think this is a complete list:

1. As Anna initially opens the diary and finds the card for the restaurant; cut to her on her bike heading for the restaurant.

2. Early the next evening as Anna rides her bike to the restaurant; the voice bridges the cut to Semyon drinking alone inside the restaurant.

3. During the scene of Nikolai having sex with the blonde prostitute.

4. Over Anna at the hospital with baby Christina. Semyon comes in and says he has translated the diary but doesn't give the translation to her.

5. Shortly thereafter, Semyon leaves, and the voice resumes over a shot of Anna, upset by his implied threats. It bridges the cut to the dining room where the mother and Stepan are translating the diary. The voice of Tatiana dissolves into that of Stepan. This signals the point at which the family members finally become aware of the specific contents of the diary: that Semyon is the one who raped Tatiana and left her pregnant with Christina.

6. A scene beginning with Nikolai in the restaurant alone, reading the diary. (Anna had given Nikolai the diary at the end of the previous scene, telling him to read it.) Semyon enters, gets the diary from him, and burns it.

7. Over a brief scene of Anna at home reading the translation of the diary. (This is immediately followed by a scene of Nikolai in his car watching Stepan go into a block of flats.) The implication is subtle, but in the most recent conversation between her and Nikolai, he has told her that she should raise Christina herself. Now perhaps she is searching the diary for evidence to justify such a decision.

8. The final voice-over passage begins as Anna sits with Christina, whom she has adopted, in the garden; the voice bridges to the restaurant with Nikolai sitting alone, a bottle of vodka at his elbow. This is, I believe, the only repeated passage, being the same part as we hear in the first instance of voice-over. The passage ends, "That is why I left. To find a better life." This is two-edged. On the one hand, Nikolai does not have the option of leaving and finding the better life that he wishes he could have with Anna—the one we've just seen her leading with her family. On the other, he has the chance to save others from the fate that Tatiana suffered.

Only after the scene in which we see Nikolai reading the diary (the sixth occurrence of Tatiana's voice-over) do we find out that he has been working against the gang—arranging for the blonde prostitute to be rescued by the police, spiriting Stepan away into hiding rather than murdering him. Yet it is not the diary's contents that affect him and cause him to do such things. Reading the diary provides a plot point, giving him the vital clue that Semyon is Christina's father, allowing him to tell the police how to test for DNA and convict Semyon of statutory rape.

The first four instances of the voice-over are not associated with anyone's reading of the diary. The last four are: Stepan translating it, Anna reading it, Nikolai reading it, and finally Nikolai apparently remembering it as he sits in place of Semyon in the restaurant. Seeing the film the first time, at the end I wondered if perhaps Tatiana's voice becomes retrospectively linked to Nikolai, who sacrifices his own chance for happiness to continue battling the system of human trafficking that had victimized her.

Watching *Eastern Promises* again, I realized that the voice-over device is not that straightforward. Yet just as learning late in the film about Nikolai's long undercover work against the *vory v zakone* shifts the implications of almost everything we have seen, so the resonance of the voice-over passages changes upon re-viewing. All the occurrences of it seem to lead up to the epilogue and to link our privileged access to Tatiana's writings to our special knowledge of Nikolai's role in so much of what has happened.

The voice-over motif has other functions. It keeps reminding us of the diary, which is crucial to the plot in several ways. Tatiana's voice provides exposition about her life and about the methods used by the Russian mafia to lure girls and women into leaving their homes. Indeed, the device is typical of the narration, which remains quite objective and informative on the whole, moving between the two central characters in an evenhanded fashion and occasionally showing the other major characters when neither of those two is present. The voice-over becomes another means that the narration uses to inform us about the one character who disappears from the scene almost immediately.

Only at the end does the narration settle with one of the characters. We have seen Anna, finally happy in motherhood after having suffered a miscarriage shortly before the action of the plot began. The film ends with Nikolai, briefly lingering over his grim situation and allowing us to picture what his life will be like. That moment, I think, was when I came to associate Tatiana's voice-over primarily with him.

Figuring Backward

Some reviewers have compared *Eastern Promises* with *A History of Violence* primarily in qualitative terms. Is the second film inferior to the first? As good? Better?

They're both very good. If more films these days were as good as either, we'd complain a lot less. Still, upon viewing each a second time in preparing to write this entry, I became convinced that *Eastern Promises* is even better than its predecessor. *A History of Violence* is a relatively simple film, and it remained much as I had remembered it. Revisiting *Eastern Promises* only a week after my first viewing, I saw far more in it.

The character of Kirill, Semyon's son and apparent heir, is more complex than one viewing fully reveals. More importantly, Nikolai's involvement in the affairs of the family's gang activities is hinted to be far more direct than his modest standing as a "driver" would indicate. Indeed, there is a strong suggestion dropped that Nikolai caused the murder of Soyka (the shocking throat-slitting in the barber shop that opens the film). In the scene after Kirill gives Nikolai a truckload of champagne, Nikolai talks with Semyon and explains that the murder had been committed because Soyka was "talking about" Kirill. It's evident that Nikolai himself could have been the source of any such notions about Soyka. There are other moments when we are led to contemplate the dense weave of possible causes and effects underlying the narrative.

It's a rich film indeed. At the beginning I cautioned that you should see it before reading this entry. If you've done that, now I suggest seeing it again.

• •

So far there is no indication that Cronenberg plans to make a third film on a related theme, so the pair remain a diptych or what is sometimes called a "duology."

Eric Dienstfrey, University of Wisconsin–Madison graduate student, responded to this entry with an intriguing suggestion about the "reversal" trait I noticed in these two films: "I think complementary films exist through most of Cronenberg's career. *Dead Ringers* and *M. Butterfly* are two that come to mind, both films being about Jeremy Irons–to reference the old Woody Allen joke–at two with himself, either as twins, or internally as both a gay and straight individual. I also like the complement between *Videodrome* and *The Dead Zone*. In *Videodrome*, Woods loses control as he becomes more and more sadistic, whereas in *The Dead Zone*, Walken loses control as he becomes more and more heroic." This sounds plausible and comes from someone who knows Cronenberg's overall career better than I do.

A third, more leisurely viewing of *Eastern Promises* on DVD confirms the accuracy of my list of Tatiana's voice-over passages. They occur in chronological order of the events of Tatiana's life. The fourth and fifth frame Semyon's visit to the hospital, the fourth being the first one in which there is a mention of a man who owns a restaurant, thus linking Semyon to her rape and prostitution. Indeed, seeing the film once more led me to realize more premises and connections–but I can't expand this into a full-fledged analysis.

A few comments on blogs took issue with my interpretation of *Eastern Promises'* closing moments. (These were ephemeral enough that I can't track them down at this point.) Their authors suggested that instead of pondering regretfully his lost love, Nikolai has become corrupt and revels in his new position as the gang's leader. Given the disagreement, one might posit that the ending is meant to be ambiguous, but I don't think that's true.

For a start, such an abrupt change from Nikolai's rescue of Christina and sad parting from Anna would not be believable. Second, such an ending would be clichéd and less effective than the interpretation I offered. It would also seem to contradict the whole premise that Nikolai has sacrificed his own happiness to continue fighting the mob. One might posit that he volunteered to work as an undercover agent for the police with the specific goal of turning double traitor and taking over the gang. But how could he predict far in advance that all his machinations could lead to his becoming the gang's boss? Why would he help free the blonde prostitute, who is, after all, one of the assets of the criminal enterprise that he would seek to rule? He also takes a considerable risk by not assassinating Stepan when ordered to. Above all, why would he show his new tattoos to the "Senior Officer," as his contact is called in the credits? Just as the new tattoos allow Semyon to try and pass off Nikolai as Kirill to the assassins in the bathhouse (and thus are the reason why Semyon lets Nikolai join the family), so they would be evidence that the police could use against Nikolai if he ever stopped working for them and truly turned criminal. There are, I think, all sorts of problems with interpreting the ending as cynical rather than tragic.

Somebody involved with the film agrees with me. When the "For Your Consideration" Oscar ads were pushing for Mortensen to be nominated as best actor, a tear was digitally added to Nikolai's cheek in a close view of him sitting as he does in the final scene of the film.

The Movie Looks Back at Us

APRIL 1, 2009

David here:

Abbas Kiarostami has the widest octave range of any filmmaker I know.

His humane dramas of Iranian life, from *The Traveler* (1974) to *The Wind Will Carry Us* (1999), have justly won acclaim on the art-house circuit. He has written scripts as well, some—like the underseen *The Journey* (1994)—that are as compelling as a Ruth Rendell thriller. He can conjure suspense out of the simplest uncertainties, such as whether an adult will rip up a child's copybook (*Where Is the Friend's Home?*, 1987) or whether a four-year-old boy locked in with his baby brother can figure out how to turn off a stove (*The Key*, 1987). Indeed, I think that one of the great accomplishments of much modern Iranian cinema, with Kiarostami in the vanguard, has been to reintroduce classic dramatic suspense into art-house moviemaking.

But at times Kiarostami has moved to an opposite pole, that of extreme minimalism and "dedramatization." The drift toward a hard-edged structure was there in *Ten* (2002), which gave us one of his drive-through dramas—people conversing in the front seat of a car—but in severe permutational form (different drivers, different passengers). Rigor was pushed to an extreme in *Five Dedicated to Ozu* (2003): five lengthy shots of water landscapes, each many minutes long, taken at different times of day. The biggest dramatic action consists of ducks walking through the frame. With Kiarostami, it seems, we cinephiles can have it all—Hitchcock and James Benning in the same filmmaker.

Now *Shirin* (a.k.a. *My Sweet Shirin*, 2008) marks another highly original exploration. I don't expect to see a better film for quite some time.

After a credit sequence presenting the classic tale *Khosrow and Shirin* in a swift series of drawings, the film severs sound from image. What we hear over the next 85 minutes is an enactment of the tale, with actors, music, and effects. But we don't see it at all. What we see are about 200 shots of female viewers, usually in single close-ups, with occasionally some men visible behind or on the screen edge. The women are looking more or less straight at the camera, and we infer that they're reacting to the drama as we hear it.

That's it. The closest analogy is probably to the celebrated sequence in *Vivre sa vie*, in which the prostitute played by Anna Karina weeps while watching *La Passion de Jeanne d'Arc*. Come to think of it, the really close analogy is Dreyer's original film, which almost never presents Jeanne and her judges in the same shot, locking her into a suffocating zone of her own.

Of course things aren't as simple as I've suggested. For one thing, what is the nature of this spectacle? Is it a play? The thunderous sound effects, sweeping score, and close miking of the actors don't suggest a theatrical production. So is it a film? True, some light spatters on the edge of the women's headscarves, as if from a projector behind them, but we don't see flickering light on their faces—the usual convention for suggesting a character is watching a film. In any case, what's the source of the occasional dripping water we hear from the right sound channel? The tale is de-realized but it remains as vivid on the soundtrack as the faces are on the image track. What the women watch is, it seems, a composite, neither theatrical nor cinematic—an "objective correlative" for an audiovisual spectacle.

Moreover, there are the faces. We see some more than once, but new ones are introduced throughout. Spatially, they float pretty free; only occasionally do we get a sense of where the women are sitting in relation to one another. All are beautiful, whether young or old. We get an encyclopedia of expressions—neutral, alert, concentrated, bemused, amused, pained, anxious. During a battle scene, faces turn away, eyes lower, and hands shift nervously. The best person to review this movie is probably Paul Ekman, world expert on the nuances of facial signaling.

The weeping starts, by my count, about thirty-eight minutes in, during a rain scene uniting the two lovers Shirin and Khosrow. Thereafter, tears run down cheeks, along jaws and mouths, down necks and nostrils. The film is an almost absurdly pure experiment in facial empathy. It arouses us by our sense of the story unfolding elsewhere, somewhere behind us, enhanced by lyrical vocalise and brusque sound effects, but above all by these eloquent expressions. It's a feast for our mirror neurons. If you're interested in reaction shots, you have to recall Dreyer remarking that "the human face is a landscape that you can never tire of exploring."

I once asked Kiarostami how he got the remarkable performances in shot/reverse-shot that we see in films like *Through the Olive Trees* (1994) and *The Taste of Cherry* (1997). He said that he simply filmed one actor saying all his lines and giving all his reactions, then filmed the other. Often the two actors were never present at the same time, especially during the car sequences. This montage-based approach, creating a synthetic space simply by cutting, has been taken to an extreme in *Shirin*, where the soundtrack supplies the reverse shot we never see. We're told that Kiarostami filmed his female actors here reacting to dots on a board above the camera! Indeed, Kiarostami claims he decided on the *Shirin* story after filming the faces. Despite that, *Shirin* becomes one of the great ensemble pieces of screen acting, although the actors almost never share a real time and space. (Take that, green-screen wizards!) Like Godard, Kiarostami has been busy reinventing the Kuleshov effect, that phenomenon encouraging us to infer a meaning solely from the linking of disparate shots.

This catalogue of female reactions to a tale of spiritual love reminds us that for all the centrality of men to his cinema, Kiarostami has also portrayed Iranian women as decisive, if sometimes mysterious, individuals. Women stubbornly go their own way in *Through the Olive Trees* and *Ten*.

The premises of *Shirin* were sketched in Kiarostami's short film *Where Is My Romeo?* in *Chacun son cinéma* (2007), in which women watch a screening of *Romeo and Juliet*. But the sentiments of that episode are given a dose of stringency here, particularly in one line Shirin utters: "Damn this man's game that they call love!"

Kiarostami built movie production into the plot of *Through the Olive Trees*. Now he has given us the first fiction film I know about the reception of a movie, or at least a heightened idea of a movie. What we see, in all these concerned, fascinated faces and the hands that flutter to the face, is what we spectators look like—from the point of view of a film.

• •

I saw *Shirin* at the 2009 Hong Kong Film Festival, and an October viewing in Chicago reinforced my sense that it's one of the most important and valuable films I saw that year. It has now come out on a British DVD, including a documentary that details the unique conditions under which the film was made.

There is also an enlightening interview with Kiarostami about the production at http://www.offscreen.com/biblio/pages/essays/shirin_kiarostami/. In it he remarks:

> Someone who had seen the movie told me, and I quote, when I was watching the film, I just wanted to see the things they were watching. Do I want to see what they were watching, I asked myself? The answer was no way, no way. I have seen those scenes again and again: horses which appear on the screen and neigh; settings which have been built on not-so-solid evidence to portray life 7,000 years ago. These decorations constantly reveal their hollow nature. I believe [*Shirin*] is new and innovative. It features things I have never had the chance to look at from a very close distance.

• •

Lessons from *Babel*

NOVEMBER 27, 2006

David here:

Whatever its faults or virtues, *Babel* seems to me to typify several trends in current cinema.

1. Network Narratives

Variety's critics call them criss-crossers; others call them thread structures or interwoven stories. I call them network narratives. This increasingly common (maybe too common) storytelling strategy has swiftly given birth to some unique conventions.

The central principle of construction is that several protagonists are given more or less the same weight as they participate in intertwining plotlines. Usually these lines affect one another to some degree. The characters might be strangers, slight acquaintances, friends, or kinfolk. The film aims to show a larger pattern underlying their individual trajectories.

Several directors have specialized in this structure, from Robert Altman and Claude Lelouch to Otar Iosseliani and Rodrigo Garcia (most recently, *Nine Lives*). I found over a hundred such films, some going back quite far (e.g., *Grand Hotel*) but most made since the 1980s. Do they reflect some social zeitgeist—our search for connections with one another? Nope, I don't think so. The most proximate and pertinent causes lie elsewhere.

There are solid production-based motives: big stars can commit to brief appearances but their names will lure audiences. In addition, the idea of human relations as a system of networks—the six-degrees-of-separation principle—has become a commonplace of popular culture, especially after branching-tree video games and the popularity of the Internet. Both industrial pressures and emerging trends in modern media have made the network format attractive, especially to the independent film sector, where small budgets are accompanied by ambitions to display *au courant* attitudes.

Alejandro González Iñárritu has made the network idea a signature element of his films. His first feature, *Amores perros*, used a common network situation, the traffic accident, to tie together three characters. We follow their story lines leading up to and away from the car crash. *21 Grams* had a smaller cast but a more scrambled structure. Now, with *Babel*, we have something easier to follow than the previous films. But it compensates by filling a broader canvas: action on several continents, themes heavy with significance about what Pico Iyer calls the "Global Soul."

We know how to read criss-crossers now, and so directors can push the boundaries on several fronts—more intricate plotting, portentous themes, spatial distance (critics called *Babel* an "epic"). Yet to keep audiences on track, filmmakers remain committed to the basic conventions as well, such as the notion of chance as hidden fate, or chaos theory's idea that the flapping of a butterfly's wings in Chile can . . .

Lesson 1: Once a formal tradition gets established, artists compete, seeking out ways to innovate—within tested boundaries. Fresh narrative strategies push the filmmaker to balance the novelty with familiarity.

2. Trilogies

The art-house cinema has long traded on the appeal of a series of films, more or less loosely joined. Satyajit Ray had his Apu trilogy, which was at least about the same character, but at about the same period there was Antonioni's triptych of *L'Avventura*, *La Notte*, and *L'Eclisse*. Not to be outdone, Bergman gave us two trilogies, one on the crisis of faith (*Through a Glass Darkly*, *Winter Light*, and *The Silence*), the other on, perhaps, the failure of human relationships under pressure (*Persona*, *Shame*, and *Hour of the Wolf*). More recently we've had Fassbinder's BRD trilogy (*The Marriage of Maria Braun*, *Veronika Voss*, *Lola*) and Kiarostami's threesome centered on the village of Koker (*Where Is the Friend's Home?*, *And Life Goes On*, *Through the Olive Trees*).

Labeling a trio of films a trilogy plays an important role in the festival/art-house market. Art films often lack established stars and don't belong to clear-cut genres (though most turn out to be melodramas or historical dramas). The big selling point is usually the director, whose body of work promises something of interest. If the body of work falls into neat periods or groupings, then that automatically creates opportunities for long-term funding and "product differentiation" from film to film. This may seem a crass way to talk about what many people regard as personal expressions of artists. But filmmakers who want to keep making films know that funding and festivals rely on marketable components like the stature of the director and her or his broader creative ambitions.

So it's not surprising that now directors are explicitly conceiving trilogies. Most of the earlier trilogies I mentioned were created ex post facto, by critics recognizing thematic links among works. It's not clear that Antonioni or Bergman or Kiarostami planned to make trilogies from the start. Often the idea of a trilogy hits the director after the first film (von Trier's *Dogville*) or the second. But now directors can deliberately launch a trilogy, as Kieślowski did with *Blue*. Angelopoulos has announced that *The Weeping Meadow* is the first film in a trilogy that will survey the troubled history of the twentieth century. Lucas Belvaux took the step of simultaneously making three features centered on one batch of characters, calling the overall result, of course, *Trilogy*. Turkish director Semih Kaplanoglu created a reverse-*Apu* by following his protagonist's life stages in reverse order (*Egg*, 2007; *Milk*, 2008; *Honey*, 2010).

On the festival circuit filmmakers have to explain themselves to critics, and Iñárritu has understood this well. He tells us that he decided to create a trilogy while making *21 Grams*, and he points out how the films are similar (network structure, overlapping time schemes) and different (degrees of linearity, changes in theme). He helps critics and viewers understand his work—at least, in the way he prefers it to be understood.

Lesson 2: Festival cinema discovered the trilogy before Hollywood did (*Star Wars*, *The Godfather*, *Pirates of the Caribbean*), and the three-movie cluster may well be the art movies' answer to a franchise.

3. Hyperrefined Technique

In *The Way Hollywood Tells It*, I comment on the tendency of contemporary American filmmakers to develop subtle, maybe unnoticeable patterns of technique that run alongside the film's story. So the three acts of Ron Howard's *The Paper* were planned to employ three different sorts of camera movement. The same tendency can be found in independent filmmaking; Darren Aronofsky's *Requiem for a Dream* coordinated its color scheme and seasons to mirror the film's act structure.

Such refinement is especially tempting in network narratives, in which every line of action can be given its signature look. The obvious example is Soderbergh's *Traffic*, which flaunts vivid color and texture differences among the plotlines.

Iñárritu has taken this tactic to a new level of complexity, as revealed in an article in the November *American Cinematographer* (Rachel K. Bosley, "Forging Connections," *AC* 87, no. 11, 36–49). For this project Iñárritu and his cinematographer Rodrigo Prieto distinguished different story threads through color, grain, film stock, film gauge, lab processing, and even aspect ratio. (They shot the Japanese sequences in anamorphic but then extracted a 1.85:1 frame out of them.) For example, we're supposed to register, albeit unconsciously, a shift when the Morocco story, shot in 16mm, shifts to 35mm when the helicopter arrives to rescue the wounded wife.

A harsher critic might claim that the ingenuity expended on these minutiae might better have been spent sharpening and deepening the plotlines themselves. But put evaluation aside. I just want to note that this commitment to "visual arcs" and subliminal tonal shifts echoing the drama shows that Hollywood is as committed to an aesthetic of unity as it ever was—maybe even more committed. This is a level of fanatical detail that supreme fussbudgets like Hitchcock, Sternberg, and (outside Hollywood) Ozu never sought to reach.

I also have to wonder: does anybody register, let alone notice, such hyperrefinements? In my multiplex, and primed by having read the *AC* article, I could spot almost none of this finesse on the screen. In the release print I saw, all the stories looked pretty much the same, and most images had the consistency of oatmeal. Prieto says that "the grain was the most important visual element of the story" (p. 42). In this respect, he got his wish; grain was about all I could see.

Lesson 3: Those who think that modern Hollywood has entered a mannerist phase can find confirmation in *Babel*.

Postscript: It would be worthwhile building a symptomatic interpretation of *Babel*. My hunch is that despite Iñárritu's claim that the film is about family and personal communication, something else is going on. After all, the drama suggests that prosperous white people have to suffer because Asian, Mexican, and North African men have guns.

But that's a whole other blog.

Even though I thought *Babel* a weak movie, it pushed several of my buttons. I had just finished my book *Poetics of Cinema*, and *Babel* nicely exemplified artistic choices that I had studied in two of the essays there: network plotting in "Mutual Friends and Chronologies of Chance" and art-house trilogies in "The Art Cinema as a Mode of Film Practice." And as I mention in the entry, my previous book *The Way Hollywood Tells It* had surveyed the trend toward using fine-grained patterns of technical choices to enhance a film's story line.

All of these options live on. In popular cinematic storytelling, *Star Wars* encouraged filmmakers to give franchises more coherence through the trilogy format, as in the *Matrix* films and Hong Kong's *Infernal Affairs* movies. Still, this is a comparatively recent trend. The idea of a trilogy arrived on critics' radar screens in the golden age of 1950s and 1960s auteurs, as I mention in the essay. After the Antonioni, Ray, and Bergman classics, there came Youssef Chahine's Alexandria trilogy (*Alexandria . . . Why?*, 1979; *An Egyptian Story*, 1982; and *Alexandria, Again and Forever*, 1989), Carlos Saura's Flamenco trilogy (*Blood Wedding*, 1981; *Carmen*, 1983; and *El amor brujo*, 1986), Aki Kaurismaki's Proletariat trilogy (*Shadows in Paradise*, 1986; *Ariel*, 1988; *The Match Factory Girl*, 1990), and Amos Gitai's series set in different Israeli cities (*Devarim*, 1995; *Yom Yom*, 1998; and *Kadosh*, 1999).

Typically, art-house trilogies don't feature continuing characters, as mainstream trilogies do, but rather develop common stylistic or thematic motifs. Angelopoulos had already completed his "trilogy of history" in the 1970s, his "trilogy of silence" in the 1980s, and his "trilogy of borders" in the 1990s. The new century saw him embark on a "Hellenic" one with *The Weeping Meadow* (2004), followed by *The Dust of Time* (2008). Deepa Mehta completed her "elemental" trilogy with *Water* (2006), which followed *Fire* (1997) and *Earth* (1998). Somewhat in between the popular genre trilogies and the art-house ones lie *The Red Riding Trilogy* (2009) and Park Chan-wook's "Revenge" trilogy (*Sympathy for Mr. Vengeance*, 2002; *Oldboy*, 2003; *Sympathy for Lady Vengeance*, 2005).

Network narratives are still with us as well. The pattern of intertwined stories reappears in romantic comedies like *Hot Summer Days* (Hong Kong, 2008), *Love Connected* (Hong Kong, 2009), and *He's Just Not That Into You* (2009). The week I'm writing this (7 February 2010) sees the opening of *Valentine's Day*, featuring sixteen lovelorn stars. Networked dramas include *Coeurs* (2006), *Snow Angels* (2007), *Blessed* (2009), and *Ajami* (2009). *American Dreamz* (2006) offers a criss-crossing *Nashville*-like political comedy. The car crash that brings disparate plotlines together has reappeared in *Normal* (2007). The butterfly-flapping motif returns in Jaco van Dormael's *Mr. Nobody* (2009), although it may have been less clichéd when that massively protracted project started.

Finally, the idea that film techniques should subtly enhance the storyline through their own "arcs" or "plots" continues to appear in the technical literature, although many such patterns go unnoticed by critics and viewers. The makers of *Sunshine* (2007) claim that they used increasingly longer lenses as the story progressed to make the space ship seem ever more claustrophobic (Jay Holben, "Let There Be Light," *American Cinematographer* 88, no. 8 [August 2007], 33). For *Revolutionary Road* (2008), cinematographer Roger Deakins shot the early parts of the story with a fixed camera, moving toward handheld shots for the climax (Rachael K. Bosley, "Close Focus," *American Cinematographer* 90, no. 1 [January 2009], 34). I argue in *The Way* that the nearest sources for this trend are film-school ideas, but the idea runs back to Eisenstein and his effort to create a supersaturated audiovisual texture. His models were Wagner and Joyce's *Ulysses*. Once more, popular cinema of our time intersects high culture in unexpected ways.

• •

Slumdogged by the Past

FEBRUARY 1, 2009

David here:

In graduate school a professor of mine claimed that one benefit of studying film history was that you're never surprised by anything that comes along.

This isn't something to tell young people. They want to be surprised, preferably every few hours. So I rejected the professor's comment. I still think it's not a solid rationale for studying film history. But I can't deny that doing historical research does give you a twinge of *déjà vu.*

For instance, the film industry's current efforts to sell IMAX and 3-D irresistibly remind me of what happened in the early 1950s, when Hollywood went over to widescreen (Cinerama, CinemaScope, and the like), stereophonic sound, and for a little while, 3-D. Then the need was to yank people away from their TV sets and barbecue pits. Now people need to be wooed from video games and the net. But the logic is the same: offer people something they can't get at home. It's 1953 once more.

So historians can't resist the "here we go again" reflex. But they shouldn't turn that into a languid "I've seen it all before." We can still genuinely be surprised. Occasionally, there are innovative movies that, no matter how much they owe to tradition, constitute milestones. In my view, Kiarostami's *Through the Olive Trees*, Hou's *City of Sadness*, Wong's *Chungking Express*, Tarr's *Sátántangó*, and Tarantino's *Pulp Fiction* are among the examples of strong and original works from the 1990s.

More often, the films we see draw on film history in milder ways. But this doesn't mean that these movies lack significance or impact. We can be agreeably surprised by the ways in which a filmmaker energizes long-standing cinematic traditions by blending them unexpectedly, tweaking them in fresh ways, setting them loose on new material. And the more you know of those traditions and conventions, the more you can appreciate how they're modified. Admiring genius shouldn't keep us from savoring ingenuity.

Which brings me to *Slumdog Millionaire*. I like the film reasonably well. Part of my enjoyment is based on seeing how conventions drawn from across film history have an enduring appeal. Many people whose judgments I respect hate the movie, and they would probably call what follows an ode to clichés. But I mean this set of notes in the same spirit as my comments on *The Dark Knight* (which I don't admire). Even if you disagree with my predilections, you may find something intriguing in *Slumdog's* ties to tradition. These ties also suggest why the movie is so ingratiating to so many.

Warning: what follows contains plot spoilers, revelatory images, and atrocious puns.

Slumdog and Pony Show

Adaptation is still king. Almost as soon as movies started telling stories, they borrowed from other media. Many of this year's Oscar candidates derive from plays, novels, and graphic novels. *Slumdog* is based on Vikas Swarup's 2005 novel *Q&A*, which provides the basic situation of a poor youth implausibly triumphing on a version of *Who Wants to be a Millionaire?* The novel also lays down the film's overall architecture: the hero narrates his past, tying each flashback to a round of the game and its relevant question. In the novel, the video replays are described, but of course they're shown in the film.

Of the many disparities between novel and movie, for now I simply note two. First, Swarup's book has several minor threads of action, but the film concentrates on Jamal's love of Latika. (The screenwriter Simon Beaufoy has melded two female characters into one.) Correspondingly, the book introduces a romance plot comparatively late, whereas the film initiates Jamal's love of Latika in their childhoods. Such choices give the film a simpler through-line. Second, *Q&A* skips back and forth through the hero's life, keying story events to the quiz questions. In contrast, the film's flashbacks proceed in strict chronological order. This is a good example of how screenwriters are inclined to adjust the plasticity of literary time to the fact that, at least in theatrical screenings, audiences can't stop and go back to check story order. Chronology is the default in classical film storytelling.

Then there's the double plotline. The streamlining of Swarup's novel points up one convention of Hollywood narrative cinema. The assortment of characters and the twists in the original novel are squeezed down to the two sorts of plotlines we find in most studio films: a line of action involving heterosexual romance and a second line of action, sometimes another romance but just as often involving work. The common work/family tension of contemporary film plotting (the cop, for instance, who neglects his wife and children) is to some extent built into the Hollywood system.

Beaufoy has sharpened the plot by giving Jamal a basic goal: to unite with Latika. The quiz episodes form a means to that end: the boy goes on the show because he knows she watches it. If placed in chronological order, the quiz-show stretches would have come late in the film and become a fairly monotonous pendant to the romance plot. One of the many effects of the flashback arrangement is to give the subsidiary goal of winning on the show more prominence, creating a parallel track for the entire film to move along and arousing anomalous suspense. (We know the outcome, but how do we get there?)

Swarup's novel begins, "I have been arrested. For winning a quiz show." We have to ask: what could make such a thing happen? Soon the police and the show's producers are wondering something more specific. How could Ram, an ignorant waiter, have gotten the answers right without cheating?

Noël Carroll proposes that narratives engage us by positing questions, either explicitly or implicitly. Stories in popular media, he suggests, induce the reader to ask rather clear-cut ones, and these will get reframed, deferred, and toyed with, but eventually answered. *Slumdog* accepts this convention, presenting a cascade of questions to link its scenes and enhance our engagement. Will Jamal and Salim get Bachchan's autograph? Will they survive the anti-Muslim riot? Will they escape the fate of the other captive beggar children? And so on.

More originally, the film cleverly melds the question-based appeal of narrative with the protocols of the game show, so that we are confronted with a multiple-choicer at the very start. How did Jamal manage to win? A title appears:

A. He cheated
B. He's lucky
C. He's a genius
D. It is written

The key question will be answered in the denouement, in a comparably impersonal register. A title is superimposed over the couple's kiss: "D. It is written." As in narrative itself, the answer comes at the end.

Flashbacks are also a long-standing storytelling device. A canonical situation is the police interrogation that frames the past events, as in *Mildred Pierce*, *The Usual Suspects*, and Bertolucci's *The Grim Reaper*. This narrating frame is comfortable and easy to assimilate, and it guides us in following the time shifts. *Slumdog*'s frame story obviously ties it to this tradition.

But 1960s cinema gave flashbacks a new force. From *Hiroshima mon amour* (1958) onward, brief and enigmatic flashbacks, interrupting the ongoing present-tense action, became common ways to engage the audience. Such is the case with the glimpse of Latika at the station that pops up during the questioning of Jamal, rendered as almost an eyeline match. At this point we don't know who she is, but the image creates curiosity that the story will eventually satisfy. Flashbacks can also remind us of

things we've seen before, as when Jamal recalls, obsessively, the night he and Salim abandoned Latika to Maman's band. The filmmakers call on these time-honored devices in the assurance that we will pick up on them immediately.

Flash-forwards are trickier, and rarer. The 1960s also saw some experimentation with images from upcoming events interrupting the story's present action. Unless you posit a character who can see the future, as in *Don't Look Now*, flash-forwards are usually felt as externally imposed, the traces of a filmmaker teasing us with images that we can't really assimilate at this point. (See *They Shoot Horses, Don't They?*) Such flash-forwards pop up during the initial police torture of Jamal. Encountering the above bathtub shot so early in the film, we might take it as a flashback, but actually it anticipates a striking image at the climax, after Jamal has been released and returned to the show. I'd argue that the shot functions thematically, as a vivid announcement of the motif of dirty money that runs through the movie and is associated with both the gangster world and the corrupt game show.

Slumdog Days

One of the most powerful ways to get the audience emotionally involved is to show your protagonist treated unfairly. This happens in spades at the start of *Slumdog*. A serious-faced boy is subjected to awful torture and then he's intimidated by unfeeling men in authority. He's mocked as a *chaiwallah* by the unctuous host of the show, and laughed at by the audience. Once Jamal's backstory starts, we see him as a kid (again running up against the law) and suffering a variety of miseries.

To keep Jamal from seeming a passive victim, he is given pluck and purpose. As a boy he resists the teacher, boldly jumps into manure, shoves through a crowd to get an autograph, and eventually becomes a brazen freelance guide to the Taj Mahal. This is the sort of tenacious, resourceful kid who could get on TV and find Salim in teeming Mumbai. The slumdog is dogged.

Our sympathies spread and divide. Latika is also introduced being treated unfairly. An orphan after the riot, she squats in the rain until Jamal makes her the Third Musketeer. By contrast, Salim is introduced as a hard case—making money off access to a toilet, selling Jamal's Bachchan autograph, resisting bringing Latika into their shelter, and eventually becoming Maman's "dog" and Latika's rapist. The double plotline gives us a hero bent on finding and rescuing his beloved; the underplot gives us a shadier figure who finds redemption by risking his life a final time to help his friends. Jamal emerges ebullient from a sea of shit, but Salim dies drowned in the money he identified with power.

Our three main characters share a childhood, and what happens to them then prefigures what they will do as grownups. This is a long-standing device of classical cinema, stretching back to the silent era. *Public Enemy* and *Angels with Dirty Faces* give us the good brother and the bad brother. *Wuthering Heights, Kings Row,* and *It's a Wonderful Life* present romances budding in childhood.

The device isn't unknown in Indian cinema either; *Parinda* (1989) motivates the character relationships through actions set in childhood. Somehow, we are drawn to seeing one's lifetime commitments etched early and fulfilled in adulthood.

This story pattern carries within it one of the great thematic oppositions of the cinema, the tension between destiny and accident. In *Slumdog, The Three Musketeers* may be introduced casually, but it will provide a template for later events. Lovers are destined to meet, even if by chance, and when chance separates them, they are destined to reunite . . . if only by chance. A plot showing children together assures us that somehow they will re-meet, and their childhood traits and desires will inform what they do as adults. *It is written.*

This theme reaffirms the psychological consistency prized by classic film dramaturgy as well. Characters are introduced doing something, as we say, "characteristic," and this first impression becomes all the more ingrained by the sense that things had to be this way. (This is the "fundamental attribution error" studied by psychologists.) What you choose—say, to pursue the love of your childhood—manifests your character. But then, your character was already defined with special purity in that childhood. Just another movie conceit? The existence of *Classmates.com* seems to suggest otherwise.

Chance needs an alibi, however. Hollywood films are filled with coincidences, and the rules of the game suggest that they need some minimal motivation. Not so much at the beginning, perhaps, because in a sense every plot is launched by a coincidence. But surely, our plausibilists ask, how could it happen that an uneducated slumdog would have just the right experiences to win the quiz? A lucky guy!

As Swarup realized, the flashback structure helps the audience by putting past experience and present quiz question in proximity for easy pickup. Yet as Beaufoy indicates in one of the most informative screenwriting interviews I know (http://creativescreenwritingmagazine.blogspot .com/2008/11/slumdog-millionaire-q.html), the device also softens the impression of an outlandishly lucky contestant. At the start we already know that Jamal has won, so the question for us is not, "how did he cheat?" but rather, "what life experience does the question tap?" Each of the links is buried in a welter of other details, any one of which could tie into the correct answer. Moreover, sometimes the question asked precedes the relevant flashback, and sometimes it follows the flashback, further camouflaging the neat meshing of past and present.

It's a diabolical contrivance. If you question Jamal's luck, you ally yourself with the overbearing authorities who suspect cheating. (You just think the film cheated.) Who wants to side with them? By the end the inevitability granted by the flashback obliges us to accept the inspector's conclusion: "It is bizarrely plausible."

The film has an even more devious out. Jamal can reason on his own, arriving at the Cambridge Circus answer. More important, his street smarts have made him such a good judge of character that he realizes that the MC is misleading him about the right answer to the penultimate question. So his winning isn't entirely coincidence. Life experience has let him suss out the interpersonal dynamics behind the apparently objective game. As for the final answer—a lucky guess? Fate?—it's a good example of how things can be written (in this case by Alexandre Dumas).

Slumdoggy Style
The whole edifice is built on a cinematic technique about a hundred years old: parallel editing. Up to the climax, we alternate between three time frames. The police interrogation takes place in the present, the game show in the recent past (shifting from the video replay to the scenes themselves), and Jamal's earlier life in the more distant past. Any one of these

time streams may be punctuated, as we've seen, by brief flashbacks. So the problem is how to manage the transitions between scenes in any one time frame and the transitions among time frames.

Needless to say, our old friend the hook—in dialogue, in imagery—is pressed into service often. A sound bridge may link two periods, with the quiz question echoing over a scene in the past. "How did you manage to get on the show?" Cut to Jamal serving tea in the call center. In one particularly smooth segue, the boys are thrown off the train as kids and roll to the ground as teenagers.

In the climax, the three time frames come into sync, creating a single ongoing present. Jamal will return to the show. The double-barreled questions are reformulated. Now we have genuine suspense: Will he win the top prize? Will Latika find him? To pose these engagingly, directors Danny Boyle and Loveleen Tandan create an old-fashioned chase to the rescue. Each major character gets a line of action, and all unwind simultaneously: Salim prepares to sacrifice himself to the gangster Khan, Latika flees through traffic, and Jamal enters the contest's final round. A fourth line of action is added, that of the public intensely following Jamal's quest for a million. He has become the emblem of the slumdog who makes good.

The rescue doesn't come off; Latika misses Jamal's phone plea for a lifeline, and he is on his own. Fortunately, he trusts in luck because "maybe it's written, no?" The lovers reunite instead at the train station, where Jamal had pledged to wait for Latika every day at 5:00. Fitting, then, that in the epilogue a crowd shows up, standing in for all of Mumbai, singing and dancing to "Jai Ho" ("Victory"). Jamal, Latika, and the multitudes disperse in a classic ending: lovers turning from the camera and walking into their future, leaving us behind.

Then there's the film's slick technique. The whole thing is presented in a rapid-fire array, with nearly 60 scenes and about 2,700 shots bombarding us in less than two hours. Critics both friendly and hostile have commented on the film's headlong pacing and flamboyant pictorial design. If some of *Slumdog*'s storytelling strategies reach back to the earliest cinema, its look and feel seem tied to the 1990s and 2000s. We get harsh cuts, distended wide-angle compositions, hurtling camerawork, canted angles, dazzling montage sequences, faces split by the screen edge, zones of colored light, slow motion, fast motion, stepped motion, and reverse motion (though seldom no motion). The pounding style, tinged with a certain cheekiness, is already there in most of Danny Boyle's previous work. Like Baz Luhrmann, he seems to think that we need to see even the simplest action from every conceivable angle (as on p. 220).

Yet the stylistic flamboyance isn't unique to him. He is recombining items on the menu of contemporary cinema, as seen in films as various as *Déjà Vu* and *City of God*. (That menu in turn isn't absolutely new either, but I've launched that case in *The Way Hollywood Tells It*.) More surprisingly, we find strong congruences between this movie's style and trends in Indian cinema as well.

Over the last twenty years Indian cinema has cultivated its own fairly flashy action style, usually in crime films. Boyle has spoken of being influenced by two Ram Gopal Varma films, *Satya* (1998) and *Company* (2002). (See http://www.vanityfair.com/online/oscars/2008/12/slumdog -millionaires-bollywood-ancestors.html.) *Company*'s thrusting wide angles, overhead shots, and pugilistic jump cuts would be right at home in *Slumdog*. (See *Company* and *Slumdog* frames, p. 222.) It seems, then, that *Slumdog*'s glazed, frenetic surface testifies to the globalization of one option for modern popular cinema. The film's style seems to me a personalized variant of what has for better or worse become an international style.

Slumdogma

I'd like to survey other ways in which the movie engages viewers, such as the scenes of running (an index of popular cinema; does anybody run in Antonioni?). But I've said enough to suggest that the film is anchored in film history in ways that are likely to promote its appeal to a broad audience. The idea of looking for appeals that cross cultures rather than divide them isn't popular with film academics right now, but a new generation of scholars is daring to say that there are universals of representation and

response. It is these that allow movies to arouse similar emotions across times and places.

Patrick Hogan has made such a case in his fine new book *Understanding Indian Movies: Culture, Cognition, and Cinematic Imagination* (2009). There he shows that much of what seems exotic in Indian cinema constitutes a local specification of factors that have a broad reach—certain plot schemes, themes, and visual and auditory techniques. Hogan, an expert in Indian history and culture, is ideally placed to balance universal appeals with matters of local knowledge that require explication for outsiders.

For my part, I'd just mention that a great deal of what seems striking in *Slumdog* has already been broached in Indian cinema. Take the matter of police brutality. The torture scene at the start might seem a piece of exhibitionism, with an outsider (Boyle? Beaufoy?) twisting local culture to Western ideas of uncivilized behavior. But look again at the gangster films I've mentioned: they contain brutal scenes of police torture, like the one on the following page from *Company*, compared to a shot from *Slumdog*.

Like Hong Kong cinema and American cinema, Indian filmmaking seems to take a jaundiced view of how faithful peace officers are to due process.

More basically, consider the representation of the Mumbai slums. Doubtless the title slants the case from the first; Beaufoy claims to have invented the word "slumdog," though Ram is called a dog at one point in the novel. The insult, and the portrayal of Mumbai, has made some critics find the film sensationalistic and patronizing. Most frequently quoted is megastar Amitabh Bachchan's blog entry: "If SM projects India as [a] Third World dirty underbelly developing nation and causes pain and disgust among nationalists and patriots, let it be known that a murky underbelly exists and thrives even in the most developed nations" (http://bigb .bigadda.com/?m=200901&paged=12).

Soon Bachchan explained that he was neutrally summarizing the comments of correspondents, not expressing his own view. In the original, he seems to have been suggesting that the poverty shown in *Slumdog* is not unique to India, and that a film portraying poverty in another country might not be given so much recognition.

It's an interesting point, although many films from other nations portray urban poverty. More generally, Indian criticisms of the image of poverty in *Slumdog* remind me of reactions to Italian neorealism from authorities concerned about Italy's image abroad. The government undersecretary Giulio Andreotti claimed that films by Rossellini, De Sica, and others were "washing Italy's dirty linen in public." Andreotti wrote that De Sica's *Umberto D* had rendered "wretched service to his fatherland, which is also the fatherland of . . . progressive social legislation." It seems that there will always be people who consider films portraying social injustice to be too negative and failing to see the bright side of things, a side that can always be found if you look hard enough.

Moreover, neorealists made a discovery that has resonated throughout festival cinema: feature kids. Along with sex, a child-centered plot is a central convention of non-Hollywood filmmaking, from *Shoeshine* and *Germany Year Zero* through *Los Olvidados* and *The 400 Blows* up to *Salaam Bombay*, numerous Iranian films, and *Ramchandi Pakistani*. Yes, *Slumdog* simplifies social problems by portraying the underclass through children's misadventures, but this narrative device is a well-tried way to secure audience understanding. We have all been children.

There is another way to consider the poverty problem. The representation of slum life, either sentimentally or scathingly, can be found in classic Indian films of the 1950s. One of my favorites of Raj Kapoor's work,

 *Boot Polish* (1954; left), tells a Dickensian tale of a brother and sister living in the slums before being rescued by a rich couple. (Interestingly, the key issue is whether to beg or do humble work.) Another example is Bimal Roy's *Do Bigha Zamin* (*Two Acres of Land*, 1953). Later, shantytown life is more harshly presented in *Chakra* (1981; p. 225), shot on location. And of course poverty in the countryside has not been overlooked by Indian filmmakers.

Slumdog may have become a flash point because more recent Indian cinema has avoided this subject. In an e-mail to me Patrick Hogan (who hasn't yet seem *Slumdog*) writes:

There was a strong progressive political orientation in Hindi cinema in the 1940s and 1950s. This declined in the 1960s until it appeared again with some works of parallel cinema. Thus there was a greater concern with the poor in the 1950s—hence the movies by Kapoor and Roy that you mention. There are some powerful works of parallel cinema that treat slum life, but they had relatively limited circulation. On the other hand, that does not mean that urban poverty disappeared entirely from mainstream cinema. At least some sense of social concern seemed to be retained in mainstream Indian culture, thus mainstream cinema, until the late 1980s.

However, at that time Nehruvian socialism was more or less entirely abandoned and replaced with neo-liberalism. In keeping with this, ideologies changed. Perhaps because the consumers of movies became the new middle classes in India and the Diaspora, there was a striking shift in what classes appeared in Hindi cinema and how classes were depicted. As many people have noted, films of the neoliberal period present images of fabulously wealthy Indians and generally focus on Indians whose standard of living is probably in the top few percentage points.... I don't believe this is simply a celebration of wealth and pandering to the self-image of the nouveau riche—though it is that. I believe it is also a celebration of neoliberal policies. Neoliberal policies have been very good for some people. But they have been very bad for others....

In this neoliberal cinema (sometimes misleadingly referred to as "globalized"), even relatively poor Indians are commonly represented as pretty comfortable. The difference in attitude is neatly represented by two films by Mani Ratnam—*Nayakan* (1987) and *Guru* (2007). The former is a representation of the difficulties of the poor in Indian society. The film already suffers from a loss of the socialist perspective of the 1950s films. Basically, it celebrates an "up from nothing" gangster for Robin Hood–like behavior. (This is an oversimplification, but gives you the idea.)

Guru, by contrast, celebrates a corrupt industrialist who liberates all of India by, in effect, following neoliberal policies against the laws of the government. Neither film offers a particularly admirable social vision. But the former shows the urban poor struggling against debilitating conditions. The latter simply shows a sea of happy capitalists and indicates that lingering socialistic views are preventing India from becoming the wealthiest nation in the world. Part of the propaganda for neoliberalism is pretending that poor people don't exist any longer—or, if they do, they are just a few who haven't yet received the benefits.

Paradoxically, then, perhaps local complaints against *Slumdog* arise because the film took up a subject that hasn't recently appeared on screens very prominently. The same point seems to be made by Indian filmmakers who deplore the fact that none of their number had the courage to make such a movie (http://indiatoday.intoday.in/site/Story/25720/LATESTHEADLINES/India+no+slumdog+to+West,+filmmakers+reply+to+Bachchan.html). The subject demands more probing, but perhaps the outsider Boyle has helped revive interest in an important strain of the native tradition!

Finally, the issue of glamorizing the exotic. Some critics call the film "poverty porn," but I don't understand the label. It implies that pornography of any sort is vulgar and distressing, but which of these critics would say that it is? Most such critics consider themselves worldly enough not to bat an eye at naughty pictures. Some even like Russ Meyer.

So is the problem that the film, like pornography, prettifies and thereby falsifies its subject? Several Indian films, like *Boot Polish*, have portrayed poverty in a sunnier light than *Slumdog*, yet I've not heard the term applied to them. Perhaps, then, the argument is that pornography exploits eroticism for money, and *Slumdog* exploits the Indian poor. Of course every commercial film could be said to exploit some subject for profit, which would make Hollywood a vast porn shop. (Some people think it is, but not typically the critics who apply the porn term to *Slumdog*.) In any case, once any commercial cinema falls under the rubric of porn, then the concept loses all specificity, if it had any to begin with.

The *Slumdog* project is an effort at crossover, and like all crossovers it can be criticized from either side. And it invites accusations of imperialism. A British director and writer use British and American money to make a film about Mumbai life. The film evokes popular Indian cinema in circumscribed ways. It gets a degree of worldwide theatrical circulation that few mainstream Indian films find. This last circumstance is unfair, I agree; I've long lamented that significant work from other nations is often ignored in mainstream U.S. culture (and it's one reason I do the sort of research I do). But I also believe that creators from one culture can do good work in portraying another one. No one protests that Milos Forman and Roman Polanski, from Communist societies, made *One Flew Over the Cuckoo's Nest* and *Chinatown*. No one sees anything intrinsically objectionable in the Pang brothers or Kitano Takeshi coming to America to make films. Most of us would have been happy had Kurosawa had a chance to make *Runaway Train* here. Conversely, Clint Eastwood receives praise for *Letters from Iwo Jima*.

Just as there is no single and correct "Indian" or "American" or "French" point of view on anything, we shouldn't deny the possibility that outsiders can present a useful perspective on a culture. This doesn't automatically make *Slumdog* a good film. It simply suggests that we shouldn't dismiss it based on easy labels or the passports of its creators.

Moreover, it isn't as if Boyle and Tandan have somehow contaminated a pristine tradition. Indian popular films have long been hybrids, borrowing from European and American cinema on many levels. Their mixture of local and international elements has helped the films travel overseas and become objects of adoration to many Westerners.

I believe we should examine films for their political presuppositions. But those presuppositions require reflection, not quick labels. If I were to sketch an ideological interpretation of *Slumdog*, I'd return to the issue of how money is represented in an economy that traffics in maimed children, virgins, and robotic employees. Money is filthy, associated with blood, death, and commercial corruption. The beggar barracks, the brothel, the call center, and the quiz show lie along a continuum. So to stay pure and childlike one must act without concern for cash. The slumdog millionaire doesn't want the treasure, only the princess, and we never see him collect his ten million rupees. (An American movie loves to see the loser write a check.) To invoke neorealism again, we seem to have something like De Sica's *Miracle in Milan*—realism of local color alongside a plot that is frankly magical.

Perhaps this quality supports the creators' claims that the film is a fairy tale. As with all fairy tales, and nearly all movies I know, dig deep enough and you'll find an ideological evasion. Still, that evasion can be more or less artful and engrossing.

So it seems to me enlightening and pleasurable to see every film as suspended in a web, with fibers connecting it to different traditions, many levels and patches of film history. Acknowledging this shows that most traditions aren't easily exhausted, and that fresh filmmaking tactics can make them live again. Thinking historically need not numb us to surprises.

• •

When this was written, print media and the net were awash in commentary on *Slumdog Millionaire*; it went on to win eight Academy Awards, including the Best Picture Oscar. See our original web entry (http://www.davidbordwell.net /blog/?p=3592) for several citations of reviews, technical discussions, political debates, scholarly investigations, and articles on the Dharavi neighborhood and Indian protests against the movie.

Noël Carroll discusses question-and-answer story patterns in *The Philosophy of Horror; or, Paradoxes of the Heart* (New York: Routledge, 1990), 130–136. On recent Indian action movies, see Lalitha Gopalan, *Cinema of Interruptions: Action Genres in Contemporary Indian Cinema* (London: British Film Institute, 2002). The quotations from Giulio Andreotti come from P. Adams Sitney, *Vital Crises in Italian Cinema: Iconography, Stylistics, Politics* (Austin: University of Texas Press, 1995), 107; and Millicent Marcus, *Italian Film in the Light of Neorealism* (Princeton, NJ: Princeton University Press, 1986), 26.

There is one fascinating fact I couldn't work into the original: the company holding rights to *Who Wants to Be a Millionaire?* helped finance the movie. If this is product placement, it's hardly the most flattering kind. It's another example, I suspect, of the catch-all opportunism of much popular entertainment.

• •

Rat Rapture

AUGUST 24, 2007

Recently we went to see *Ratatouille* and loved it. We thought it was the best Hollywood movie we've seen this summer.

KT: Last October, in the infancy of this blog, I posted an entry on *Cars* (http://www.davidbordwell.net/blog/?p=16). There I said, "For me, part of the fun of watching a Pixar film is to try and figure out what technical challenge the filmmakers have set themselves this time. Every film pushes the limits of computer animation in one major area, so that the studio has been perpetually on the cutting edge." For *Cars* it was the dazzling displays of light and reflections in the shiny surfaces of the characters.

I treat figuring out the main self-imposed challenge in a new Pixar film as a game, and I avoid reading any statements about the films by their makers ahead of time.

At first glance *Ratatouille* might seem to be "about" fur. True, there are lots of rats with impressively rendered fur—but fur was the big challenge way back in *Monsters, Inc.* Surely Pixar wasn't repeating itself. To be sure, *Monsters, Inc.*, contained only one major furry character, Sulley, and his fur was the long wispy type that some stuffed animals have. Difficult to render, no doubt, but different from the rats' fur, which is dense, short, and has to ripple with the movements of the animals.

Not only that, but in *Ratatouille*, we see furry rats in all sorts of situations: just running around, crawling out of water and various other liquids, and in one virtuoso throwaway shot, emerging all fluffed up from a dishwasher. It's all very impressive, but I didn't think that was the main technical feat that the filmmakers were aiming at.

I quickly became aware that there was something different about the settings. Pixar films always have eye-catching settings: the beautiful and convincing underwater seascapes of *Finding Nemo*, the huge vistas of the factory in *Monsters, Inc.*, the stylized domestic settings in the *The Incredibles*.

The Incredibles, the first film that Brad Bird directed for Pixar, was deliberately cartoony looking, evoking the streamlined Populuxe look of 1950s cartoons. *Ratatouille*, his second effort, takes a very different approach. Here the settings are far more realistic and three-dimensional, approaching photo-realism in some of the Parisian street scenes. Often our vantage point moves rapidly through these settings, twisting, turning, and plunging from high-angle to low-angle framings in a second. In the scene where the protagonist Remy is swept away from his family through the sewers until he emerges in Paris, the twists and turns of the pipes sweep by. Likewise, the camera explores the crevices of the restaurant's crowded pantry.

The settings have a tangible and immediate presence beyond what we have seen in previous Pixar films, partly because so many objects in the surroundings are pulled into the action. Ingredients sit in bowls and jars that take up considerable portions of the kitchen set, and the rat dashes among them, sniffing to find the ones he needs for a new concoction. The lessons learned in *Cars* return here to make the shiny copper cooking utensils reflect their surroundings. The brick arch and floor tiles of the restaurant kitchen were individually tweaked, so that they don't have the uniformity that CGI tends to give repetitive patterns. Dense combinations of bricks, tiles, wood panels, carpets, patterned wallpaper, glass, and Venetian blinds make every shot too busy for the eye to take in fully.

A delightful demonstration of all these features and more is given in the "Ratatouile QuickTime Virtual Tour" (http://movies.aol.com/movie -photo-bts/ratatouille-quicktime-virtual-tour). A 360-degree spherical space allows you to look up at the ceiling and down at the floor as well as scan the walls.

DB: Two things, one general and one specific to *Ratatouille*:

1. The idea of explaining artists' works in terms of problems and solutions is common in art history and musicology, but not so common in film studies. Clearly, though, sometimes filmmakers face common problems and compete to solve them, or to find different problems they can solve.

I sometimes try to imagine what animators for other Hollywood studios thought when they walked out of *Snow White and the Seven Dwarfs*.

Did the talents at Warner, Fleischer, et al., just throw up their hands in despair? Disney must have been the Pixar of its day, challenging its rivals with a dazzling series of achievements along many dimensions. Disney had solved so many problems—of rendering color and depth, of catching detail and voluminous movement, of blending pathos with comedy—that the others could hardly compete in the same race. So it seems that they carved out other niches. Fleischer, though trying its hand at feature cartoons as well, concentrated on the familiar and presold comic-strip world of Popeye. Warner avoided child-oriented sentiment and offered more insolent and whacked-out entertainment, personified in Bugs and Daffy. In today's CGI realm, Pixar seems to set the pace, staking its claim before anybody else has realized the territory has opened up—though Aardman consistently offers something different.

2. Along with the problems that you've mentioned, I was struck by what we might call a general task facing all animators: the need to display a cinematic sophistication that fits contemporary tastes in live-action movies. So the pacing has to be fast (here, an average shot length of about 3.5 seconds), though it isn't frantic. Today's movies are overstuffed with details, so this is too; but here many stand out sharply. Central are all the minutiae of food and its preparation, which you mention below. A friend's son, who is a chef, noticed the burn mark on Colette's right forearm—a combat wound of the professional cook. Instead of the heavy satire and flatulence of the Shrek cycle, Pixar always gives us something that would engage us even if it weren't animated.

Every director, I think, should study this film for lessons in making movement expressive. The velocity of our rats' scampering depends on the surface they cross, and the differences in acceleration and braking are vivid. The vertigo-inducing river turbulence that carries Remy away from his clan displays the old Disney genius in rendering the behavior of water. There's a caricatural difference in body language among all the characters, from the cadaverous Ego to the heaving movements of pudgy Emile and the spasmodic twirling of Linguini when Remy is at the controls. Shot scale is always well judged. When there's a moment of uncertainty about whether the kitchen team will support Linguini, the pause is accentuated by the fierce Horst taking a step forward toward the boy, in medium close-up. Will this be the signal for the others to join him? The framing conceals the key piece of information: Horst has stripped off his apron, and only when he lifts it into the frame and proffers it to Linguini do we realize that he's walking out (see following page). Perhaps the visual reversals of silent filmmaking survive best today in animation.

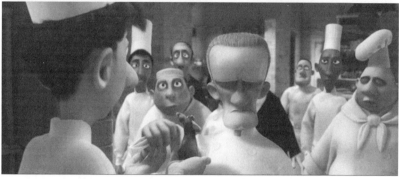

KT: A secondary but still important challenge seemed to be the effort to find ways of rendering the textures of surfaces that are difficult to capture in animation. Most obviously the food—slices of carrots and tomatoes, stalks of celery—must look realistic and attractive if we are to believe that the dishes Remy devises are truly as scrumptious as the characters find them. (The film wisely sticks to soups, desserts, and, yes, ratatouille, sidestepping the problematic notion of an animal cooking other animals.)

Once you decide what you think the Pixar crew was working on extra hard in their newest film, it's usually easy to find supporting evidence in interviews with the top people involved. For some reason Bird was reluctant to talk much about the big technical challenges for *Ratatouille*, but he gave a good summary in an interview on *Collider.com* (http://www .collider.com/entertainment/interviews/article.asp/aid/4739/tcid/1).

I think our goal is to get the impression of something rather than perfect photographic reality. It's to get the feeling of something so I think that our challenge was the computer basically wants to do things that are clean and perfect and don't have any history to them. If you want to do something that's different than that you have to put that information in there and the computer kind of fights you. It really doesn't want to do that and Paris is a very rich city that has a lot of history to it and it's lived in. Everything's beautiful but it's lived in. It has history to it, so it has imperfections and it's part of why it's beautiful is you can feel the history in every little nook and cranny. For us every single bit of that has to be put in there. We can't go somewhere and film something. If there's a crack in there, we have to design the crack and if you noticed the tiles on the floor of the restaurant, they're not perfectly flat, they're like slightly angled differently, and they catch light differently. Somebody has to sit there and angle them all separately.

DB: This relates back to the idea that an animated film has to offer its own equivalent of what live-action film has led viewers to expect. Since at least *Alien* and *Blade Runner*, we've come to equate realism with a worn-out world. No more spanking-clean spaceships, but rather creaky Gothic ones; no more shiny futures, only dilapidated ones. Bird acknowledges that once his team opts for more detailed settings, they have to look lived-in, rather than providing the rather generic locales we find in *Toy Story* and even *The Incredibles*. But then the food contrasts with this air of casual imperfection; it looks pristine.

KT: Speaking of food, in another interview (http://movies.about.com /od/ratatouille/a/ratatbbo61307.htm), Bird expands on the difficulties of rendering it:

There was quite a bit of effort expended to make the food look delicious. Because if one of the things your movie is about is gourmet food, then you can't have it not look delicious. And computers aren't really very interested in making things look delicious. They're interested in things looking clean and things looking geometrically precise, and usually hard not squishy— not tactile. Computers are great for perfection. They're not great at organic things. We had to work really hard to get the food to look like you could taste it and smell it and enjoy it.

The interviews I've read don't mention it, but the film also takes a small but impressive step toward solving the ever-difficult problem of rendering human skin. Most of the characters are given the usual smooth skin that we have come to expect in computer-animated films.

DB: Agreed! One of the things that put me off CGI animation years ago was the overpolished look of CGI surfaces. Volume without texture always looked plastic to me. But in *Ratatouille*, the Pixar team has made great progress in dirtying up the surfaces. That kitchen is full of spills and stains, but the faces are still pretty balloon-like, except for that villainous chef Skinner. He's the most cartoony character, I suppose, and the range of expressions he passes through just in delivering a single line had me in stitches. The Termite Terrace legacy lives on in him.

KT: Yes, Skinner must have inspired the filmmakers. His face gets very sophisticated treatment. In most character animation, eyes and eyebrows are the main means of creating expressions in the upper half of the face. Several times, however, Skinner comes into extreme close-up, so that his expressions of rage and shock are complete with elaborate forehead wrinkles. There's even a patch of pores on his nose. That degree of detail is used sparingly in this film, but perhaps we see a sign of things to come as the Pixar animators set up new hurdles to jump.

· ·

For an interesting, more thematically oriented discussion of *Ratatouille*, see Michael J. Anderson and Lisa K. Broad's entry on the *Tativille* blog (http://tativille.blogspot .com/2007/07/new-animation-ratatouille-co-written.html). Bill Desowitz has a lively and informative feature on the film, including behind-the-scenes interview material, at *Animation World Network* (http://www.awn.com/articles/production/iratatouillei -pixar-style-ibon-appetiti).

Pixar continues to tackle difficult challenges. Just watching *WALL·E* (2008), anyone but an expert would be hard put to say what the new challenge was. Publicity for the film emphasized the difficulties of using long stretches of action with two central characters who don't speak. But that's a storytelling challenge, not a technical one.

For *WALL·E*, the filmmakers "reinvented" their virtual camera to behave like a real camera. It was programmed to imitate such features as an anamorphic lens and depth of field based on the f-stops. Lighting and other factors in live-action cinematography were included. The resulting film felt as if it had been recorded by a real camera in actual three-dimensional space. See Bill Desowitz's detailed discussion on *Animation World Network* (http://www.awn.com/articles/production /hello-iwall-ei-pixar-reaches-stars).

For *Up* (2009), the Pixar filmmakers took the logical next step, making the film in 3-D—a format posing its own battery of problems. We discuss that film briefly in another entry (http://www.davidbordwell.net/blog/?p=5398).

· ·

A Welcome Basterdization

SEPTEMBER 12, 2009

David here:

It's a measure of the changes wrought by the Internet that *Inglourious Basterds* has in about a month amassed a daunting volume of serious commentary. Without benefit of DVD (let's be charitable and assume no BitTorrenting), dozens of online writers have dug deep into this movie. As if to demonstrate the virtues of crowdsourcing, this flurry of critical discussion has shown that most professional movie reviewers have tired ideas, know little about film history, and are constrained by the length limits and looming deadlines of print publication. At this point, I'm very glad I'm not writing a book on Tarantino. The sort of secondary sources that normally take years to accrete have piled up in a few weeks, and the pile can only grow bigger, faster.

So what is there left for me to say? A little, though I can't be sure every point isn't made somewhere else. In any case, surely you've seen the movie, so I don't have to warn you about spoilers, do I?

Since I thought *Death Proof* merely offered proof of the director's creative death, I went to *Inglourious Basterds* with low expectations. I came out thinking that it was the most audacious and ambitious American movie I saw this summer.

To deal with the current controversy immediately: I didn't think its counterhistory was intrinsically offensive or immoral, since I remembered those what-if-Germany-had-won counterfactuals in Deighton's novel *SS-GB* and Brownlow's film *It Happened Here* (1966). Did those express defeatism or an inability to counter the Nazi threat? So why not have a band of vindictive Jews seeking to match the Nazis in ruthlessness (except that their targets, so far as we see, are only soldiers and collaborationists)? We call it fiction.

You can argue that a revenge plot should carry some signals of the cost to the avenger, but I'm sufficiently convinced that tit-for-tat is embedded in human nature and will always be perceived, however recklessly, as virtuous. In any case, the movie's emblem of vengeance, the powerful image of Shosanna laughing mockingly as she goes up in flames along with the audience, carries the strategic ambiguity of a lot of cunning popular art. The shot is a glorying in payback, a Jeanne d'Arc martyrdom, and a reminder of the fate of Jews elsewhere at that moment. It doesn't permit a single easy reading.

Granted, there are some low-jinks, like the misspelled title; is it a joke on Tarantino's notorious spelling malfunctions? Yet the movie seemed to me Tarantino's most mature (to use a term of praise that he hates) since *Jackie Brown*. I say that not because his other work is juvenile, which it's not (except for *Death Proof*). I call *Inglourious Basterds* mature because it exploits his strengths in fresh but recognizable ways.

First, strengths of structure. Tarantino's conception of storytelling owes at least as much to popular literature, particularly *policiers*, as it does to current conventions of screenwriting.

Take his penchant for repeating scenes from different viewpoints. In Elmore Leonard's novel *Get Shorty*, chapter 2 ends with Harry, seeing Chili at his desk, exclaiming, "Jesus Christ!" Chapter 3 consists of the first stretch of their conversation. Chapter 4 starts with Karen approaching Harry's office and hearing him say, "Jesus Christ!" This overlapping-scene strategy, sketched in *Reservoir Dogs*, gets elaborated in *Pulp Fiction* and *Jackie Brown*.

Likewise, thrillers and crime novels commonly show how distant lines of action unexpectedly intersect. In Peter Abrahams's *Hard Rain*, the agent who becomes the hero tells the story of two coal miners, Bazak and Vaclav, who meet after tunneling from two ends of the field. Needless to say, *Hard Rain*'s own plot enacts the same pattern. Charles Willeford's chance-driven, parallel-action novel *Sideswipe* could be a model for the structure of *Pulp Fiction*. So it should be no surprise that *Inglourious Basterds*, labeling its long sequences "chapters," should rely on the stepwise convergence of Shosanna's plotline and the Basterds' guerrilla operations, with the UK Operation Kino serving as the first sign of a merger.

The film is built on large-scale alternation of the principal forces: Shosanna (chapter 1), the Basterds (2), Shosanna again (3), the Basterds again (4), and finally the two strands knotting at the screening of *Nation's Pride* (5). Landa also knits the two strands together, of course, starting when he investigates the tavern shootout at the end of (4). In chapter 5 the alternation gets carried by classic crosscutting. We shift to and fro among Shosanna's plot, the capture of Raine and Utivich, the conflagration in the auditorium, and the deal struck between Landa and the U.S. command. Yet right to the end both Shosanna and the Basterds have no awareness of each other's plan: only we can grasp the double dose of Jewish vengeance. More than in most films, but typical for Tarantino, we're aware of the plot's abstract architecture.

Then there are strengths of texture—the moment-by-moment un-folding of the action. Again pulp fiction offers some models.

In *Get Shorty*, Leonard develops the scene I mentioned above in an extraordinary way. Chili, Harry, and Karen talk through the night about Chili's purpose and about the mores of the movie industry. Their conversation runs for a remarkable seven chapters and sixty pages, interrupted only by a brief flashback. When I met Leonard at a book-signing event, I asked him why he took up a fifth of the novel with a single scene. He said that he hadn't realized it consumed so much space because it was "fun to write."

Tarantino can lay bare his chapter-block architecture because his scenes are devoted to this sort of prolongation. You may remember the bursts of violence, but what he fashions most lovingly is buildup. Here the spirit of Leone hovers over our director. In each entry of the *Dollars* trilogy, the rituals of the Western get more and more stretched out, filled with microscopic gestures and eye-flicks. In the parched and dusty prairie Eastwood's lips stick slightly together, and they peel apart when he speaks. This becomes a major event. I'm a primary-document witness to the fact that 1969 cinephiles were stunned by the long opening scene of *Once Upon a Time in the West*, which after painstakingly establishing the tics of several characters ends by eliminating them. Later, John Woo gained fame by dwelling on Homeric preparations for combat and endlessly extended bouts of gunplay. From these masters Tarantino evidently learned the power of the slow crescendo and the sustained aria.

Leone's and Woo's amped-up passages rely chiefly on imagery and music. Tarantino is no slouch in either department, but he relies, like his beloved pulp writers, on talk. As everyone has noticed, the conversations in *Basterds* go on a very long time. In an era when scenes are supposed to run two to three minutes on average, Tarantino has only a couple this brief. The introduction at LaPadite's farm runs over eighteen minutes, and the more complicated chapter 2, with intercut flashbacks and flash-forwards, runs about the same length. Thereafter scenes last anywhere between four and twenty-four minutes, and chapter 5's crosscut climax consumes a stunning thirty-seven minutes. All but the last depend completely on dialogue. Leonard would probably consider them to have been fun to write.

Talk in Tarantino comes in two main varieties: banter and intimidation. At the coffee shop the Reservoir Dogs squabble and soliloquize; later exchanges will be conducted at gunpoint. En route to the preppies' apartment, Jules and Vincent chat casually; when they arrive, the talk turns threatening. If *Death Proof* is ruled by banter among equals, *Inglourious Basterds* goes to the other extreme. Here talk is a struggle between the powerful and the powerless.

As Jim Emerson points out, nearly every scene is an interrogation. This entails that someone in authority (Landa, Aldo, Hitler, the Germans who question Archie's accent in the tavern, Zoller) is trying to pry information out of someone else. Intimidation through interrogation gives every scene an urgent shape. Now Tarantino's digressions (three daughters, rats and squirrels, a card game, the correct pronunciation of Italian) don't read as self-indulgence, but rather as feints in a confidence game. Tarantino's tendency to write endless scenes, something he confesses in his recent *Creative Screenwriting* interview on the film, is here harnessed to more classic scene structure.

To keep us focused on the lines and the actors delivering them, Tarantino has adopted a classical approach to style. He shoots with a single camera, so every composition is calculated. "I'm not Mr. Coverage," he remarked in 1994, "I shoot one thing specifically and that's all I get." He forswears handheld grab-and-go. In *Basterds* he locks his camera down, or puts it on a dolly or crane. Cinematographer Robert Richardson says that there is only one Steadicam shot in the film.

We don't usually call Tarantino tactful, but his technique can be surprisingly discreet. He has the confidence to let key dialogue play offscreen: in the café when Landa arrives at Goebbels's lunch, we stay fastened on Shosanna, a good old Hitchcockian ploy that ratchets up the tension. Although Tarantino cuts rapidly throughout each chapter (on average every 5.6 seconds), he repeats setups quite a bit. This permits a simple change of angle or shot scale to mark a beat or shift the drama to a new level.

He can bury details on the fringes of the shot. A cut to a tight close-up of LaPadite shows him tossing his match into an ashtray sitting beside

Landa's cap, which bears the insignia of a skull and crossbones. It's out of focus and on the edge of the screen, but the glimpse of it increases our worry that LaPadite is indeed harboring a Jewish family. As in *Jackie Brown*, another film that extends its scenes through detailing of performance, lighting, and setting, there seems no doubt that Tarantino, for all his PoMo reputation, appreciates some traditional Hollywood virtues.

He can inflect them, however. Richardson finds that Tarantino has an unusual approach to the anamorphic format. "I naturally move [the framing of characters] to one side or the other, especially when shooting anamorphic, whereas Quentin enjoys dead-center framing. For singles in particular, we're just cutting dead-center framing from one side to the other, with the actors looking just past the barrel of the lens."

I noticed this tendency most in the reverse angles. Tarantino's two-shots tend to be simple and symmetrical, shooting the characters in profile. But in over-the-shoulder shots, about half the frame is unoccupied—as if Tarantino were compensating, like his 1970s mentors, for an eventual TV pan-and-scan version of the scene (see following page).

Or take the cliché of arcing the camera around a group of chatting people, picking up one after the other. Tarantino didn't invent this, but the opening scene of *Reservoir Dogs* probably helped popularize it. In chapter 5 he uses the technique in the lobby of the Le Gamaar cinema, only to break its momentum by having the camera trail Landa when he lurches out of the circle and retreats, in a paroxysm of giggles, after Bridget says she broke her leg while mountain climbing.

There are many other intriguing touches, like the mixed typography of the opening credits, all of which seem to use fonts derived from 1970s paperback novels. Or the reference to *The Saint in New York*, perhaps

less important for its plot parallels than for the fact that author Leslie Charteris's later Saint novel, *Prelude to War* (1938), was banned in Germany and Italy for its attacks on fascism (even warning about the camps). So is reading a Saint novel a covert act of defiance on Shosanna's part? Later, she applies makeup in fierce strokes, like an American Indian, reminding us that Raine's Basterds model their tactics on the Apache.

Perhaps most striking is the dairy motif, from the glass of milk in chapter 1 to Landa's ordering a glass for Shosanna in chapter 3. Is this a hint that he suspects her of being the girl who fled the massacre? Or is it a test he offers to any French national he meets? In the restaurant scene, the extreme close-ups of the crème fraiche may underscore the possibility that Landa is looking for signs that she won't eat dairy products not prepared according to Orthodox dietary rules. The hunch that this is a test is supported by the somewhat resigned way she swallows the strudel and then sighs. Few filmmakers today would trust audiences to imagine this possibility on their own; instead we'd get Landa's explanation to an underling. ("So here's a quick way to find out if we have a Jew . . .")

Another nest of details involves the film-within-the-film, *Nation's Pride*. Many online critics have noticed that it provides the sort of film that *Basterds* refuses to be: we never see our squad in the sort of *Merrill's Marauders* skirmishes we probably expected going in. What I find intriguing about the movie, credited to Eli Roth, is that despite some anachronisms it exemplifies the sort of confrontational cinema we find in the silent Soviet pictures. Surprisingly, this was a tradition that Goebbels admired. Eisenstein's *Battleship Potemkin*, he claimed, "was so well made that it could make a Bolshevist out of anyone without a firm philosophical footing." So *Nation's Pride*, in the portions screened in Shosanna's theater and in fuller form on the DVD supplement, provides a Nazified homage to Eisenstein. A baby carriage rolls away from a mother, a soldier suffers an assault to the eye reminiscent of the wounding of the schoolteacher on the Odessa Steps, and even Soviet-style axial cut-ins are used for kinetic impact (see following page).

This pastiche of agitprop culminates in the sort of to-camera address we find in Dovzhenko. Zoller shouts, "Who wants to send a message

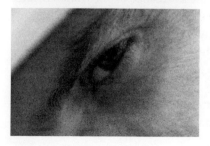

to Germany?" But this is followed by Shosanna's spliced-in close-up addressing the audience in her theater. She makes her own confrontational cinema.

Several years ago the film theorist Noël Carroll speculated that the Movie Brats of the 1970s sought to create a shared culture of media savvy that would replace a traditional culture based on Judeo-Christian religion, classical mythology, and official history. For the baby boomers, knowledge of the Bible and iconography of American history would be replaced by deep familiarity with movies, pop music, and TV. This secular sacred would bind the audience in a new set of traditions.

On this path, Scorsese, Spielberg, and Lucas didn't go as far as Tarantino has. In his films every situation or character name or line of dialogue feels like a citation, a link in a web of pop-culture associations. (Aldo Raine = Aldo Ray = Bruce Willis, whom Tarantino once compared to Aldo Ray.) The only other filmmaker I know who has achieved this supersaturated cross-referencing is Godard, another exponent of the vivid-moments model (though he uses it to create a more fragmentary whole). Tarantino is the most visible evidence of what Carroll called "the future of allusion."

But it's too limiting to see

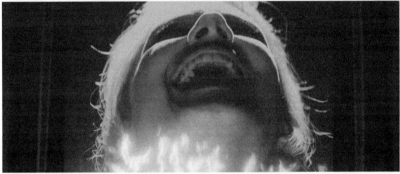

Tarantino's films as merely anthologies of references. I think he wants more.

Many viewers seem to assume that Tarantino's film is somewhat cold. The Basterds are grotesques, parodies of men on a mission; Shosanna, though in a sympathetic position, must maintain a frosty demeanor. Even revenge, so central to films that Tarantino admires, is served frigid here, a purely formal postulate, like the urge for vengeance animating classic kung-fu films.

There is cinema that asks you to empathize with its characters, like *How Green Was My Valley* (1941). Then there is cinema that aims to thrill you with a cascade of vivid moments, like *Citizen Kane* (1941). I think that

Tarantino's films mostly tilt to the vivid-moment pole, seeking to win us through their immediate verve, the way film noir and the musical and the action movie often do. The young man arrested by great bits from blaxploitation and biker movies sees cinema not as merely piling up cinephiliac references—though that's surely part of it—but as a flow of tingle-inducing gestures, turns of phrase, shot changes, musical entrances. There can be pure pleasure in having time to see how actors move, or savor their lines, or simply fill up physical space by being centered in the anamorphic frame. Our fascination with Landa comes, I suspect, from the spectacle of a man who is utterly enjoying himself every second.

We might be tempted to claim that this effort to create what Jim Emerson calls "movie-movie moments" actually breaks the film's overall unity. But Tarantino keeps nearly everything in check by the architectural clarity of his plot. The carving of the swastika on Landa's brow sets you squirming, but it reveals itself as the culmination of a process we have seen piecemeal up to now. It's the last in a string of firecracker bursts that have kept the film humming along.

So I'm not convinced that *Inglourious Basterds* lacks emotion. The emotions Tarantino aims for will arise not from character "identification" but from the overall structure and texture of the work. We are to be stirred, startled, astonished by a procession of splendors big and small. It's the tradition (again) of Eisenstein, particularly in the *Ivan* films, but also of Leone and, in another register, Greenaway. Formal virtuosity isn't necessarily soulless; it can yield aesthetic rapture.

· ·

The best of the online response to *Inglourious Basterds* is typified by the writing of the indefatigable Jim Emerson (http://blogs.suntimes.com/scanners/2009/08 /some_ways_to_watch_inglourious.html) and his well-informed readers, who furnished a book's worth of commentary and critique. For exhaustive coverage of things Tarantino, visit *The Archives* (http://www.tarantino.info/). The range and depth of the ideas on display in these web locations show up the superficiality of most print-based critics.

On Tarantino's time-shuffling and its relation to crime fiction, see my *The Way Hollywood Tells It*, 90–91. In chapter 7 of *Film Art*, Kristin and I provide an analysis of the replayed scene in *Jackie Brown*. Tarantino's comments on writing the *Basterds* script are in Jeff Goldsmith's article "Glorious," in *Creative Screenwriting* 16, no. 4 (July/August 2009), 20–29. His comments on coverage come from Gavin Smith, "When You Know You're in Good Hands," in *Quentin Tarantino Interviews*, ed. Gerry Peary (Jackson: University Press of Mississippi, 1998), 102. Robert

Richardson discusses filming *Basterds* in Benjamin Bergery, "A Nazi's Worst Nightmare," *American Cinematographer* 90, no. 9 (September 2009); the quotation here is from p. 47. This feature is available online at http://findarticles.com/p/articles /mi_7119/is_200909/ai_n39230243/?tag=content;col1.

In a supplement to the *Inglourious Basterds* Special Edition DVD, Tarantino notes that his protracted scenes tend to smuggle in key bits of exposition. "Part of my plan, my method, is to bury [exposition] in so much minutiae that you don't realize you're being told an important plot point, until it becomes important" (disc 2, "Roundtable Discussion with Quentin Tarantino, Brad Pitt, and Elvis Mitchell," 28:50).

Goebbels's remark on *Battleship Potemkin* is quoted in Klaus Kreimeier, *The UFA Story: A History of Germany's Greatest Film Company*, trans. Robert and Rita Kimber (New York: Hill and Wang, 1996), 207. For background on Goebbels's agenda for German cinema, summed up by Lt. Archie Hicox, see Eric Rentschler, *The Ministry of Illusion: Nazi Cinema and Its Afterlife* (Cambridge: Harvard University Press, 1996). I talk about axial cutting at http://www.davidbordwell.net /blog/?p=6136.

Noël Carroll's comments about popular entertainment as a secular alternative to shared religious culture are in "The Future of Allusion: Hollywood in the Seventies (and Beyond)," in his *Interpreting the Moving Image* (Cambridge: Cambridge University Press, 1998), 244, 261–63. On the idea of an emotionally arousing cinema that doesn't rely on attachment to character psychology, see my *The Cinema of Eisenstein*.

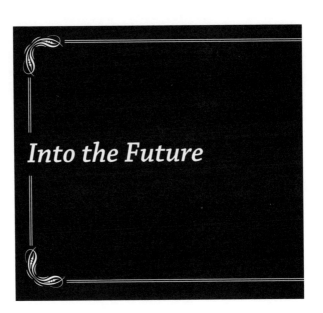

Into the Future

New Media and Old Storytelling

MAY 13, 2007

David asks:

To what extent has the DVD changed viewing habits and movie story-telling?

In a theater, the movie rolls on, unaffected by anything you may do. But with a DVD you can pause the film, run fast-forward, skip to a particular second, shuffle chapters, even play the thing in reverse.

Most minimally, the DVD offers greater convenience. You can halt the film to answer a phone call or zip back to replay a bit you've missed. But some of us wonder if this new interactivity harbors more radical implications. Does the new flexibility of use allow us to experience the film in new ways?

In a mystery film, say there's a clue at the half-hour mark. In a theatrical screening, we're pressed forward with no time to ponder it. Watching the film on DVD lets us halt the film, ponder the clue as long as we like, and maybe track patiently back to earlier scenes to test our suspicions about what that clue means. Or suppose you decide to sample the film, browsing through the opening bits of several chapters? More radically, suppose we decide to watch the DVD in fast-motion reverse. Nothing stops us, and we'd have an experience of the story very different from that of someone who watched the film in the normal order. Doesn't this all suggest that it's hard to generalize about what the "ordinary" viewer's experience of a movie might be nowadays?

Now consider the craft of fictional filmmaking. The movie's creators make choices about what story information to impart, when to impart it, and how to impart it. They assume that the viewer follows the story in the order mandated by theatrical projection—scene 1, then 2, 3, and onward. Likewise, the pace of uptake is set by the film; no slowing down or speeding up at the viewer's will. But given the new conditions of home-video consumption, these assumptions may be wrong. So shouldn't the filmmakers take those conditions into account? And more specifically, haven't some filmmakers already taken them into account? In other words, hasn't the DVD transformed cinematic storytelling?

This question is important to me. I've long argued, along with Kristin, that mainstream U.S. filmmaking, dubbed long ago "classical Hollywood cinema," has cultivated a sturdy and pervasive tradition of storytelling. That tradition depends on clearly defined characters pursuing well-defined goals. This commitment in turn creates a plot that displays linear cause and effect: in pursuing goals, the protagonist makes one thing happen, and that makes something else happen, which in turn triggers something else. Moreover, the mainstream tradition lays these actions and reactions along a fairly rigid structural layout. And this tradition depends on a system of narration that constantly reiterates the characters' traits, their goals, important motifs, and the overall circumstances of the action.

But now home video allows our consumption to be highly nonlinear. By skipping or skimming DVD chapters, we may not register the plot or narration as the makers intended. Doesn't this make hash of goal-directed action, character arcs, and all the other features of classical storytelling? Might we not be moving toward a "post-classical" cinema?

Movie as Book

Let's tackle the question first from the standpoint of the viewer. I think we can get help by recognizing this basic point: the DVD made a movie more like a book.

This sounds odd, because we think of digital media as replacing print. Yet consider the similarities. You can read a book any way you please, skimming or skipping, forward or backward. You can read the chapters, or even the sentences, in any order you choose. You can dwell on a particular page, paragraph, or phrase for as long as you like. You can go back and reread passages you've read before, and you can jump ahead to the ending. You can put the book down at a particular point and return to it an hour or a year later; the bookmark is the ultimate pause command.

We tacitly acknowledge the resemblance between the DVD and the book when we call the segments on a DVD its *chapters*, the list of chapters an *index*, and the process of composing the DVD its *authoring*.

With these similarities in mind, we can ask, how many people, on first contact, would sit down to watch a film in a nonlinear way? My hunch: just about as many who would buy or borrow a book and then proceed to read it in a nonlinear way. Granted, if you have a nonfiction book in hand, you might move straight to the chapters that seem most interesting. Similarly, with a DVD documentary on penguins, some viewers might want to move straight to the chapter labeled "Mating Habits."

With a fictional film, though, we're much less inclined to graze and browse. Some viewers might skip to a chapter opening or two, but I expect that soon they'd settle down to watching the show at the order and pace of a theatrical screening. This is more or less what happens with print fiction. True, we might sample a novel, but I'd bet the portion we're most likely to sample is the opening chapter. The person who reads a novel will proceed in linear order in order to *follow the story*. It's a revealing phrase: we're following a path laid down for us, not racing ahead or falling back.

This isn't to say that all consumers of fiction move at the same pace or read the same way. I'm just indicating that following the mandated order, page by page or shot by shot, is the default that people adhere to in the overwhelming majority of cases.

This suggests that pausing is the most common way we play an interactive role. When reading a book you might call out to your friend and re-read a particularly striking description or funny dialogue exchange. When watching a film, you might stop and replay a passage to enjoy it again. Another common act is probably quickly "paging back"—rereading or reviewing a bit that just preceded the pause to remind ourselves of what's going on at the moment.

Our purpose in starting a book or film at the beginning is to get into the story world and start to think and feel in relation to the information we get about it. But we don't have to take that as our primary purpose. More extreme acts of "creative" spectatorship are tied to different purposes than learning about the story world. I suppose that teenage boys might well rent 300 when it comes out on DVD and fast-forward looking only for the scenes showing carnage or naked ladies . . . the same way that my high-school contemporaries rummaged through Terry Southern's *Candy* digging out the good parts. But this doesn't seem to be a radically new way of using any medium, because the purpose—scanning a text for immediate gratification rather than narrative involvement—was common well before DVD.

Of course we students of cinema use the DVD commands in order to study a film, spooling back and forth to analyze it. But that usage isn't a radical reworking of consumption either. Typically before we start to analyze a movie, we've already experienced it in the ordinary beginning-to-end way. Students of literature execute the same sort of back-and-forth moves studying a text that they've read before.

Finally, I'd suggest that a highly unorthodox mode of consumption, like setting out to watch a film in reverse at 8x speed, would become quite boring fast. As with so many things in life, just because you can do something doesn't mean you'd enjoy it.

Speculation 1: The actual uses that people make of DVD interactivity are limited; traditional beginning-to-end consumption is the default.

Speculation 2: Pausing, paging back, and scanning for the good bits suggest that the most frequent DVD interactivity is familiar from other media, particularly books.

Guided Interactivity

Let's now consider things from the side of the creators. Knowing that films are seen on DVD, don't filmmakers adjust their art and craft to this new medium? Of course they can provide revised versions, or directors' cuts, along with alternative endings, deleted scenes, and other material that shed light on the film and the production process. But does the DVD format change the very act of conceiving and executing the story presented by the film?

Yes, in certain respects. The possibility of rewatching a film with little fuss encourages ambitious filmmakers to "load every rift with ore," to pack in details that might not be noticed on a single viewing. One example is the 8:2 motif in *Magnolia*. Likewise, the looping plotlines of *Donnie Darko* and the reverse-order one of *Memento* are amenable to being picked apart after several viewings. But before home video, you as a viewer could scrutinize such movies by just going back to the theater and watching the film over and over, very attentively.

Clumsy as it seems, film nerds of my generation did this. I remember my thrill as a junior in college when I discovered, after rerunning a 16mm print of *Citizen Kane* on my apartment wall, the snowstorm paperweight that Kane clutches on his deathbed sitting on Susan's vanity table the night he first meets her. Welles had, as it were, planted this clue for attentive viewers to spot. When we were lucky, we might get a film on a flatbed viewer and go through it reel by reel. Granted, the random-access aspect of DVD allows this sort of micro-analysis to be done much more easily, but it's not different in kind from rolling up your sleeves and threading up a 16mm print one more time.

I'd add that this sort of scrutiny enriches the film in a very traditional way. Films that sustain this sort of attention, from Buster Keaton silents to *Hiroshima mon amour* and *The Silence of the Lambs*, long predate the arrival of DVD. Throughout *Play Time* Tati sprinkled details and gags that reward many viewings. When Paul Thomas Anderson and Christopher Nolan bury details in their films, or when *The Simpsons* flashes a jokey sign past us, they're practicing a time-honored strategy of teasing the viewer to return to the work to get something more out of it. Having the DVD at your disposal makes it easier to find half-hidden motifs, jokes, ironies, and the like, but all of these are traditional elements of films both classical and nonclassical.

There are, though, more radical cases. The experimental novelist Michel Butor pointed out that the fact that the book is an object to be manipulated at will harbors the possibilities of innovative storytelling. He pursued those in works like *La Modification* (1957) and *Degrés* (1960) and theorized about them in an essay, "The Book as Object."[1] Along the same lines, once a film becomes a booklike object, it can be composed to encourage multiple replays not merely to appreciate little touches but just to make bare sense of what's going on in it.

Memento and *Primer* would seem to be instances. Their makers seem to have designed the films to encourage admirers' extensive, not to say obsessive, re-viewings. Again, however, the DVD serves not as a unique format for the film but as a tool that makes analyzing the plots a lot easier than would several visits to the theater.

There are other possibilities tied to the format itself. The DVD of Max Allan Collins's *Real Time: Siege at Lucas Street Market* (2001) was designed to permit the viewer some choice of camera angle in certain scenes. At a few points we're permitted to enlarge the monitors of different surveillance cameras in order to follow one or another strand of action. (Actually, I couldn't get this feature to work on my players.) Still, in *Real Time*, the plot action is clear and redundant in the classical manner, so even if you don't enlarge the screens, maybe you won't miss much.

Butor suggested that since a book is an object, all in hand at once, a plot could be composed to permit many, equally valid points of entry and exit. Such seems to have been achieved by the DVD version of Greg Marcks's *11:14*. The film is a network narrative, following five characters in a small town as their lives intertwine. The plot is broken into five segments, each one following a character up to the critical moment given in

254 | PART SIX: INTO THE FUTURE

the title. It's a clever and enjoyable piece of work. In carrying it to DVD, Marcks chaptered it so that you could skip among storylines at will. He explains in an e-mail to me: "It's a feature on the DVD that I called 'character jump,' which allows you to jump to what another character is doing at that same moment in time. Theoretically you could watch the film in an endless circuitous loop because the end is simultaneous with the beginning."

During some scenes of *11:14*, a JUMP icon appears, and if you press Enter, the scene switches to another character's storyline—either earlier or later in the theatrical version's running time. Once in that story, the icon stays on for a bit so that you can return to your point of departure if you want. Presumably for reasons of engineering and disc space, the number of JUMP options remains fairly limited. Still, it's a fascinating prospect, and it does seem to offer the possibility of your restructuring the plot in fresh ways.

Even in *11:14*, however, the story possibilities are closed. As in a *Choose Your Own Adventure* book, you're hopping among trajectories that are already designed. The opening remains the opening for every option; no Butor-style starting in the middle. Furthermore, the trajectories themselves are linear, running along a cause-effect pattern very familiar to us from classically constructed stories.[2] We often find this linearity in branching or multiple-draft narratives. Even the reverse-order disjunctions of *Memento* sort out along lines to be found in film noir.

Let's also recall a simple point. Even though the book format offers the sort of mind-bending manipulations Butor celebrates, most literary fiction remains traditionally plotted and narrated. Likewise, we should expect that the arrival of the DVD permits filmmakers who want to tell orthodox stories in orthodox ways to keep on doing so. The line of least resistance is straightforward linear presentation.

Speculation 3: The ease of DVD replay can encourage filmmakers to pack their films with more details that repay rewatching. The result might be films that are "hyperclassical," to use a term I suggest in *The Way Hollywood Tells It*—films that are even more tightly woven than we tend to find in the studio years.

Speculation 4: Some filmmakers have made their storylines harder to follow on a single viewing, encouraging DVD replays so we can figure out what's going on. This strategy makes the films less classical in construction, to a greater or lesser extent.

Speculation 5: A few filmmakers have utilized DVD features to allow greater interactivity than a theatrical screening would grant. In most cases, however, this interactivity rests upon classical guidelines—protagonists with goals, confronting obstacles, conflicting with others, and arriving at a definite conclusion along a linear path.

A Stubborn Structure

Once upon a time, roughly between the 1920s and the 1960s, movie theaters had a policy of continuous admissions. Metropolitan theaters were sometimes very crowded and patrons had to wait in line outside for seats to be freed up. (Hence the need for ushers to find vacant seats during the screening.) You might enter in the middle of the movie and watch the film through to the end, sit through shorts and perhaps another feature, and then stay for the opening of the initial film. Hence the expression, "This is where we came in." Doubtless many people planned to see films from beginning to end, but a lot also arrived in medias res.

Someone might speculate that this manner of viewing would encourage filmmakers to indulge in slack plotting. After all, if viewers can come in at any point, a vaudeville-like cascade of acts and incidents—what people are now calling a "cinema of attractions"—would be most satisfying. In fact, however, Hollywood feature filmmakers told complex, linear stories of the sort I've already mentioned. They didn't seem to care if viewers were entering midway.

But they really had no choice. If the filmmakers wanted to tell a fairly coherent story, how could they cater to a viewer who might enter at any moment? The only feasible plan, then and now, is just to go ahead and present a story in the linear way, but make sure that it's presented so clearly that even a viewer entering in the middle can pick up what's happening. That was, and still is, the default practice. The redundancy of Hollywood storytelling, bent on clear and cogent presentation of the action, is the most effective response to fragmentary viewing.

Hollywood films have been shown in picture palaces, rural playhouses, college classrooms, churches, military bases, and submarines. They've appeared on TV, in drive-in theaters, on airline screens, on computer monitors, and now on iPods. In design and execution, the films have stayed remarkably stable. They have relied on our understanding of general principles of storytelling and more specific ones typical of Hollywood. In most cases, this default will stay in place. It works very well, and there's no alternative that can be customized to all the different ways in which viewers can consume the movie.

Speculation 6: Odd as it sounds, fragmented viewing conditions can encourage coherent storytelling.

Speculation 7: We can't easily draw conclusions about how films are constructed on the basis of how they're presented and consumed. Changes in viewing practices don't automatically entail changes in storytelling.

I'd just add that even in the age of digital media, spectators enjoy greatest freedom not in the way that they manipulate films but in the ways they can interpret them. But even an epic blog has to stop somewhere, so I'll leave that matter for another time.

Notes

1. Translated in his English-language collection *Inventory* (New York: Simon and Schuster, 1968), 39–56.
2. Marcks's DVD version has allowed us to create a Griffith-style crosscutting of plot strands. Interestingly, network narratives are constructed in two main ways: crosscutting the story lines (as in *Short Cuts*) or presenting them in blocks that we must synchronize in our heads (as in *Pulp Fiction* and *Go*). Marks's theatrical version gives us the block version of *11:14*, while the DVD reveals one possibility of an intercut one.

• •

Both journalists and academics greeted the arrival of the DVD with claims that nonlinear storytelling and at-will viewing would soon become the norm. This entry tries to offer a calmer account. Since it was written, there have been a few more films that allow multiple points of entry, such as *The Onyx Project* (2006) and *Late Fragment* (2008). They are tied to the DVD format rather than commercial theatrical screening, and so far they have not created a significant trend.

On the whole, the possibility of branching structures has entered mainstream films via time-travel plots. These suggest alternative paths through the story world by having characters skip back to crucial moments of decision. Of course the viewer has no say in how or when those jumps occur, and they will be patterned for the usual purposes of arousing curiosity, suspense, surprise, and emotional impact. *Back to the Future Part II* (1989) seems to have been influential in this trend, and its central conceit crops up in films as different as *The Butterfly Effect* (2004) and the Japanese anime *The Girl Who Leapt through Time* (2006). Perhaps the ultimate example is *Primer*, which multiplies turning points by looping back and forth. Its baffling time structure is analyzed in a useful article available at http://en.wikipedia.org/wiki/Primer_(film), while a mind-boggling anatomy of the film's time frames can be found at http://neuwanstein.fw.hu/primer_timeline.html.

Just as Hollywood films of the 1960s absorbed stylistic devices from broadcast television, such as the zoom and the handheld camera, video has inspired filmmakers to explore new possibilities of visual storytelling. One can't deny that DVD viewing habits have shaped film style. The fashion for "ramping" action, from normal to slow to fast, was facilitated by computer post-production but was legible to viewers as analogous to what they could do with their remote controls. Similarly, films like *Sliding Doors* (1998), *Déjà Vu* (2006), and *Vantage Point* (2008) mimic video search with fast-motion and instant-replay techniques. As I indicated in the essay, however, such films still rely on traditional assumptions about character goals, conflict, and causal progression.

This essay appeared in shorter form in Phillip Lopate, ed., *American Movie Critics: From the Silents Until Now*, expanded edition (New York: Library of America, 2006), 724–29.

The Celestial Multiplex

MARCH 27, 2007

Kristin here:

The Internet is mind-bogglingly huge, and a lot of people seem to think that most of the texts and images and sound-recordings ever created are now available on it—or will be soon. In relation to music downloading, the idea got termed "the Celestial Jukebox," and a lot of people believe in it. University libraries are noticeably emptier than they were in my graduate-school days, since students assume they can find all the research materials they need by Googling comfortably in their own rooms.

A lot depends on what you're working on. While I was writing *The Frodo Franchise*, studying the ongoing *Lord of the Rings* phenomenon would have been impossible without the Internet. A big portion of its endnotes are citations to URLs. On the other hand, my previous book, *Herr Lubitsch Goes to Hollywood*, a monograph on the stylistic and technical aspects of Ernst Lubitsch's silent features (Amsterdam University Press, 2005), has not a single Internet reference. Lubitsch must be investigated in archives and libraries, where one finds the films and the old books and periodicals vital to such a project.

Vast though it is, the Internet is tiny in comparison with the real world. Only a minuscule fraction of all the books, paintings, music, photographs, and so on, are online. Belief in a Celestial Jukebox usually works largely because people tend to think about the types of texts and images and sounds that they know about and want access to. Yes, more is being put into digital form at a great rate, but more new stuff is being made and old stuff being discovered. There will never come a time when everything is available.

Even so, every now and then someone proclaims that in the not-too-distant future all the movies ever made will be downloadable for a small fee, from a sort of Celestial Multiplex. A. O. Scott declared this in "The Shape of Cinema, Transformed at the Click of a Mouse" (*New York Times*, March 18, http://www.nytimes.com/2007/03/18/movies/18scot.html): "It is now possible to imagine—to expect—that before too long the entire surviving history of movies will be open for browsing and sampling at the click of a mouse for a few PayPal dollars."

Not only that, but Scott goes on, "This aspect of the online viewing experience is not, in itself, especially revolutionary." He's more interested in the idea that online distribution will allow filmmakers to sell their creations directly to viewers. That would be significant, no doubt, but as a film historian, I'm still gaping at that line about "the entire surviving history of movies." Such availability would not only be "revolutionary"; it would be downright miraculous. It's impossible. It just isn't going to happen.

I will give Scott credit for specifying "surviving" films. Other pundits tend to say "all films," ignoring the sad fact that great swaths of our cinematic heritage, especially in hot, humid climates like that of India, have deteriorated and are irretrievably lost.

Critic Dave Kehr has already pointed out (in a blog entry no longer online) some of the problems with Scott's claims, mainly the overwhelming financial support that would be needed: "Tony Scott's optimism struck me as, well, a little optimistic." On the line about "the entire surviving history of movies," Kehr suggests, "That's reckoning without the cost of preparing a film for digital distribution—the same mistake made by the author of the recent vogue book 'The Long Tail'—which, depending on how much restoration is necessary, can run up to $50,000 a title. None of the studios is likely to pay that much money to put anything other than the most popular titles in their libraries online." As Kehr says, the numbers of films awaiting restoration and scanning isn't in the hundreds, as Scott casually says. No, it's in the tens of thousands even if we just count features. It's more like hundreds of thousands or more likely millions if we count all the surviving shorts, instructional films, ads, porn, everything made in every country of the world. To see how elaborate the preservation of even one short medical teaching film can be, have a look at this story on the Johns Hopkins University news site: http://www.jhu.edu/~gazette /2003/21jul03/21film.html.

Putting aside the need for restoration, the unending flood of new films presents a daunting prospect. To help put the situation in perspective, let's glance over the total number of feature films produced worldwide during some representative years from recent decades (culled from *Screen Digest*'s "World Film Production/Distribution" reports, which it publishes each June):

1970: 3,512
1980: 3,710
1990: 4,645
2000: 3,782
2005: 4,603

For me the numbers conjure up the last shot of the artifacts warehouse in *Raiders of the Lost Ark*, but with stack upon stack, row upon row of film cans.

Scott isn't the first commentator to prophesy that all films will eventually be on the Internet. It's an idea that crops up now and then, and it would be useful to look more closely at why it's a wild exaggeration. It's not just the money or the huge volume of film involved, though either of those factors would be prohibitive in itself. There are all sorts of other reasons why the practical digital downloading of films will never come close to providing us with even a substantial slice of cinema.

Coincidentally, two experts on this subject, Michael Pogorzelski, director of the film archive of the Academy of Motion Picture Arts and Sciences, and Schawn Belston, vice president, film preservation and asset management for Twentieth Century Fox, visited Madison this past week. Mike got his MA here in the Department of Communication Arts and now returns about once a year to show off the latest restored print that he has worked on. Schawn isn't an alum, but he has visited often enough that most students probably think he is. The two brought us the superb new print of *Leave Her to Heaven* that Fox and the Academy have recently collaborated on.

I figured it would be enlightening to sit down with these two and talk about why the Internet is never going to allow us to watch just anything our hearts desire. They kindly agreed, and with my trusty recorder in tow we went for burgers—and fried cheese curds, a commodity not available in Los Angeles—at the Plaza Tavern. I'm grateful for the fascinating insights they provided into some of the less obvious obstacles to putting films on the Internet en masse.

No Coordinating Body

Before we launch in, though, one point needs to be made: there is no single leader or group or entity out there organizing some giant program to systematically put all surviving movies on the Internet. There isn't a set of guidelines or principles. There's no list of all surviving films. How would we even know if the goal of putting them all up had been achieved? When the last archivist to leave turned out the light, locked the door, and went looking for a new line of work?

Many of the film prints that would be the basis for such transfers are sitting in the libraries of the studios that own them or in the collections of public and private archives. The studios would make films available online for profit. The archives might be nonprofit organizations, but they still would need to fund their online projects in some fashion, either by government support, from private grants, or by charging a fee for downloads. Most archives are more concerned about getting the money to conserve or restore aging, unique prints than about making them widely available. Preservation is an urgent matter, and making the resulting copies universally available for public entertainment or education is decidedly a secondary consideration. So far archives have mainly put up a few early shorts to promote their own preservation accomplishments.

Mike works for a nonprofit archive, Schawn for a studio, so together they provide a good overview of some key problems facing the creation of an ideal, comprehensive collection of movies for download.

Money

People who claim that all surviving films could simply be put on the Internet don't go into the technology and expenses of how that could be done.

Of course, Schawn says, studios want to "digitize the library." That phrase is highly imprecise, however. He specifies, "For the purposes of this idea of media being online, available, downloadable, streamable, whatever, that's something that we're dealing with now using existing video masters. So there isn't an extra cost to quote, unquote, digitize. But there is a cost to make the compression master, what we're calling at Fox a 'mezzanine file,' which is basically a 50-megabit file. That's the highest-quality 'low-quality' version of the content from which you can derive all of the different flavors of compression for the various websites that have downloadable media.

"There's a huge problem with this, in that Amazon, iTunes, and Google all have a slightly different technical specification of how they need the files delivered to them. If you don't have this kind of mezzanine file, you have to make a different compressed version for each one of these, which costs something, certainly. It's not incredibly expensive, but it's not free.

"So why? What's the motivation to us to compress at Fox the entire library? I don't know. Are we going to sell enough copies of *Lucky Nick Cain* [a 1951 George Raft film] compressed on iTunes to cover the costs of making the compression? I don't think so."

Compatibility and the Onrush of Technology

Schawn's mention of the variety of files needed by the big download services raises the problem of compatibility. It's not just a matter of supplying the files and then forgetting about the whole thing, assuming that the film is available to anybody forever. What about new standards and formats?

Schawn says, "Just as with consumer video, the standard changes, so what used to be acceptable yesterday isn't acceptable now in terms of technical quality." As time passes, plug-ins make access faster and cheaper, and eventually the original files don't look good enough. He points out that currently iTunes can't download HD (high definition). If it becomes possible later, "if you want to get *24* in HD, what Fox will have to do is go and re-deliver all the files in HD." And presumably re-deliver again when the next big format revolution occurs.

Mike explains further, "Using the mezzanine file, you would just have to continue to reformat it to whatever the players demand. The lowest of the low quality will keep going up as people have broadband and can handle larger chunks of data faster."

What about the film you've already downloaded? You acquire films using plug-ins, which change. Think how often you're told that an update is now available. If you go ahead and keep updating, the changes accumulate. Eventually you may not be able to play the download you paid for. QuickTime, for instance, will have moved way beyond the technology as it existed when you made your purchase.

Schawn and Mike both point out that at this stage in the history of downloading, the level of quality is still pretty bad in comparison with prints of films in theaters or on DVDs. It would be nice to think that the virtual film archive could provide sounds and images worthy of the movies themselves, but that will take a long, long time—not the "before too long" that Scott envisions.

Copyright

I raised another matter: "But what about copyright? Every time I hear something about restoration or bringing something out on DVD, it's, 'Well, there are rights problems.' And some of those rights problems don't get resolved. I assume that quite a few films that they blithely believe can be slapped up for downloading can't be slapped up."

Schawn: "Sure, and there are often not any kinds of provisions in the contract about Internet distribution—obviously! So you're right, how do you deal with that?"

He points to *Viva Zapata* as a film that Fox has restored but can't make available due to rights issues. The potential sales are not thought to warrant paying to resolve those issues. "I'm sure there are lots of titles in everybody's libraries that you can't just pop up on the Internet and start selling."

The copyright barrier is worse for nonstudio archives, which seldom own the exhibition or distribution rights to the films they protect. Usually—though not invariably—the studios do not object to archives owning and preserving prints. Making money through showing them or selling copies would be quite another matter.

Mike describes the online presence of archival prints. "On a much smaller scale, this is being attempted in the archive world already, like on Rick Prelinger's site [*Prelinger Archives*, http://www.archive.org/details /prelinger] or on the Library of Congress's site [http://www.loc.gov/rr /mopic/ndlmps.html], where they've put up dozens of moving-image files. True, it's not independent cinema, and it's mostly commercials and the paper prints that have recently been restored. On Prelinger's site it's all the industrial films that he's collected over the years. That has seen a good amount of traffic, but it hasn't created new audiences for these films, I would argue. At least, not on a huge scale."

Prelinger's site contains only public-domain items, including the ever-popular *Duck and Cover*, allowing him to avoid the problem of copyright. Similarly, the Library of Congress gives access primarily to films in the pre-1915 era.

Suppose an archive and a film studio both have good-quality prints of a minor American film made in the 1940s. The archive does not have the legal right to put it online, and if the studio decides that it does not have the financial incentive to do so, that film will not be made available for downloading. A private collector might possibly create a file and make it available, but he or she would risk being threatened by the copyright-holder.

Piracy

We briefly discussed the methods used to prevent pirated copies being made from downloaded films. Like DVDs, downloads can be pirated, with people sending copies to their friends or even offering downloads for a fee in competition with the copyright holder. Copy-protection codes might make it necessary for a purchaser to keep a downloaded copy only on a hard drive without being able to burn it onto a DVD. Another type of code could erase the file once the film had been viewed once or twice. That's not exactly conducive to the ideal archive of world cinema, where we would hope to be able to study a film in detail if we so choose.

One might think that piracy protection mainly applies to studios, with their need to make money. Mike points out, though, that the need for such protection "even applies to the archival model, too. For films that you mention that have gone out of copyright . . . there's still the same costs associated with putting [online] a silent film that no one owns—digitizing it, creating the compressed master that goes on the web—and they aren't the kinds of subjects that people are going to get rich on at all, so there isn't a lot of piracy. You don't hear many archivists complaining, 'Hey, you took my 1911 Lubin film, damn you! You can't put that on your website. That belongs on the archive's website.' But that scenario becomes more of a likelihood for more popular titles. The obscure 1911 Lubin film is on one extreme, but *Birth of a Nation*, a well-known silent film a lot more people would like to see, is on the other. Let's say the highest-quality copy is on the Museum of Modern Art's website and can be easily lifted and posted on your own site. And even if you just say, 'Oh, I'll charge 99 cents or I'll charge 50 cents to stream it,' it's still going to be someone taking over something that the archive put all of the high-end effort and money into doing. Frankly, I think unless it's an archive with a national mandate and a little bit higher budget to digitize and to put the contents of their archives online, there's not going to be any motivation to make that high-end investment up front."

Thus an archive may simply not bother to put a film on the Internet because it can't guarantee recouping the costs that would be generated.

Language and Cultural Barriers

Scott's notion of easy access to all of surviving world cinema implicitly depends on an idea that all these films are either English-language or already subtitled or dubbed for English-speaking users.

That's not true for a start, so there would remain a great deal of work to translate films that have never been released in English-language markets. That's another huge, expensive task.

Then there's the opposite side of that coin. For truly complete access, everyone in the world, whatever language they speak, would be able to download and appreciate every film. Of course, there are billions of people without computers or Internet access, and it looks unlikely that being able to go online will become universal anytime soon. For figures on numbers of people with Internet access, check https://www.cia.gov/library/publications/the-world-factbook/rankorder/2153rank.html; percentages can be calculated by clicking on each country and finding the total population. In Tajikistan, for example, .07 percent of the population was online in 2005. One has to assume that a lot of connections in some of those countries are dial-up, so downloading films would be almost impossible.

So let's just say that for the foreseeable future downloadable films would "only" need to be subtitled in the languages of countries or regions where significant numbers of people can use PayPal, iTunes, Netflix, and similar services.

In our conversation, Schawn pointed out that digital compression files entail huge numbers of versions, with different soundtracks dubbed in or different subtitles added. Technically it's possible to do all that translation. Still, "it's very complicated. So for worldwide distribution of anything—like you're talking about your silent film—if you're in Pakistan, do you get the American version of the movie or do you get the version of the movie with the intertitles appropriate to wherever it is that you're showing it? If so, that quickly compounds the amount of stuff that's digitized."

I responded, "Yeah, or a 1930s Japanese film put on the Internet for downloading, subtitled in every language where there are people that can pay for it. The more you think about it, the more absurd it becomes."

Scott must be implying as well that there is some single "original" version of a film and that that version would be the one available in this ideal collection in cyberspace. Yet any archivist or film historian knows that multiple versions of a given film are typically made, depending partly on the censorship laws of the different countries where it is originally shown. In making downloadable files available, does a studio or archive use only the original version of a film made for its country of origin and thus risk having it include material offensive to viewers in some places where it might be downloaded? Or does a whole slew of different versions, one acceptable in, say, Iran, another inoffensive to the Danes, and still another compatible with Senegalese social mores, get put online? How could one even gather all such versions and digitize them? National film archives tend to have government mandates to concentrate primarily on preserving their own countries' films. Not every version of every film gets saved.

The Bottom Line

For all the reasons noted here and others as well, film availability for download will follow pretty much the same economic principles that have governed film sales in other media. Mike's opinion is, "Whether they're from an archive or a studio, I think things will start going online in the same pace that they came onto DVD, in an eight-to-ten-year cycle. And there still will be large gaps."

Schawn interjects, "Just as there are on DVD."

Mike concludes, "There's stuff that will never go online. Yeah, just as on DVD."

• •

This entry prompted two immediate and dramatically opposed reactions. One attacked my entire piece as "illogical." It was posted on the *Cinematical* website (http://www.cinematical.com/) by Ryan Stewart. His basic claim was that Scott had not meant literally all movies—instructional films, ads, travelogues, and so on—but only "movie-movies," presumably mainstream commercial and art cinema that real people want to see. Stewart passes in silence over the fact that the organization of my piece, logical or not, was based on a conversation with two major archivists, both of whom restore "movie-movies."

Stewart claims, "If I wanted, I'm sure I could go to the New York Public Library and microfiche an article from the early 80s explaining why all the movies we grew up with won't ever be transferred to home video." Of course, commentators like him don't often go to libraries and "microfiche" things. He seems unaware of the irony here: those putative prognosticators were right. A lot of the movies "we" grew up with still are not on home video and never will be.

I mention this piece here because, as the prolific Anonymous once put it, "the confidence of ignorance will always overcome the indecision of knowledge," but that doesn't mean that ignorance should go unchallenged. I fear that this dismissive attitude is fairly common among film fans, awed by the wide range of films available in digital forms and unaware of the far vaster, largely unseen holdings of film archives and studios.

Stewart also faults my use of the word "complete," saying that online film access "wouldn't be any more 'complete' than the book libraries of Oxford or Harvard are 'complete.'" I never heard that those libraries or any other on earth claims to be complete. But A. O. Scott said "the entire surviving history of movies." I take it that's roughly synonymous with "complete surviving history of movies." Stewart prefers "comprehensive" and concludes, "I would imagine that 20 years from now, a comprehensive online library of films will be readily available to those who can pay. Hopefully, we'll also have done away with the traditional small computer screen by then, and we'll be able to blow up those films we download to wall-size after we pay our 99 spacebucks."

Stewart can go on imagining. Even if we settle for a comprehensive library of films (by whose definition?), for all the reasons Mike, Schawn, and I raised, that is not going to happen. And those people who say that "movie-movies" are all that is necessary for completeness are essentially saying that as long as the movies they personally want to watch are available, the ones that others might want to see don't matter. But archives do preserve films of all types, and they have a particular duty to preserve those that neither big companies nor solitary film fans would pay attention to.

In contrast, shortly after we posted the entry, Alexander Horwath, director of the Austrian Film Museum, asked if he could include it in the collection *Film Curatorship: Archives, Museums, and the Digital Marketplace*, which he and three other archive heads were preparing. (In 2008, the book appeared, with "The Celestial Multiplex" on pages 216 to 221, from SYNEMA, Vienna; the Austrian Film Museum and Le Giornate del Cinema Muto, the Italian silent-film festival, cosponsored it.)

Ryan Stewart's biographical blurb on Cinematical explains much about the state of film writing on the Internet:

Ryan Stewart is a reporter for Dow Jones. He did one film review for *Time Out New York* five years ago, which also makes him a certified film critic. He was born the same year *Superman* came out, but unlike Superman, he did not crash land into Kansas. His favorite film is *Vivre Sa Vie*. He also enjoys anything by Jean Renoir, Billy Wilder or Josef von Sternberg. Ryan has an apartment in a bad neighborhood, and was recently called away from watching *Hiroshima Mon Amour* at 11:00 at night in order to convince a police officer that he was not involved in the spray-painting of a car.

Luckily for Stewart, his favorite films and filmmakers happen to be those readily available on DVD and other new-media formats.

Finally, a few specific points. I mentioned that the cost of subtitling films creates a prohibitive barrier. In some cases, filmmakers solicit volunteers to provide subtitles for online films. Nina Paley has done so for *Sita Sings the Blues* (see the next entry, "Take My Film, Please"). Yet even with the possibility of volunteers, the result would remain patchy and probably limited to the most widely used languages. Volunteers, however selfless and enthusiastic, could never provide intertitles for every film currently online, let alone those that potentially could be there.

Scott makes the point that the Internet will allow for the distribution of movies online. True. Paley's *Sita Sings the Blues* is unusual, in that she offered the film for free initially (again, see "Take My Film, Please"). The rental option via download or streaming rather than DVD-in-the-mail is growing on Netflix, which may have helped make sales of physical discs hit a plateau. Given how much studios make on DVDs, the struggle over the division of online rental fees will no doubt be long and bumpy.

This entry avoided touching on the "darknet," where many copyrighted films are available for illegal downloading. Undoubtedly this sphere expands the number of films online, but it still will never include all films or even all "movie-movies," due to the constraints we discussed. Most obviously, there are hundreds of thousands of films sitting in locked archive vaults from which no digital copies have been made.

By 2008, the percentage of Tajikistan's population online had grown to .08 percent.

• •

Take My Film, Please

MAY 7, 2009

Kristin here:

Nina Paley's animated feature *Sita Sings the Blues* was one of the highlights of the 2009 Ebertfest. Afterward I had the privilege of moderating the on-stage discussion with the director and University of Illinois film professor Richard Leskovsky, who has a special interest in animation.

Sita has not had a regular theatrical release, though Nina has made it available to theaters, festivals, and everyone with access to a high-speed Internet link. She gives it for free to anyone who wants it, believing that people who see it will pass the word along and that as the film becomes more well known, it will become more valuable as well. Income should flow in. Nina is confident, some might say cocky, about this. The thing is, she may be right. *Sita* is a terrific film, and I can well imagine a groundswell of interest gradually building. Indeed, it's happening already. Here I am, blogging about it, and others are as well. Nonbloggers are e-mailing their friends. Festivals have booked it up to the end of this year and beyond.

Roger Ebert found *Sita* early on, and the program notes reprinted his online review (http://rogerebert.suntimes.com/apps/pbcs.dll/article?AID =/20090429/REVIEWS/904229995/1023), which begins:

I got a DVD in the mail, an animated film titled "Sita Sings the Blues." It was a version of the epic Indian tale of *Ramayana* set to the 1920's jazz vocals of Annette Hanshaw. Uh, huh. I carefully filed it with other movies I will watch when they introduce the 8-day week. Then I was told I must see it.

I began. I was enchanted. I was swept away. I was smiling from one end of the film to the other. It is astonishingly original. It brings together four entirely separate elements and combines them into a great whimsical chord.

The four elements are a sketchily animated account of the breakup of Nina's marriage; the tale of Rama and Sita from the Indian epic, the *Ramayana*; musical numbers that all borrow recordings of Ms. Hanshaw; and three shadow-puppet narrators who try, not always successfully, to recall the details of the *Ramayana* and its background history. As Roger says, these ingredients blend marvelously.

The timing of the Ebertfest screening was fortunate. Within the next few weeks, the DVD release is due. Of course, you can already watch it online or burn your own DVD. But for those who can't or don't want to, you can buy the DVD package, complete with what is described on the film's website as a pre-downloaded copy of the film.

As Roger's review says, Nina is a hometown girl (from the Champaign-Urbana area, where Ebertfest is held). She started out doing comic strips and then made some animated shorts before progressing to *Sita*, her first feature. Her father taught at the University of Illinois. Her mother was an administrator there. Both have supported her in the making and distribution of *Sita*, and both were present throughout the festival.

Here's a transcript of our conversation. Applause, laughter, and a fast-talking film director at times defeated my efforts to catch every word of my recording, so some details have been lost.

KT: I know you want to talk about how you've been getting the film out to the public, but I'd like to start off by talking about the film itself. A lot of people think that you were pushing a lot of buttons and somehow the computer was generating the images. But obviously you were generating them yourself by painting and collage and so forth. Could you just start with the process of what you did before you put this material into the computer and then what you did afterwards?

NP: Well, there are a whole bunch of different styles and techniques used in the film. The style of the musical numbers—actually I drew that in Flash using a lot of really simple tools, so the perfect circles have a smoothness that you don't get by hand. By the way, I want to mention that what you saw was not 35mm. You saw HD-cam, and there are actually 35mm prints of this, and seeing it here was very strange. It was unusually solid, rock solid, a little bit troublingly solid, although that is the ideal that film technology has been striving for. But 35mm prints have all these scratches and splices, and grain and a kind of warmth that moves around, which is almost like a kind of very desirable filter that really warms up the film. So watching it in 35mm is different. I was noticing how computery it looked on the HD projection at this particular size, because I was looking for imperfections that simply weren't there.

But anyway, yeah, I did some paintings on parchment paper. To me, some things were simple, because I only had me working on the animation, and I used as many computer shortcuts as I possibly could. Most of the technique was what's called "cut-outs," so I made pieces of things, moved them around, and the computer does what's called "tweening" [i.e., "in-betweening," filling in the frames between key points]. There's a little bit of full animation in there. It would take a long time to say everything that I did.

KT: Yeah, but every bit of that visual material was something that you put into the computer in some fashion, so that—

NP: The computer didn't draw it, that's for sure. I drew it, whether I started with paper or drawing on a little [digital] graphics tablet, or eventually I got what's called a Cintiq, which is a monitor you can draw on. You can draw straight into a program through the monitor, and so what's on the monitor—it tricks you into thinking you're actually drawing on the screen, but it went through both my hand and the computer.

KT: Is this the kind of thing you teach? Do your students learn how to do this kind of animation?

NP: No. I'd love to teach this. Right now I'm teaching visual storytelling, which is a much more basic class, and I taught something called "classic film and video" for a while at Parsons [the New School for Design]. I actually really like to teach artists. I'm teaching people who already know what they want to say and already have a voice and just need a little bit of technical [help]—it's slightly faster if they ask me rather than reading a manual. I learned by reading manuals.

RL: You're a woman artist making an animated feature. Actually one of the very first animated features, done ten years before *Snow White and the Seven Dwarfs*, was Lotte Reiniger's *The Adventures of Prince Ahmed*, which also deals with Eastern myths. You actually did a little bit of cut-out animation, too, with the shadow puppets. That brings a nice circularity—

NP: Well, hopefully this isn't the last one!

KT: Was that the silent film that you referred to in your film?

NP: I still haven't seen that film. First of all, everything has influenced me, because everything influences everything else. Culture, language, so there's a language of cell phones, a language of animation that comes from every piece of animation that's been shared ever. So even if I haven't been directly influenced by something, I haven't seen the actual film, I will have been indirectly influenced by it simply keeping my eyes open.

RL: All the Annette Hanshaw songs are accompanied with the Flash animation, but it looked like there were a couple of different styles of Indian art represented there, from different periods. Tell us a little bit about what the choice was.

NP: The *Ramayana* is thousands of years old, and it also covers an enormous chunk of geography. It's very popular not just in India but also in Cambodia, Thailand, Polynesia, Indonesia—this huge swath of South and Southeast Asia and parts of China. So there's just this enormous range of art styles that have come up around it, and the styles I used in the film were influenced by just a tiny, tiny sample of that. Obviously shadow puppets. The designs were derived from puppets from Indonesia, Korea, Thailand, Malaysia, and also India. There's a whole slew of paintings. There's lots of *Ramayana* paintings that were actually commissioned by Muslim [inaudible] who had money. There were collages of these traditional arts. Everything went into the hopper, all going into my head. Everything goes in there, grinds up, and comes out.

KT: Traditionally in animation the entire soundtrack is done first, which is not the way it's done in regular live-action filmmaking, but of course it's virtually impossible to synchronize cartoons if you have someone doing the voices after the animation is done. So could you tell us a little about the soundtrack and how much of it you had ready by the time you started the visuals?

NP: Well, I should say, the whole production, it's not like I had everything ready when I started the visuals. The way you're supposed to make a film, first you're supposed to write a treatment, and then you're supposed to write a script, and then if it's animation, you're supposed to have everything designed and do breakdowns and storyboards and this and that. Then at the very end you animate it.

I didn't have to do that, because it was just me working and it was with a computer. So I came up with things as I was going along. The whole structure of the story was there, because the *Ramayana* is this very well-established story that's been told billions of times. I knew that story. I also had the songs, so the first thing that I synchronized and edited was the songs. As I was working on those, I was figuring out how the rest of the film was going to come together. [Then there were] the three narrators, who were just friends of mine who I convinced to go into a recording studio, and I asked some questions about the *Ramayana*. They were all very busy and went, "Oh, I should have read more before." The conversation that they had was actually quite typical, because I had so many conversations with so many Indians. It was just uncanny; they really captured the twenty-first century zeitgeist of *Ramayana*, I guess.

RL: That intermission was a bit daring.

NP: I should mention that the 35mm print, depending on where you see it, it has surround sound, and the HD only has stereo. If you see it on 35mm, depending on what speaker you're near, [during the intermission] you'll hear different complete conversations coming out of each. Some of those conversations are extremely funny. I recommend the left rear speaker. There is Will Franken, who's a distribution executive, talking about how unsellable the film is. And there are people on the front right speaking Hindi. I think they're saying, "I thought this was a children's film."

So, yes, intermission. Old American musicals had intermissions. I was watching some of them while I was working on the film, and sure enough, two-thirds of the way through, intermission comes up. Bollywood films still have intermissions—a three- or four-hour-long Bollywood film has a little gap. So it was a tribute to both old American musical films and all Bollywood films. When I showed the film in Livingston, New Jersey, to an audience of primarily Indian-Americans, during intermission they just left for 15 minutes. And they missed my favorite part of the film, which is the part that comes a minute after the intermission.

KT: I can second that statement about the 35mm, because I was lucky enough to see this film three weeks ago in 35mm at the Wisconsin Film

Festival, and it's a different experience. I've enjoyed both of them, but I think there are definite advantages to 35.

It's actually much easier for most people to see this film on a computer screen or television, because you chose a very unusual way to disseminate the film to the public. Can you talk a little about that?

NP: Why, yes, I can! You can see this film for free online if you go to sitasingstheblues.com and follow a variety of links and get the film. You can get everything from a streaming version from New York Public Television to a 200-gigabyte file from which you can make your own 35mm print if you have $30,000 to download it. Briefly, every file I have for the film is either online now or it's going to go online. It's a completely decentralized distribution model. People have compared it to Radiohead's English model [for their *In Rainbows* album, 2007], but that's different, because that relied on a single, central location where you got the audio, and it was tracked. It was simply what you decided to pay.

Mine is totally decentralized. I shouldn't even call it "mine" anymore. It's yours. This film belongs to you and everybody else in the world. The audience, you and the rest of the world, is actually the distributor of the film. So I'm not maintaining a server or host or anything like that. Everyone else is. We put it on archive.org, a fabulous website, and encourage people to BitTorrent it and share it. That's what's happening, and we hope people do it more. There are also broadcast versions, which you can download. If anyone here is from a television station, you can broadcast this for free.

Which begs the question, why is Nina Paley giving her work away for free? Doesn't she want to get money? The answer is yes, I want to get money, and I believe that I will get money. I think I am getting money from this, because the more people share the film, the more valuable the film becomes. I have told people after screenings that they can get the film for free online, but I have some DVDs which I sell for twenty bucks, and here for twenty-five bucks—the Virginia [Theatre] is still remodeling, so [the extra five dollars] is for the Virginia.

I should also mention regarding DVDs that we, my mom—oh, I should mention my mom! Sorry, I thank my parents, of course, who gave me the gift of life and all that, but my mom, who gave *Sita Sings the Blues* the gift of being its festival-relations manager, which is a huge, huge job. For those who don't know, my mom was the main administrator of the math department of the University of Illinois and is a spreadsheet master and business-communications master and stuff like that and has been just essential to the film having such a successful festival life. So, thank you, mom! [Applause.]

Anyway, I have made thousands of festival screeners so that festivals will have something to preview, and we're down to the last 35, or at least we were this morning, and we handed them to the people in the Virginia, and that's it for DVDs until a few weeks from now I'll have the new purchasable DVD edition available.

RL: Will there be special features?

NP: Because the film is free, people can subtitle it freely, and the new one will have some subtitles. There's gonna be more subtitles online. It's been translated into French and Hebrew and Spanish and Italian and pirate. [Applause.] The thing is, the film is now halfway. It will just continue growing, so whatever the DVD is, it's just snatched off the stuff we have as of this week. So it'll be the film; it'll be a bonus feature called *Fetch*, a film I made; it'll be some subtitles; I think there'll be a couple different audio options.

It'll be a very nice package, because basically what I'm selling is packaging for the film. If you have a computer, you've got your own packaging. You just download it. But many people just the same want an actual printed package. There'll be two editions. There's the artist's edition, a limited edition of 4,999 DVDs, because for every five thousand DVDs I sell, I have to pay the licensers more money. You may think that's too bad, and it's OK if the other DVD distributors pay the licensers more money, but I paid $5,000 in order to decriminalize the film, so that I wouldn't go to jail.

JEAN PALEY, FROM THE AUDIENCE: Fifty thousand!

NP: Fifty thousand, yeah. Fifty thousand dollars is enough.

KT: Which is for the song rights.

NP: Yes. Those old songs. I cannot thank Roger enough for writing about this film. Also, after he wrote about it on his blog, my colleague, a professor of copyright law here, said, "Does he know about the copyright issue of the songs?" The film uses old songs that were written and performed in the late 1920s. Had they been from 1923, they would be in public domain now. When they were written, they were supposed to be in public domain in the 1980s, but there have been these continuous, retroactive copyright extensions, so they may never enter the public domain.

We were so relieved that Roger agreed that what copyright law has become is really not serving culture or people. These copyright extensions have really gotten way out of control. [Applause.] They [inaudible] me so much that I actually question copyright fundamentally, but even those who don't agree, I think, [would agree] that retroactively assigning copyrights is not actually acting as an incentive for dead artists to create more art.

Whereas, these songs. It's a scandal, these beautiful songs! Many people have never heard of them until seeing my film. That's just a crime. She was a huge seller in the twenties. Huge! Why is it that we can't hear her music? It's because all the rights are controlled by corporations, and anybody who dares to share Annette Hanshaw's music is risking a lawsuit or jail. As I did. As I decided I was willing to do. I didn't realize I was doing civil disobedience at the time. I didn't realize how severe the possible punishments were for doing this kind of thing, but even had I known I would have done it anyway. I have no regrets. Now, I'm turning into a full-time free-culture activist. [Applause.]

Some of you may know my dad is a retired math professor here. I grew up in this science and engineering culture. In all these books about copyright, people always talk about scientists and how scientists share information. How it's really important, this really strong ethic of sharing information. Scientists seek to discover some really great information to share it with the community, and that actually benefits the contributing scientist.

As an artist, it's actually exactly the same. My status vastly increases as I share this film. But I think it's quite possible that the way I was growing up here formed me that way, to see it this way. A lot of artists don't see it this way. People see it as property. I just wanted to share what I've been thinking about a lot. [Applause.]

RL: Has your film prompted an Annette Hanshaw revival?

NP: Not an official one. I should mention that the only reason that these songs exist in a form in which we can hear them at all is because of the efforts of underground record collectors, because the corporations that have the official rights to control this music hadn't done it. They actually scrapped the masters. There's no surviving masters of Annette Hanshaw's recordings, because they were so very valuable that in the forties they were sent for scrap metal. And yet somehow it would be theft if somebody in America released her recordings today.

But yeah, there's this wonderful network of record collectors who just preserved her stuff on lacquer, and that's how I originally heard her songs. I was staying in the home of a record collector, and he actually had Annette Hanshaw on 78s. And this is the tip of the iceberg. There's so much amazing culture that we've forgotten all about and can't get at. There's this wealth of films that's just sitting there, that nobody can restore, because if you restore a film you don't have the rights to, you can get sued for showing it! And it's very expensive to restore films, so the result is, nobody wants to touch it. Everyone is scared, and our cinematic history is disintegrating. It doesn't last. Records actually last longer than film.

KT: We should point out that you have a very informative website, *nina paley.com*.

NP: Yeah, it's now *blog.ninapaley.com*, and there's also *sitasingstheblues .com*, and I'm also artist-in-residence at *QuestionCopyright.org*.

KT: Most of the ways to get the film out to people that you've talked about would be DVDs or downloaded copies, but your film is still being shown in a lot of festivals, well into the future.

NP: Yeah, festivals and also cinemas. Hurray for independent cinemas! I support them, and they support me. [Applause.] There's some great cinemas programming it. It's going to be in Chicago at the Gene Siskel Film Center, very soon. And it's going to be in Vancouver. It's going to be in some other cities. And there's no real time limit. There's no advertising for this film, no paid advertising. The audience is also the public-relations department, so it's gone completely by word of mouth, word of web, word of blog. There's absolutely no end time. It can be screened anytime. There are some prints circulating right now, and hopefully any cinema that has a little off time and wants to give it a shot, can program it.

KT: Your mother was telling me that the film will be probably in two hundred festivals.

NP: Not two hundred. I think it's been in a hundred.

KT: Well, there's a long list on your website that goes into 2010, I think, so [to audience] you want to tell your friends who live in those various cities, see it on the big screen!

[Mother knows best: the list of screenings and festivals on the film's website numbered exactly 200 as of May 4.]

NP: When I decided to give it away free online, what finally made me realize this was viable was when I realized that this didn't mean it wouldn't be seen on the big screen, that the Internet is not a replacement for a theater. It's a complement. Many people will see it online and go, "Wow, I wish I could see this on the big screen!" And so they can, and some people like to see it more than once. Another thing is, you see it online, and that increases the demand for the DVDs. So it's the opposite of what the record and movie industries say. Actually, the more shared something is, the more demand there is for it. [Applause.]

RL: Are you doing this for your short films, too?

NP: I would like it for the short films. It's simply a matter of time. I want to do it with my comic strips. I'm still seeking a volunteer, although someone contacted me from the U[niversity] of I[llinois], I think from the library, whom I need to call. Maybe everything will be scanned and uploaded right here from Urbana, which would be awesome. But yeah, I want to go back. Just as Congress is retroactively extending copyrights, I'm retroactively de-copyrighting all of my stuff and sharing it, because that will make it more valuable. Imagine some original comic strip that everybody knows. That's much more valuable to people than a comic strip that no one's ever seen. Andy Warhol, for example. Some Warhol print just fetched some huge price at auction. There was a photo of it up in the newspaper. We all know what Andy Warhol's prints look like, even though most of us have never seen them in the flesh. We all know that they're worth a lot, 'cause they're famous. They're famous because people reproduce images of them.

• •

For our main entry on Ebertfest 2009, see http://www.davidbordwell.net /blog/?p=4441. Nina mentions using a "Cintiq" in her work; for images and a description, go to the company's website: http://www.wacom.com/cintiq/index.php.

Sita Sings the Blues continues to play in theaters, and there are additional ways to obtain a personal copy. Shortly after Ebertfest, the DVD which Nina mentioned in the Q&A was directly available from Cafe Press (http://www.cafepress.com/) (along with a range of T-shirts and other merchandise); it came in a square cardboard folder. In July 2009, a DVD (NTSC but with no region coding) with a more conventional upright plastic holder was released on Amazon and started renting on Netflix. Nina's blog, http://blog.ninapaley.com/, is updated regularly. It posts notices of showings at festivals and in theaters, as well as new ways to Sita-ize your viewing, including cell-phone downloads.

As of February 2010, the list of festival screenings had risen to 246.

• •

Index